D1193899

BAPTISM
IN THE THOUGHT OF
ST. PAUL

BAPTISM
IN THE THOUGHT OF
ST. PAUL

A Study in Pauline Theology by
RUDOLF SCHNACKENBURG

Translated by
G. R. BEASLEY-MURRAY

HERDER AND HERDER

1964
HERDER AND HERDER NEW YORK
232 Madison Avenue, New York 10016

English translation of "DAS HEILSGESCHEHEN BEI DER TAUFE NACH DEM APOSTEL PAULUS" *by* G. R. Beasley-Murray.

Nihil Obstat: Henricus F. Davis, S.T.D.
censor deputatus

Imprimatur: ✠ Franciscus
Archiepiscopus Birmingamiensis

Datum Birmingamiae, 27a Aprilis, 1964.

Library of Congress Catalog Card Number: 64-25228

First published 1964 in Great Britain
Printed in the United States of America

CONTENTS PART ONE

Exegetical Foundation

EXAMINATION OF THE PAULINE BAPTISMAL SAYINGS

CONTENTS PART TWO

Biblical-Theological Construction

THE SALVATION-EVENT AT BAPTISM IN THE CONTEXT OF THE PAULINE THEOLOGY

Author's Preface

The present work is a drastically revised new edition of a dissertation that was published by K. Zink of München in 1950 under the title, *Das Heilsgeschehen bei der Taufe nach dem Apostel Paulus.* The work was prepared in the years 1946–1947 and suffered by reason of the imperfect communications between libraries that still existed in the immediate post-war years. Meanwhile much labour has been expended on baptism in primitive Christianity and a rich literature has appeared. From this I have learned not a little and corrected many of my views. If I venture to allow the work to appear now in a fresh edition, that is due to encouragement given me by my friends Prof. G. D. Kilpatrick (Oxford) and Dr. G. R. Beasley-Murray (London), who have also smoothed the way for this book to be issued by the publishing house of Basil Blackwell, Oxford. I am constrained at this point to express my sincere thanks to the colleagues I have mentioned. Dr. Beasley-Murray has undertaken the arduous task of translating into English my work in its new form; for this service I owe him my profound thanks. I am also grateful to the publisher for his readiness to set the work before the English-speaking public.

The book does not repudiate the Roman Catholic standpoint, but an endeavour is made in it to investigate the Pauline texts, according to the rules of the historical-critical method which all scholars in the New Testament field are obliged to observe, and to elucidate them in the framework of the Pauline world of thought. That it may be received as a contribution to the understanding of the Apostle's theology is the desire of

THE AUTHOR

Würzburg, June 1961.

Translator's Preface

THE appearance of a book on baptism, written by a Roman Catholic New Testament scholar and translated by a Baptist New Testament teacher, is sufficiently unusual to call for comment.

The original publication of the book caused considerable controversy on the Continent, and it is not impossible that it may provoke discussion in the English-speaking world. At the outset, therefore, it would seem needful, in the interests of both author and translator, for it to be clearly stated that their co-operation is under no circumstances to be construed as indicating that the author leans to Baptist views, or that the translator inclines to Roman Catholic interpretations of baptism. The author has stated in his preface that he has endeavoured to follow the historical-critical method 'which all scholars in the New Testament field are obliged to observe'. The results obtained by a distinguished Roman Catholic scholar, using this common method of Biblical scholarship on a theme of importance to all Christian people, will be of interest to Protestants and Roman Catholics alike: the former may be surprised that a Roman Catholic theologian should express himself in the manner found at times in this book; the latter will undoubtedly be stimulated by the freshness of approach to the subject.

Inevitably I myself would find it necessary constantly to express myself differently from the author. Yet my first impression on reading this book remains, that no treatment known to me of Paul's teaching on baptism is so profound as that contained within these pages. For this reason I was happy to offer my services in making it available to English readers and I am glad to share its insights with all fellow-believers in Christ.

THE TRANSLATOR

London, Easter 1962.

ABBREVIATIONS

AC = F. J. Dölger, Antike und Christentum, 5 Bde 1929ff

ALW = Archiv für Liturgiewissenschaft, Regensburg

BenMon = Benediktinische Monatsschrift, Beuron

BFchTh = Beiträge zur Förderung christlicher Theologie, Gütersloh

Bibl = Biblica, Rom

BSt = Biblische Studien, Freiburg i. Br.

BZ = Biblische Zeitschrift, Paderborn

BZfr = Biblische Zeitfragen, Münster

CSEL = Corpus scriptorum ecclesiasticorum latinorum, Wien

DAL = Dictionnaire d'Archéologie chrétienne et de Liturgie, Paris

DB = Dictionnaire de la Bible, Paris (Suppl. = Supplément)

DThC = Dictionnaire de Théologie catholique, Paris

EphThLov = Ephemerides theologicae Lovanienses, Löwen

EvTh = Evangelische Theologie, München

FRLANT = Forschungen zur Religion und Literatur des A und NT, Göttingen

GCS = Griechische christliche Schriftsteller, hrsg. v. d. Preussischen Akademie zu Berlin

GGM = O. Casel, Glaube, Gnosis, Mysterium (Münster 1941)

HRE = Realencyklopädie für protestantische Theologie und Kirche, 3. Aufl. hrsg. v. A. Hauck, Leipzig

JBL = Journal of Biblical Literature, Philadelphia

JLW = Jahrbuch für Liturgiewissenschaft, Münster

JThSt = Journal of Theological Studies, Oxford

LThK = Lexikon für Theologie und Kirche, Freiburg

MüThZ = Münchener Theologische Zeitschrift

NTD = Das Neue Testament deutsch, Neues Göttinger Bibelwerk

NtlAbh = Neutestamentliche Abhandlungen, Münster

NTS = New Testament Studies, Cambridge

PL = Migne, Patrologia, series latina

PG = Migne, Patrologia, series graeca

PRE = Paulys Realencyklopädie der klassischen Altertumswissenschaft, fortgeführt von Wissowa-Kroll u. a., Stuttgart

RB = Revue biblique, Paris

RGG = Religion in Geschichte und Gegenwart, 2. Aufl., Tübingen

RGH = K. Prümm, Religionsgeschichtliches Handbuch (Freiburg 1943)

RHPhR = Revue d'Histoire et de Philosophie Religieuses, Paris

SAB = Sitzungsberichte der Preussischen Akademie der Wissenschaften zu Berlin, Phil.-hist. Klasse

SAH = Sitzungsberichte der Heidelberger Akademie der Wissenschaften, Phil.-hist. Klasse

StTh = Studia Theologica, Lund

ThBl = Theologische Blätter, Leipzig

ThGl = Theologie und Glaube, Paderborn

ThLZ = Theologische Literaturzeitung, Leipzig

ThRdsch = Theologische Rundschau, Neue Folge, Tübingen

ThRev	= Theologische Revue, Münster
ThSt	= Theological Studies, Baltimore
ThStKr	= Theologische Studien und Kritiken, Gotha
ThW	= Theologisches Wörterbuch zum NT, hrsg. v. G. Kittel, bisher 4 Bde, 1933 ff
ThZ	= Theologische Zeitschrift, Basel
TU	= Texte und Untersuchungen, Leipzig
ZKTh	= Zeitschrift für katholische Theologie, Innsbruck
ZNW	= Zeitschrift für die neutestamentliche Wissenschaft, Giessen
ZsyTh	= Zeitschrift für systematische Theologie, Berlin

PART ONE

Exegetical Foundation

EXAMINATION OF THE PAULINE BAPTISMAL SAYINGS

CHAPTER ONE

Baptism as a Bath

(ἀπολούεσθαι, λουτρόν)

§1. BAPTISM AS BATH OF CLEANSING

OF all expressions which Paul uses in connection with baptism ἀπολούεσθαι indicates the closest link with the material of baptism, the water. Washing or cleansing is one of the most primitive uses of water; it appears to be basic for the conceptions of baptism which were current even in pre-Christian times and over wide areas of the ancient world. In the Pauline letters we meet ἀπολούεσθαι only in 1 Cor. vi. 11. It is not immediately apparent that the expression here necessarily relates to baptism. Two considerations spring to mind that militate against it: (i) λούεσθαι is used in the LXX for the Jewish cultic cleansings;[1] therefore in 1 Cor. vi. 11 it could be simply a picture for cleansing from sins; (ii) the middle voice is striking, for elsewhere in Paul Christian baptism is described with passive verbs. Nevertheless other considerations make the connection with baptism plain: (i) a comparison with Acts xxii. 16 shows that this picture does relate to baptism. Ἀπολούεσθαι, however, has not become a mere synonym for baptism; it retains its pictorial significance. Baptism bespeaks a comprehensive act of reception (Acts ii. 41), whereas washing singles out a particular effect that then takes place, that is, cleansing from sins. (ii) As to the middle voice, it can scarcely be maintained, with Johannes Weiss, ad loc, that it expresses the action of man in contrast to the action of God. In Acts xxii. 16 the causative meaning is plain: 'Get baptized and washed!';[2] it is possible that in our passage this significance is intended. The passive of λούω and ἀπολούω does not occur in the New Testament.[3] (iii) The aorists support a once for all, foundational act in the past, hence there could be an overtone here: 'At one time you used to be like that; but then you had yourselves washed....'

Alongside the more negative idea of washing away the defilement of

[1] See especially Lev. viii. 6; xi. 40 (along with πλύνειν); xiv. 8–9; xv. 5–6, etc.

[2] Blass-Debrunner, par. 317; Bauer, *Wörterbuch*, see under ἀπολούω.

[3] Also ὁ λελουμένος Jn. xiii. 10 and οἱ λελουμένοι Heb. x. 22 are to be understood as middle voice, cf. Bauer, op. cit. Sp. 950f, see under λούω 2a β and b; A. Oepke in *ThW* IV, 306–8.

sin stands ἡγιάσθητε, which describes the positive effect of salvation. Corresponding to its root in the O.T. concept of holiness, this expression originally denotes a removal from the realm of the profane; it has a close relation to the sacrificial cult, which may still be traced in Paul (Rom. xv. 16).[4] The passive lays emphasis on the divine activity: 'You did not consecrate yourselves to God, but God cleansed you from all your sin and drew you into His holy sphere of life; you have become ἅγιοι'. The passage reflects the strong tension of the holiness effected in the Corinthians through the Holy Spirit and the unholiness of their conduct. Instead of suffering injury and permitting themselves to be robbed, they themselves do injury and rob, and that moreover in relation to brethren (*vv.* 7–8). The Apostle therefore gives them a powerful motive for action of another order: 'You have become holy', and by that he means, 'Act in a fashion corresponding to your capacity as God's holy ones'. The concept ἁγιασμός actually is adapted to this connection of equipment of spiritual being and moral outworking, cf. 1 Thess. iv. 3–7 and 2 Thess. ii. 13f. The discrepancy between what is and what ought to be threatens to break the Apostle's heart and moves him to the rhetorically stressed description (observe the threefold intensifying ἀλλά) of the wonderful saving event, which the children of his care have experienced. The affinity between sacrament and ethic is palpable through the choice of expression and the tone of the passage, rather than through its precise wording.

A third expression ἐδικαιώθητε represents the high point of the saying; it is the standing term for justification in the Letter to the Romans and is a picture taken from the life of the courts.[5] Its position *after* ἡγιάσθητε is remarkable, but here it is at the opposite pole to ἄδικοι, *v.* 9. The Apostle desires to say: 'It is unthinkable that you as ἄδικοι should not inherit the kingdom of God, since you have become δίκαιοι through the divine act of grace (=ἐδικαιώθητε)'. It is precisely when the change of the ἄδικοι to δίκαιοι is considered[6] that the tension, already remarked on in connection with ἡγιάσθητε, and the exhortation that springs from it, receives its intensity: 'As those who have become righteous, show the fruits of the divine righteousness in your conduct.'

This 'impressive conclusion' (Lietzmann) confirms that Paul is thinking of baptism, at which the name of Jesus is invoked and the Spirit of God is imparted (cf. Acts ii. 38). The name of Jesus and the

[4] Cf. O. Procksch in *ThW* I, 114; P. Feine, *Theologie*, 257; R. Asting, *Die Heiligkeit im Urchristentum* (FRLANT, NF 29), Göttingen 1930, 29ff. 213.

[5] E. Tobac, op. cit. 211–3; G. Schrenk, *ThW* II, 219f.

[6] This is stressed also by W. Heitmüller, *Namen Jesu*, 321; J. Weiss ad loc; Asting, op. cit. 214; Bultmann, *Theologie*, 329.

Spirit of God do not stand on the same plane, as though the name effects in a magical way the new Christian life that the Spirit of God produces.[7] The baptized become the property of Jesus through calling on the name of Jesus, while the Spirit of God is bestowed as a gift on them (Rom. v. 5: τοῦ δοθέντος ἡμῖν) and at the same time effects holiness and justification. The concluding formula has a certain triadic sound, without however formally attesting the Trinity.[8]

Thus the verse, starting out from the figure of cleansing in the bath of water, does in fact describe the great soteriological effects of baptism. It suggests to us that in employing this image the Apostle is adhering to the primitive Christian teaching and proclamation of baptism; but before we test this supposition further we should consider another passage that contains the same picture, Eph. v. 26.

In Eph. v. 26 baptism again is not expressly mentioned, but a connection lies at hand through the expression τῷ λουτρῷ τοῦ ὕδατος. The writer[9] sets as an example before the eyes of men the willingness of Christ to suffer for the Church. He then applies the image of marriage to the relationship of Christ and the Church. Baptism becomes the cleansing bath that Christ prepares for his Church.[10] In *v.* 27 the author portrays the care of Christ for his Church. The Lord desires to make her wholly 'radiant' (ἔνδοξος), 'without stain or wrinkle or the like'. Is all that the effect of the 'bath of water'? No, this description goes further; 'wrinkle' is 'a manifestation of age' (von Henle, Meinertz). The ἵνα sentence *v.* 27a thus depends not only on the phrase καθαρίσας κτλ which immediately precedes, but is subordinate to the entire ἵνα-sentence of *v.* 26. In fact it develops ἁγιάσῃ. On the other hand καθαρίσας continues its effect in σπίλον: the bath cleanses from the stains. The author was manifestly not satisfied with depicting the immediate effect of the bath, or with the recollection of the 'cleansing' of the Church in accordance with the background already mentioned. Christ's surrender

[7] W. Heitmüller, op. cit. 75; W. Bousset ad loc.

[8] So Theodoret ad loc (ed. Noesselt III. 196f); P. Gächter, 'Zum Pneumabegriff des hl. Paulus', *ZKTh* 53 (1929), 386–408, esp. 390.

[9] As to the question of the Pauline authorship of Ephesians, still strongly contested, see the more recent works of Introduction by M. Meinertz, *Einleitung*, 145f; A. Wikenhauser, 304–7; further E. Percy, *Die Probleme der Kolosser- und Epheserbrief*, Lund 1946. A different opinion is represented by C. L. Mitton, *The Epistle to the Ephesians, its authorship, origin and purpose*, Oxford 1951; G. Schille, 'Der Autor des Epheserbriefes', *ThLZ* 82 (1957), cols. 325–34. H. J. Cadbury gives a careful assessment, 'The Dilemma of Ephesians', *NTS* 5 (1958–9), 91–102.

[10] The 'bath of water' has been linked with the bride's bath, common among the heathen in ancient times, see O. Casel, 'Die Taufe als Brautbad der Kirche', *JLW* 5 (1925), 144–7; M. Meinertz and J. Huby ad loc. H. Schlier explains the passage from Gnostic ideas, *Christus und die Kirche*, 72f, and *Der Brief an die Epheser*, 264–76. If the conceptual background of this or that kind is to be presumed, the test itself is developed entirely from the Christian teaching of salvation.

to death (*v.* 25) brought richer blessing, and that for all time. 'Stain or wrinkle or the like' is a negative portrayal (ἀλλ' ἵνα) of ἔνδοξον and is intended to illustrate the fundamental, all embracing care of the Lord. Thus the author uses the bath at most as a point of departure. He desires to avoid the impression of speaking of something that once happened and has passed away.

In general our passage does not lay stress on the figure but on the fact. Powerful sentiments attach to ἑαυτὸν παρέδωκεν ὑπὲρ αὐτῆς which Paul understands of the sacrificial death of Christ on the cross (Rom. iv. 25, viii. 32, Gal. ii. 20, Eph. v. 2). Everywhere the lines of actuality burst through the picture of the bath of water. 'Αγιάσῃ *v.* 26, ἁγία καὶ ἄμωμος *v.* 27, the addition ἐν ῥήματι to λουτρῷ τοῦ ὕδατος *v.* 26, can only be understood in the light of the theological ideas which prompt the writer.

Exegetically the addition ἐν ῥήματι calls for attention. Whether the expression is connected with ἁγιάσῃ (cf. Jn. xvii. 17) or with καθαρίσας (cf. Jn. xv. 3) or should be closely attached to τῷ λουτρῷ τοῦ ὕδατος (Belser, Schlier), depends on how one understands ῥῆμα. If it is interpreted as 'teaching, gospel' (Jerome,[11] Estius, etc.) it will be linked to ἁγιάσῃ. But in this case an explanatory addition should be made to ῥῆμα: cf. τῆς πίστεως, Rom. x. 8; τὸ εὐαγγελισθέν, 1 Pt. i. 25. For the Christian teaching or for the gospel Paul uses ὁ λόγος, ὁ λόγος τοῦ θεοῦ, ὁ λόγος τοῦ κυρίου.[12] Accordingly the old Greek expositors, followed by most Catholic scholars in recent times, think in terms of the baptismal formula. This gives a good sense, but the lack of the article suggests that the author wanted to say quite generally, 'Water alone is not effective; the cleansing and sanctifying power proceed from the word' (cf. Jn. vi. 63). Grammatically ἐν ῥήματι is best linked with τῷ λουτρῷ τοῦ ὕδατος; the expression then denotes the accompanying circumstance, the fashion and the manner in which the bath of water becomes effective.[13]

It is incorrect to postulate[14] that the baptism of death is in view here in the same manner as it is in Rom. vi. The surrender of Christ to death (*v.* 25) is the presupposition for the cleansing and sanctification which the Church experiences; but the bath itself has the meaning of washing clean. Similarly the pictorial character of our passage has nothing to do with regeneration,[15] the raising to a new or 'higher' life.

[11] Pl. 26, 532. D: *Sanctificet verbo doctrinae.*
[12] Cf. G. Kittel *ThW* IV. 115–7.
[13] Cf. Blass-Debr. par. 219. 4; Schlier ad loc.
[14] Cf. Dibelius, Haupt ad loc.
[15] Meinertz ad loc refers to Tit. iii. 5.

What is new and unusual is the idea that the Church as a whole has received this bath. In Eph. iv. 4 the author views baptism as a means of securing the Church's unity (cf. I. Cor xii. 13). The entire Church has received *one* baptism; following on the sacrificial death of Jesus, and based upon it, this indicates the deep concern of the Lord for his Church. In Eph. v. 26 baptism gains a more profound significance: it is not only a lustration but a spring of divine glory, not a mere means that lies to hand but the work of Christ himself.

But where is the source for considering baptism as a bath? A whole series of N.T. texts points to the primitive Apostolic proclamation of the gospel. In his sermon at Pentecost Peter emphasizes in general terms the necessity of baptism 'for the forgiveness of sins' (Acts. ii. 38), and Acts xxii. 16 throws into relief the idea that lies behind it: forgiveness of sins ensues from the means of washing employed, which, although applied to the body, effects the cleansing of the inner man. We cannot know all the elements of the instruction that Philip gave the Ethiopian eunuch; but that it included the necessity of water baptism is to be deduced from the spontaneous cry of the catechumen: 'See, there is water! What hinders me from being baptized?' (Acts viii. 36).

On the other hand the washing away of sins does not represent the whole significance of becoming a Christian. The reception of the Spirit must also be included, as Acts ii. 38 shows. This, together with the administration of baptism 'in the name of the Lord Jesus' (Acts viii. 16, x. 48, xix. 5), essentially distinguishes the Christian initiation rite from Jewish proselyte baptism, which incidentally was also closely linked with circumcision.[16] At proselyte baptism many of the commands of the Tora were again read out to the baptized,[17] and from this time on they were to form the essence of his mode of life, his obligations and expectations. Christian baptism had a different point of emphasis. What the fulfilment of the Mosaic and Rabbinic prescriptions was to the Jews, that faith in his Lord is to the Christian candidate for baptism. Moreover the Holy Spirit is bestowed on him as the divine 'gift', and for him

[16] bJebamoth 46 a/b (Goldschmidt, Kl. Ausg. IV. 469ff) and 47b (Goldschmidt 474), Gerim I, 6 (Polster in *Angelos* 2 (1926), 5). Cf. the exposition of Polster, op. cit. 23f; further J. Thomas, *Le Mouvement Baptiste* 356–76. Thomas contends that proselyte baptism did not arise till the end of the 1st century A.D. J. Jeremias on the other hand has adduced weighty grounds for a pre-Christian origin of proselyte baptism, see 'Proselytentaufe und Neues Testament', *ThZ* 5 (1949), 233–46; *Die Kindertaufe in den ersten vier Jahrhunderten*, 23–34. He strongly stresses the contacts between primitive Christian baptism and proselyte baptism, op. cit. 34–44. See further Marsh, op. cit. 10–13; Flemington, op. cit. 3–11; T. F. Torrance, 'Proselyte Baptism', *NTS* I (1954–5), 150–4; T. M. Taylor, 'The Beginnings of Jewish Proselyte Baptism', *NTS* 2 (1955–6), 193–8.

[17] bJebamoth 47a (Goldschmidt IV, 473) and 47b (Goldschmidt IV, 474); Gerim I, 3–4 (Polster 3 and exposition 21–23).

it is the assurance of his new life and deliverance. We may observe here a mark of connection between Paul and the primitive Apostolic preaching of salvation, for in his teaching these two other characteristics are also found linked with baptism: its administration in the name of Jesus (1 Cor. i. 13) and the working of the Spirit (1 Cor. vi. 11, xii. 13).

The Christian bath of cleansing stands both in contact and in contrast with the baptism of John.[18] The washing away of sins indicates an area of common significance. The baptism of John also was a βάπτισμα μετανοίας (Acts xix. 4); whether this expression connotes a purely symbolic or a sacramental-realistic interpretation, whether thus the Johannine circle believed in a cleansing of the heart through repentance alone or also through the rite of baptism can no longer certainly be ascertained.[19] Over against the baptism of John the distinguishing mark of Christian baptism is its administration εἰς τὸ ὄνομα τοῦ κυρίου Ἰησοῦ (Acts xix. 5) and the reception of the Spirit attaching to it, a feature which John himself, the preacher of repentance, had excluded from his baptism (Mk. i. 8 par, Jn. i. 33).

The idea of cleansing in baptism also forms a bridge to ancient and widespread views of baptism in heathenism.[20] Since however Judaism with its many washings and bathings proffers the best illustrative material for instruction, there is no need to have recourse to pagan Hellenistic and syncretistic sources. And yet Judaism was hardly the immediate occasion for the baptismal practice of the primitive Church, for the Christian sacrament was distinct from all Jewish baptisms.

Heb. vi. 2 βαπτισμῶν διδαχή cannot denote simply the teaching about Christian baptism, which was only one and was administered but once; moreover everywhere else in the N.T. it is designated by βάπτισμα. Βαπτισμοί in Mk. vii. 4, 8 are the ritual washings which the law prescribed for Levitical uncleanness, and Heb. ix. 10 speaks in the same sense of 'various washings'. The expression in

[18] A. Oepke in *ThW* I, 535, 4–6 roots the baptism of John in proselyte baptism. J. Coppens. Art. 'Baptême' in *DB* Suppl. I, col. 893f, considers that to be possible, J. Thomas, op. cit., 373f, opposes it. See further the exhaustive discussion in Marsh, op. cit. 15–82; C. H. Kraeling, *John the Baptist*, New York—London 1951, 95–122. On the relation of John's baptism to the Essene immersions, cf. J. Gnilka, 'Die essenischen Tauchbäder und die Johannestaufe', *Revue de Qumran* 3 (1961).

[19] J. Coppens ascribes to it only a symbolic value for the conviction of repentance, op. cit. col. 894; J. Gewiess judges of the matter less certainly, op. cit. 125. A. Oepke contends more decisively for the realistic sacramental interpretation, *ThW* I, 535, 29–31. Both Marsh, op. cit. 39–44, and Kraeling, op. cit. 120–2, oppose the sacramental view of John's baptism.

[20] Tertullian already knew that, *De bapt.* 5, but he made a sharp separation between them. Leipoldt presumes a strong heathen influence on primitive Christian baptism, *Die urchristlichen Taufe*, 38–59. J. Coppens opposes it, op. cit. cols. 903–7 and (on 1 Cor. vi. 11) 915, sub 4; further J. Thomas, op. cit. 288–339. Cf. also E. Fascher in PRE 2. Reihe, IV (Stuttgart 1932), col. 2512, 10–28.

Heb. vi. 2 cannot signify anything other than that the instruction of catechumens included teaching on the difference between Christian baptism and these purely ritual rinsings and bathings. The Christian bath of water washed away the stain of sin; it gained such power through the bloody sacrificial death of Christ on the cross (cf. Tit. ii. 14; Heb. ix. 14; 1 Pt. i. 18). Thus Christian baptism preserves its own independent significance.

The assurance with which the primitive Church from the beginning developed its teaching on baptism makes a special commission of Christ in the sense of Mt. xxviii. 19 necessary. We must therefore seek in Christ himself the real roots of the basic views of the primitive Church on baptism.

The manner in which the idea of cleansing was further developed in the Church is illustrated by 1 Pt. iii. 21; Christian baptism does not cleanse physical dirt but rather creates a good conscience; it is the great means of deliverance and so a type contrasting with the destructive waters of the Flood. In later times reflection on the element of the water increased and the content of the symbol was correspondingly filled out. This is particularly marked in Tertullian's writing, *De baptismo*. In his day the exorcisms played a great role. Nevertheless there is not a shred of evidence in the N.T. for the belief that cleansing from sin was a deduction from the expulsion of demons performed by means of the water of baptism.[21] The conception remains bound to that of a simple washing away; the cleansing power of the water, not its exorcistic effects, is still the dominant point of view in the later time.[22]

Thus Paul's concept of cleansing belongs to the broad stream of the primitive Christian tradition. Within it, however, the Apostle maintains his freedom to mould it according to his convictions.

[21] W. Heitmüller, *Im Namen Jesu* 280, cf. 307f; *Taufe* II, 9. When Heitmüller maintains that in the eyes of the post-apostolic time sin is a kind of spirit-possession (307), he does so in accordance with his mode of interpreting the text in the most material-magical way possible. Cf. also Bultmann, *Theol.* 126 and 137. Undoubtedly this early period gave more place to the influence of demons, cf. F. J. Dölger, *Der Exorcismus im altchristl. Taufritual*, Paderborn 1909, 25–38. But if sin and spirit-possession were believed to be connected, that does not mean they were identical. Hence the exhortation to flee from evil works *in order that* the devil might not be able to creep in, cf. Barn. 2. 10; 4. 10; *Hermas*, m. V, i, 2–4; XII, 5. 4. Sin itself was reckoned as 'lawlessness' (ἀνομία), cf. Barn. 4. 1; 10. 4, 8; 14. 5 etc.; *Hermas*, *v.* III, 6. 4; m. X, 3, 2; s. VIII, 10, 3; *Did.* 16. 4. Cf. J. Weiss in HRE IV, 409, 27–36: 'Naturally they (the demons) also seduce men to sin (Enoch 69. 4, 6), although this aspect is decidedly secondary to the physical and material harm they do'.

[22] Justin, I *Apol.* 61. 6–8 applies Is. i. 16ff to baptism: λούσασθε, καθαροὶ γίνεσθε κτλ. Tertullian begins his treatise on baptism with the words: Felix sacramentum aquae nostrae, quia ablutis delictis pristinae caecitatis in vitam aeternam liberamur. In ch. 5 also he refers to the cleansing power of the water (Reifferscheid-Wissowa I, 205. 6–9). Cf. further *De pudic.* 16 (Reiff.-Wiss. 252. 30–253. 2) and *De paenit.* 6 (Oehler I, 655. 14–17); Cyprian, De *domin. orat.* 12 (Hartel I, 275. 1–15). Note also Ignatius, *Ephesians* 18. 2: (Ἰησοῦς) ἐβαπτίσθη, ἵνα τῷ πάθει τὸ ὕδωρ καθαρίσῃ. Cf. P. Lundberg, op. cit. 189, n. 1; A. Benoit, op. cit. 59–69.

§2. BAPTISM AS BATH OF REGENERATION

The designation of baptism as a bath (λουτρόν) is found also in Tit. iii. 5, but in a different connection from that in Eph. v. 26. With the addition of παλιγγενεσίας an expression occurs in this Pastoral Epistle[23] that plays a significant role in profane literature and in the piety of the Mysteries.[24] A second expression is adjoined to it in Tit. iii. 5: καὶ ἀνακαινώσεως πνεύματος ἁγίου. Is this intended to supply a closer definition, 'bath of regeneration', or does it denote a second means of consecration alongside baptism? Without doubt it serves solely to characterize the saving event that takes place at 'regeneration', for the primitive Church knew only baptism as a decisive means of deliverance, cf. Acts ii. 38, xvi. 31, 33, Jn. iii. 3–5, 1 Pt. iii. 20f, Mk. xvi. 16. Linguistically παλιγγενεσία and ἀνακαίνωσις belong closely together. To the πάλιν corresponds the ἀνά, and the active form καίνωσις (from καινόω) postulates a creative activity in contrast to διαφθείρειν (cf. 2 Cor. iv. 16), hence it could supply a suitable complement to the idea of a γενεσία. Since the Holy Spirit, however, is bestowed for the *first* time in the bath of baptism, the ἀνά can signify only a transformation (cf. Rom. xii. 2) which the creative Spirit of God himself achieves. In this sense ἀνακαινίζειν τὸ πνεῦμα or τὰ πνεύματα in Hermas, s. VIII 6. 3, IX 14. 3 means 'to give a new spirit'.[25] The expression also occurs in the Jewish missionary writing Joseph and Aseneth,[26] and the idea is not foreign to the Qumran literature.[27] That a special outpouring of the Spirit apart from the bath of regeneration is not contemplated follows from the dependence of both on the one chief verb ἔσωσεν. Accordingly πνεύματος ἁγίου is, as Belser and M. Dibelius ad loc rightly emphasize, a genitive of cause.

The expression παλιγγενεσία is found again in the N.T. in Mt. xix. 28 in an eschatological-cosmic sense, where it signifies the new creation of the world in the future aeon, an idea that has come from Jewish apocalyptic thought.[28] In employing it for the renewal of the redeemed

[23] On the question of the Pauline authorship of the Pastoral Epistles see the introductory works of Meinertz 169–71; Wikenhauser 318–24; W. Michaelis (*Einleitung in das Nt*, Bern 21954) 238–59. Further K. Grayston-G. Herdan, 'The Authorship of the Pastorals in the Light of Statistical Linguistics', *NTS* 6 (1959–60) 1–15.

[24] Cf. Bauer, *Wörterbuch* col. 1201f; further J. Dey, op. cit. 4–32.

[25] Cf. Bauer, *Wörterbuch* col. 110, see under ἀνακαινίζω.

[26] Joseph prays (ch. 8) ἀνακαίνισον αὐτὴν τῷ πνεύματί σου τῷ ἁγίῳ (P. Batiffol, *Studia patristica* 1–2, Paris 1889–90, 49f). He then promises Aseneth (ch. 15): 'Απὸ δὲ τῆς ἡμέρας ταύτης ἀνακαινισθήσῃ κὰι ἀναπλασθήσῃ, καὶ ἀναζωοποιηθήσῃ (Batiffol, 61).

[27] Cf. E. Sjöberg, 'Wiedergeburt und Neuschöpfung im palästinischen Judentum', *StTh* 4 (1950) 44–85, especially 70–74; G. Schneider, Die Idee der Neuschöpfung beim Apostel Paulus und ihr religionsgeschichtlicher Hintergrund, in *Trierer Theol. Zeitschr.* 68 (1959) 257–70.

[28] G. Schürer, *Gesch. der jud. Volkes im Zeitalter Jesu Christi* 4II, 636–8; Bousset-Gressmann, op. cit. 280–2; G. F. Moore, op. cit. 303–5; P. Volz, *Eschatol.* 338–40; E. Sjöberg, op. cit.

individual, Tit. iii. 5 is peculiar; but before analogies in extra-biblical, pagan testimonies are examined we should enquire whether similar conceptions in the field of the N.T. literature illuminate the idea. The classical baptismal passage Jn. iii. 5 likewise employs the image of a begetting, and that a begetting 'from above'; it originates in the divine-transcendent sphere, in contrast to the fleshly-earthly, and its principle is the *Pneuma*. According to 1 Pt. i. 3, God has 'newly begotten us' (ἀναγεννήσας) to a living hope through the resurrection of Jesus from the dead. Christians are ἀναγεγεννημένοι, not from corruptible but from incorruptible seed through the living and abiding word of God (i. 23, cf. Jas. i. 18). Here the idea of 'new begetting' is more strongly influenced by the analogy of natural begetting[29] than it is in Jn. iii. The supernatural agent that functions therein is the Spirit-filled word of God—similarly as in Eph. v. 26, only that in 1 Peter it is not its cleansing but its procreative power that is said to be active. Justin expresses himself in an even less veiled manner in I *Apol.* 61. 10. He adduces the following points of comparison between the 'first begetting' and the ἀναγεννηθῆναι: (i) moist seed and water; (ii) necessary beginning and free choice; (iii) unconscious event and understanding accomplishment; (iv) birth to a life of evil doing and bad habits and remission of sins and a change of mind. It will be observed that the comparison gains in increasing fulness.

Are we justified in regarding a similar view as lying behind the unique expression παλιγγενεσία in Tit. iii. 5? If the ἀνακαίνωσις πνεύματος ἁγίου is explanatory then (i) it has to do with the creation of a new man (καινός) in another (ἀνά) 'begetting', and (ii) an event that is effected by the Holy Spirit (πνεύματος ἁγίου). (iii) This extraordinary event ensues in a bath (λουτρόν). The element of water is brought into view, yet in such a manner that the Holy Spirit appears as the essential element. Thus we find associated the two constitutive elements, water and Spirit, just as in Jn. iii. 5, and the emphasis on the Spirit as in Jn. iii. 6–8. The πάλιν in our expression, however, in distinction to the ἄνωθεν of Jn. iii. 3, demands an unambiguous rendering in a temporal sense: we have to do with a 're-birth'. Through the Spirit this begetting is recognized to be one of a quite new kind, namely a supernatural. The image is not so fully exploited as in 1 Peter or by Justin, but that it has gone far beyond 1 Cor. vi. 11, Eph. v. 26 is only too plain.

Having concluded this exegetical elucidation, supported by the N.T. texts themselves, we may profitably turn to a consideration of the

[29] It is better therefore to speak of 'begetting'. The idea of birth is found only in the *misunderstanding* of Nicodemus, Jn. iii. 4b.

evidence from the religious world in which the Church was set. Whereas it was precisely the concept of 'regeneration' that adherents of the 'religious-historical school' regarded as proof of the nearness of Pauline Christianity to non-Christian Hellenism, there have never lacked voices urging a consideration of the comparable views in Judaism. If the Rabbinical proof-texts for proselyte baptism as a 'new creation' do not offer completely satisfactory parallels, yet we do possess in the Qumran writings (cf. also Joseph and Aseneth) valuable comparative material, for the conception of a (present) 'renewal of spirit' is to be met also in them.

Among the ideas of the Mystery religions concerning regeneration W. Heitmüller urged that two forms be distinguished, one having in view a process of dying and rising, the other the idea of begetting.[30] He subsumes both under the dominant conception of deification. In Tit. iii. 5 only the idea of begetting comes into consideration. If the writer of the Letter had wished to develop ideas of dying and rising with Christ, as in Rom. vi. 1–11, he would have done this more plainly (cf. 2 Tim. ii. 11). The flowing and fading transitions of Mystery thinking are foreign to Paul.

> That various conceptions could be conjoined in water rites has been demonstrated by H. Bonnet in connection with the Egyptian cultus.[31] The rich symbolic significance of water evidently moved the religious power of imagination in ever changing ways. Many old rites could no longer be understood and they received new interpretations. In any case, the thought characteristic of the Mysteries loves a certain fulness and indistinctness. Bonnet considers that originally the images of the gods were washed and from this 'toilet' the conception of cleansing was developed with increasing strength. Next to the image of the god stood the king as representative of the people and of the sacred, revered dead. Inscriptions are to be found like this: 'I cleanse you with life and salvation'.[32] The idea of living water as available to the dead is known. The libation on the grave of a dead man is intended to symbolize that the water penetrates again the shrivelled, dried body of the deceased and brings him to new life.[33] It is even viewed as an effluence from Osiris himself.[34]

[30] *Taufe* II, 23.
[31] 'Die Symbolik der Reinigung im ägyptischen Kult', *Angelos* 1 (1925) 103–21; cf. also F. L. Dölger, 'Nilwasser und Taufwasser' (*AC* 5 (1936), 153–87, esp. 166f.)
[32] Op. cit. 107.
[33] Op. cit. 116.
[34] Op. cit. 118.

The Pauline thought, as indeed the N.T. as a whole, is distinguished by the fact that it is not concerned with constantly fluctuating ideas inspired by the symbolism of the water. Paul holds certain clearly defined teaching, and he links it with symbols and symbolic events when the opportunity offers itself; but with him the didactic content remains the chief thing. In Tit. iii. 5 salvation through the Saviour-God (σωτήρ *v.* 4-ἔσωσεν *v.* 5), and hence the great event through which the world in principle was snatched from ruin, is primary. This deliverance becomes effective for the individual believer in the bath of baptism. If the latter can be considered as a 'living water', the picture is nevertheless not elaborately illuminated nor decked out with fantasy. Rather the theological meaning is immediately brought to view, viz. the transformation wrought by the Holy Spirit. In order to show the effect of this divine principle in its fulness, the next verse describes how God has richly poured out this Spirit upon Christians. The primitive Church, accordingly, is most deeply affected by its experience of receiving the Spirit, i.e. by the reality and not by the symbol. The author of the Letter to Titus in *v.* 6 simply betrays his familiarity with the primitive Apostolic kerygma.

Many sayings which are cited in connection with the Hellenistic idea of regeneration have terminological echoes in the N.T. texts we have mentioned. The famous inscription: *taurobolio criobolioq(ue) in aeternum renatus*[35] reminds us of the conception of eternal life which forms the high point and conclusion of the movement of thought in Tit. iii. 7—but it may be influenced by Christian sources.[36] Moreover the *tauro-* or *criobolion* of the Attis worship was not a water but a blood baptism. In the initiation into the worship of Isis, as Apuleius, so far as the promised silence does not bind him, describes in detail in his *Metamorphoses* XI. 1–30, mention is made both of a bath and a washing through the priest,[37] as also of the effect of regeneration.[38] But the two things do not immediately hang together. The baptism at the beginning of the initiation was a bath of cleansing (*sacerdos ... purissime circumrorans abluit*). The ensuing consecration, wherein the initiate was 'in a certain manner born again', consisted probably of a visionary (or mystic-theatrical) wandering through the realm of the dead, a journey through the 'elements', and the entry into heaven with a view of the

[35] CIL. VI. 510; see in N. Turchi, *Fontes* p. 249 (no. 289).

[36] It dates from the year 376 A.D.; cf. Jacono, op. cit. 385; Dey, op. cit. 73. According to A. Dieterich, *Eine Mithrasliturgie* 163, the *taurobolium* consecration ensued 'mostly at 20 years of age', a repetition of it in any case took place, cf. Dey. op. cit. 74f.

[37] *Metam.* XI. 23 (Turchi 208. 20–24).

[38] *Metam.* XI. 21 (Turchi 207. 3–10).

upper gods.[39] According to Tertullian the reception into the worship of Mithras was also by means of a bath.[40] Nevertheless this also, as in the Isis consecration and in the Mystery cults generally, is to be understood as an introductory bath of cleansing.[41] The baths at the beginning of the Apollinarian and Pelusian games had the same significance, even though Tertullian adds the expression 'regeneration'.[42] The conception of regeneration in the so-called 'Mithras liturgy' culminated in an ecstatic vision of God, for which the *mystes* ascended in a kind of journey to heaven,[43] hence it stands in no relation, at least originally, to baptism, which always remains a bath of water. Philo of Alexandria[44] and the Hermetic mysticism[45] know of no sacramental or mystery rite for the attainment of the 'vision of God' or 'regeneration'. The idea of regeneration in any one of these forms, linked with the bath of baptism, would have introduced something quite new into the Pauline conception of baptism. M. Dibelius, who otherwise admits the influence of the Mystery piety on Paul, justly emphasizes that Tit. iii. 5 knows nothing of ecstasy, and further that regeneration is considered not as a prerogative of certain mystics but as the fundamental experience of all Christians.[46]

In the view of K. Prümm, it is a serious mistake to look on the notion

[39] Cf. M. Dibelius, *Die Isisweihe bei Apuleius* 6, 19–28; Gressmann, *Die orientalischen Religionen* 42f; F. Cumont, *Die orientalischen Religionen* 92 and n. 106 (p. 249f).

[40] *De bapt.* 5 (Reiff.-Wiss. 204, 30f); on the other hand the textual criticism of F. J. Dölger in AC I. 143–59 has been accepted for *Iudis Appollinaribus* et *Eleusiniis* (Reiff.-Wiss. 205. 3); cf. A. Oepke in *ThW* I, 528, n. 6 and Dey, op. cit. 102f.

[41] Cf. F. Cumont, *Die Mysterien des Mithra* 144: 'As with certain Gnostics, the lustration doubtless had different effects in the various stages of consecration, and could, according to occasion, consist of a simple sprinkling with consecrated water or of a real bath, as in the Isis cult'; Dey, op. cit. 101. Concerning the indispensable presupposition of cultic cleansing, cf. Th. Hopfner in PRE XVI 1330f. For the whole question see also Prümm, *RGH* 295–7.

[42] *De bapt.* 5 (Reiff.-Wiss 205. 4). Cf. Dey, op, cit. 103: 'The regeneration will not signify more than this; the freeing from sin can be understood as a renewal'. It did not have to do with consecration.

[43] Cf. especially the conclusion (Dieterich, *Eine Mithrasliturgie* 14f). Dey interprets thus: the regeneration 'consists of this, that his (the mystic's) human and natural power departs from him and instead higher powers are given him. They are powers of the Spirit which make one capable of vision, and whereas the physical power disappears a new birth in the Spirit ensues' (108f).

[44] On this strongly contested problem. cf. esp. W. Völker, *Fortschritt und Vollendung bei Philo v. Alex.* Leipzig 1938, 283ff. Völker provides a survey of the opinions of the scholars. He himself does not regard Philo as an ecstatic but only as a pious man who strives after perfection, and a philosopher who employs to some extent mystic and mystery modes of expression (314). For the opposite viewpoint cf. Bousset-Gressmann, *Rel. d. Judentums* 449ff.

[45] This literature knows a 'birth in the Spirit', attained through ecstasy. Cf. the 13th book of the Corp. Hermet; XIII, 3 (Nock-Festuguière I. 201): (ὁρῶν ...) ἐμαυτὸν ἐξελήλυθα εἰς ἀθάνατον σῶμα· Καί εἰμι νῦν οὐχ ὁ πρίν, ἀλλ' ἐγεννήθην ἐν νῷ; XIII. 13 (Nock-Fest. I. 206): πάτερ, τὸ πᾶν ὁρῶ καὶ ἐμαυτὸν ἐν τῷ νοΐ. Cf. on this A. Wikenhauser, *Christusmystik*, 119–23; Dey, op. cit. 117–25; H. Jonas, *Gnosis und spätantiker Geist* (FRLANT, NF 33), Göttingen 1934, 200–3.

[46] *Handb. z. N.T.* 1931, p. 95 (in the excursus).

of regeneration as the leading element in the Apostle's teaching on redemption and baptism.[47] The singular expression in Tit. iii. 5, without exhausting its significance any further, does not give a right to attribute to Paul a close affinity with the piety of the Mysteries or with philosophic mysticism. At most a terminological dependence may be admitted,[48] but the language of Christian thought immediately appears beside it by way of explanation.[49]

In connection with 2 Cor. v. 17 (cf. Gal. vi. 15) we come upon the expression 'new creature = new man', which is 'taken over from the language of the (Rabbinic) schools'.[50] The heathen proselyte after his baptism is reckoned as a new born child. On that basis certain principles controlling the rights of marriage and the family are derived;[51] but that is not all the consequence of *baptism*. The new creation idea is a comparison to depict the complete break of the proselyte with his former life, but it is not a picture of baptism. No (sacramental) saving effects are ascribed to the latter.[52] The decisive initiation rite for the proselyte was originally circumcision, and the accompanying baptism served to remove the (levitical) uncleanness of the heathen. In the first Christian century the bath did indeed develop from being an accompanying feature to the primary matter,[53] yet without losing its real significance. The rabbinic concept of the 'new creature' remains a kind of theological-juristic fiction which stands in no closer relation to the immersion rite. Nevertheless the Jewish-Rabbinic idea, that the proselyte attains a wholly new existence through his conversion, creates a good foundation for the Pauline view that baptism makes a new man. Paul fills it with a new content.

[47] *Christlicher Glaube und altheidn.* Welt II 276. Cf. the survey of the religious-historical discussion on this question which Prümm offers in the following pages.

[48] The thesis of Dey, op. cit. 157–76, that Paul attained to this expression in the process of his own development of thought, cannot wholly carry conviction and takes too little account of the significance of the term.

[49] In the post-Apostolic period we find the thought of regeneration in Barn. 6. 11–14; 16, 8; Justin, *Apol.* 61. 3, 10, 66. 1; *Dial* 138. 2; and especially in Irenaeus. Cf. A. von Harnack, *Die Terminologie der Wiedergeburt und verwandter Erlebnisse in der ältesten Kirche* (TU 42. 3), Leipzig 1918, 97ff; A. Benoit, op. cit. 40f, 163f. 197–201. In the Greek Fathers the idea became predominant with the penetrating of Greek philosophy through the Alexandrines.

[50] Cf. Billerbeck II, 421–3, III, 519; for 'new birth' through repentance, Moore, *Judaism* I, 533.

[51] bJebamoth 22a; 62a; 97b (Goldschmidt IV, 386, 528, 661).

[52] Cf. V. Jacono, 'La παλιγγενεσία in S. Paolo e nell' ambiente pagano', *Bibl.* 15 (1934), 396f, n. 3; Dey op. cit. 160. Cf. E. Sjöberg in *StTh.* 4 (1950) 50: 'Circumcision and baptism do not in themselves effect the change. They are signs of the conversion and belong indissolubly to it, but they have no sacramental effect'. Contra J. Jeremias, *Die Kindertaufe* 34–44. The decisive factor in the 'renewal', according to the Jewish view, is conversion: cf. Joseph and Aseneth 15: (Gott) ἀνακαινίζει πάντα μετανοήσαντα (Batiffol p. 61).

[53] J. Jeremias, 'Der Ursprung der Johannestaufe', *ZNW* 28 (1929) 313; Billerbeck I, 102–8. Moreover see p. 8, n. 19.

The Qumran texts offer fresh aspects of this question. According to the testimony of the Hodajoth the divine Spirit is bestowed on the one entering the Qumran community, and He imparts to him the true knowledge that comes from God.[54] The worshipper then prays: 'Having received the gift of insight I have known Thee, my God, thanks to the Spirit which Thou hast given to me; and I have received what is trustworthy concerning Thy wonderful mystery, thanks to Thy Holy Spirit' (1 QH XII, 11f; cf. XIII, 18f, XIV, 25). This bestowal of the Spirit results in the entry into the community, for only in it is the true knowledge of God possible. No other occasion can be intended in the statement: 'Thou hast cleansed the perverted spirit from great wickedness, that he may betake himself to the station with the host of the saints' (1 QH III, 21f), or in another place: 'For the sake of Thy glory Thou hast cleansed this man from sin ... that he may be cleansed with the sons of Thy truth and in the lot of the people of Thy saints, to raise out of the dust the "worm of the dead" (,) . . . to be renewed with all that exists' (1 QH XI, 10ff). The thought of cleansing is here linked with the gift of the Spirit (cf. also 1 QH XIV, 11f, XVII, 26). With O. Betz it would seem that in the belief of the Qumran group a threefold gift of the Spirit can be received: one at birth, a further one at the entry into the community and finally an eschatological bestowal (for the last cf. 1 Qs. IV. 20f).[55] The natural provision of the divine Spirit succumbs to the weakness and defilement that are due to the evil of the 'flesh'; but the entry into the band of the 'saints' cleanses from all wickedness and bestows new Holy Spirit; this bestowal of the Spirit will find its perfection at the eschatological outpouring of the Spirit. The same view is found also in the Jewish missionary writing Joseph and Aseneth, which probably originates from the first century B.C.: 'Thou the most high and mighty God, who quickenest the universe and callest out of darkness into light, out of error into truth and out of death into life, bless this virgin, quicken her and renew her through Thy Holy Spirit.'[56]

Admitting the close approximation of Christian teaching to these Jewish ideas, the differences must nevertheless not be overlooked. The gift of the Spirit to the Christian is exclusively bound to baptism. Of a provision of the divine Spirit from birth, or of a defilement of this original Spirit, we hear nothing in the N.T.[57] There is no proof that the

[54] Cf. E. Sjöberg, 'Neuschöpfung in den Toten-Meer-Rollen', in *StTh.* 9 (1955) 131–6.

[55] O. Betz. *NTS* (1956–7) 324f.

[56] Batiffol, p. 49, translation after Riessler, *Altjüdisches Schrifttum* 505f.

[57] O. Betz (*NTS* 3, 324) would understand Tit. iii. 5 in a manner corresponding to the Qumran view as a renewal of the Spirit already present; but that is as good as excluded by *v.* 6.

Qumran community knew an initiatory baptism similar to the Christian one; the frequent ablutions have another significance: they serve the cultic purity and presuppose also adherence to the community and the possession of the Spirit.[58]

Many ideas in Judaism, therefore, lie at hand to aid the Pauline view of baptism as a 'new creation' or 'renewal through Holy Spirit', and the chief root of the concept will have to be sought here; but baptism as παλιγγενεσία is not fully and completely explained thereby. The possibility remains open that through this Hellenistic expression a bridge to the pagan world of thought may be constructed, precisely in the late Epistle to Titus.

[58] O. Betz endeavours to prove a baptism at the reception into the Qumran community, 'Die Proselytentaufe der Qumransekte und die Taufe im NT', *Revue de Qumran* 1 (1958–9) 213–34. Against this see J. Gnilka, op. cit.; the same in *BZ* (NF) 5 (1961) 44–47.

CHAPTER TWO

Baptism as Assignment to Christ and Incorporation in Christ

§3. BAPTISM IN THE NAME OF CHRIST

In contrast to the baptismal conceptions so far considered the expression βαπτίζειν εἰς τὸ ὄνομα τοῦ Χριστοῦ brings the baptized into immediate relation to Christ himself. Admittedly this expression does not occur verbatim, but Paul's denial that the Corinthians were baptized in *his* name is an indirect declaration that they were baptized in Christ's name, and indeed in his alone (1 Cor. i. 13). Since Christology (and the soteriology bound up with it) is the heart of Pauline theology, we can hope to gain a clearer understanding of the Apostle's view of the sacrament along this line. Unfortunately the textual material at our disposition is restricted to the single passage 1 Cor. i. 13, 15; but Paul adduces this mode of expression as something on which the Corinthians require no further explanation. It is therefore not unimportant to establish its meaning, and this passage is well suited for the purpose.

Divisions have broken out in the Corinthian Church. Four groups are named. Their precise characteristics are not significant for us here; we are concerned only with their possible connection with baptism. Each group attaches itself to a particular person and feels that it belongs to him, as the genitives in *v.* 12 show. Paul, Apollos, Cephas and Christ are all in a similar way the heads of the parties, and the slogan of each is (ἕκαστος ὑμῶν λέγει): 'I belong to Paul, etc'. Of course, the adherents of the first three groups do not deny the place of Christ as Mediator of salvation; otherwise Paul would not have spoken simply of σχίσματα (1 Cor. i. 10) but of false teachers, as in Eph. iv. 14 or Col. ii. 8. But he sees in their behaviour a practical disparagement of the unique significance of Christ. 'The really offensive element of the whole business lay in the fact that they made men rivals of Christ, or at least that they were in danger of doing so' (Bachmann on 1 Cor. i. 13). Positively the meaning of the three questions may be paraphrased in the following manner:

i. Christ is undivided and indivisible;

ii. Christ alone died for you and therefore you belong to Christ alone, cf. 1 Cor. iii. 23, vi. 19, 2 Cor. x. 7;

iii. You were baptized in the name of Christ (and in the name of no other).

The first sentence (*v.* 13a) proceeds from the idea that the community as a whole represents 'the Christ' and therefore must not be divided.

Μεμέρισται is not always explained in the same way.[1] Yet the connection with σχίσματα (*v.* 10) justifies those scholars who translate it by 'divided'.[2] By 'Christ' is meant the Body of Christ, since the community as a whole is in view here (cf. the same expression in 1 Cor. xii. 12).[3] The article also is to be observed; the anarthrous Χριστοῦ (*v.* 12) is evidently to be understood as a mere name along with other names (Παύλου κτλ. *v.* 13b); but *v.* 13a denotes the reality of 'the Christ'.

Verse 13b brings another argument. The Apostle adduces the group that calls itself after him. He makes it clear from his own 'party', which in fact he desires to recognize as little as he does the others, that they are ascribing to a human person a significance that belongs to Christ alone. 'Has perchance Paul been crucified for you?' Through the death on the cross Christ bought them for Himself (cf. 1 Cor. vi. 19f).

In *v.* 13c Paul adduces baptism as a third proof. Baptism 'in the name of Christ' makes it impossible for them to feel bound to any other than Christ. The 'name' (Jesus Christ) that was invoked over them[4] denotes the Lord to whom they exclusively belong from the time of their baptism.

Since Heitmüller it has been common to explain the formula εἰς τὸ ὄνομα in the light of its usage in the papyri, where it means 'to the account of'. In commercial life it denoted payment to the

[1] Robertson-Plummer reproduce it as 'divided among' (has been appointed, i.e. given to someone as his separate share), Schlatter as 'distributed', 'as if Christ could be apportioned out' (*Paulus, der Bote Jesu*, 73).

[2] Bachmann, Cornely, J. Weiss, Sickenberger, Allo, Huby and the majority. Cornely rightly refers to Mk. iii. 26.

[3] L. Cerfaux, *La théologie de l'Église suivant S. Paul*, Paris 1942, p. 218, n. 1, followed by Huby (on xii. 12, p. 288, n. 1), thinks that the Pauline formula indicates not that Christians form a mystical 'Christ' but that Christians possess a mystical identity with the personal Christ. That 'the Christ'='the Body of Christ' (cf. 1 Cor. xii. 27) stands in closest connection with the personal Christ is obvious. But how Paul interprets the relation of this ecclesiological 'Body of Christ' to the 'Body of Christ' that died on the cross and was raised is not clear from 1 Cor. xii. Cf. further § 13.

[4] So Heitmüller, *Im Namen Jesu*, 168; Bachmann, Bousset, J. Weiss, Sickenberger ad loc. Other Catholic exegetes hesitate because of the Trinitarian baptismal formula (attested in Mt. xxviii. 19, Did. vii. 1. 3, Justin, I. *Apol.* 61. 3). Thomas Aquinas, like many theologians of early and late scholasticism, admits that the baptismal formula 'in the name of Jesus' was current in the earliest period and that 'ex speciali ordinatione Spiritus Sancti' (in 1 Cor. i. Lect. II. 3, ed Vives. I, 253a).

account of the person whose name was written above it.[5] Yet the formula when linked with βαπτίζειν must surely be derived from the language of the Rabbinic schools as the translation of לְשֵׁם. It indicated to what purpose an ablution took place.[6] The naming of a person had the meaning of attaching the baptized to this person so that the baptized belonged to him. This is confirmed by exegesis; for the consequence and effect of baptism 'in the name' of Christ may be gathered from a consideration of Paul's assertion, 'you belong to Christ' (ὑμεῖς δὲ Χριστοῦ, 1 Cor. iii. 23, the same genitive as in i. 12). In that case a close connection with *v.* 13b results: Christ died for the Corinthians, He acquired them for Himself, and in baptism they are made over to Him.

Thus the formula expresses a binding to Christ, but the nature of the relation is not more closely defined. From other passages it may be gathered that Paul understands the *koinonia* of the baptized with Christ as realistic, spiritual and personal, established through the divine πνεῦμα (cf. Gal. iii. 27, 1 Cor. xii. 13); but there is nothing mystical in the formula itself. 'No mystic ideas whatsoever are bound up with the expression; the juristic interpretation approximates more closely to its intention.'[7]

From the Apostle's affirmation that he baptized nobody in Corinth, apart from a few exceptions, some exegetes draw the conclusion that in Corinth a specially close and mystic bond between the baptizer and the baptized was believed to exist.[8] But Paul himself gives the ground of his satisfaction in *v.* 15: the idea should not gain currency that the Corinthians were baptized in *his* name.[9] By this means he simply strengthens his argument: a man belongs to the one in whose name he is baptized as to his master.

The conclusion, sometimes drawn from *v.* 17a, that Paul esteemed baptism as of small account,[10] is also false. Baptism is the last and not least link in this short chain of proof. In it he sets baptism next to the cross. In his churches all were baptized, and on this fact he built his

[5] Cf. Heitmüller, *Im Namen Jesu*, 102–9; Deissmann, *Licht vom Osten*, 97f; F. Preisigke, *Wörterbuch* II, 185f.

[6] H. Bietenhard in *ThW* V, 274, 21–275, 33; for the ablution 267, 31ff.

[7] H. Bietenhard, op. cit. 274, 38f.

[8] J. Weiss, Bousset, Lietzmann. They compare with this the custom attested for heathen cults, of calling the initiating priest 'Father'.

[9] Verse 15 is an impossible supposition—a pure *Irrealis*. The actual slogans are in *v.* 12. On the linguistic side, how actual objections are adduced, cf. Rom. iii. 8, vi. 1, 1 Cor. vi. 12a, x. 23, etc.

[10] Cf. H. Weinel, *Bibl. Theol.* 251; Bousset, Lietzmann ad loc; to the contrary J. Weiss, Schlatter, H. D. Wendland, J. Héring etc. ad loc.

teaching of the Body of Christ (1 Cor. xii. 13, Gal. iii. 27f), which dominates his theology of the Church. He did not attempt to remove baptism to a distance from his theological construction, as if it were a foreign body, or to push it in a spare room, as it were; rather he was increasingly concerned to make it a corner stone of his Christ-related doctrine of salvation. Next to this soteriological line, which finds its high point in Rom. vi. 1–11, is the ecclesiological, which rates baptism as the basis of the unity of the Christian Church and of all the churches together. This line reaches its summit in Eph. iv. 5, where baptism is counted among the foundational principles of the unity of the Church life: *one* Lord, *one* faith, *one* baptism.

Thus it is seen that the Apostle was well able to insert the current practice of baptism, including the formula 'in' or 'to the name of Jesus', into his theological world of thought.[11] Moreover baptism did not come into rivalry with his doctrine of the saving power of faith; both remained duly ordered to each other, as will be seen later. For him the formula βαπτίζειν εἰς τὸ ὄνομα Χριστοῦ was not the means of expressing the unique and deepest characteristic of baptism, but it did afford a possibility of building it into his Christocentric doctrine of salvation.

§4. THE CONTESTED EXPRESSION βαπτίζειν εἰς Χριστόν

Two interpretations of the expression βαπτίζειν εἰς Χριστόν (Gal. iii. 27, Rom. vi. 3a) stand in irreconcilable opposition. The one allows εἰς to reproduce only an outer relation, like εἰς τὸ ὄνομα, the other holds to the spacial idea, and so obtains a deeper mystical significance. Whereas the majority earlier inclined to the former view, the second has won many adherents in more recent times.[12]

There can be no doubt that the *concluding* statement of Gal iii. 27b, Χριστὸν ἐνεδύσασθε, describes a profound ontological relation to Christ. Does the *first* clause ὅσοι ... εἰς Χριστὸν ἐβαπτίσθητε also signify a mystical 'immersion into Christ'? The fundamental question must be raised at this point: is this mystical-symbolic meaning necessarily given with the linguistic form βαπτίζειν εἰς? If so it must also be postulated for Rom. vi. 3—an important decision for our investigation.

[11] H. J. Holtzmann, *Lehrbuch der ntl. Theologie*, II, 208, considers that there are 'many incongruities' in the Apostle's teaching on baptism, but he admits that he 'mastered the difficulties'.

[12] Chrysostom on Rom. vi. 3: 'What does it mean, "We are baptized into his death"? That we also die as He died; for the cross is baptism. What the cross and the grave were for Christ that baptism is for us' (In Rom. hom. X—Mont. IX, 535 DE). Aquinas also shows reserve: 'In Christo Jesu, id est in quadam conformitate ad Christum Jesum (Gal. iii. 24); in morte ipsius baptisati sumus, id est in similitudinem mortis eius, quasi ipsam mortem Christi in nobis repraesentantes (2 Cor. iv. 10)' (lect. I in Rom. vi, ed. Vives I, 92).

F. Prat affirms that through baptism εἰς Χριστόν the baptized is not alone subjected like a slave to his owner, or a hireling to the employer who hires him, rather he is incorporated in him, immersed in him as in a new element, becomes a part of him, a second 'self'.[13] Many scholars express themselves similarly.[14] They are fond of appealing to the etymological meaning of βαπτίζειν = 'immerse'.[15] They also find support in the local significance, which is still presumed in Mk. i. 9 (εἰς τὸν Ἰορδάνην), cf. Jn. ix. 7.[16]

A. Oepke represents the contrary opinion. He urges, 'Its interpretation in the sense of a mystically interpreted baptismal medium is everywhere and in every respect to be refused'.[17] Others would confirm his view.[18]

That βαπτίζειν, the intensive of βάπτειν, necessarily includes the idea of immersion is not demonstrable. In profane Greek βαπτίζειν has preponderately taken over the transferred sense, 'destroy', and in the passive, 'perish';[19] in the N.T., however, it is mostly[20] applied in the technical sense 'baptize' (72 times), while for 'immerse' βάπτειν appears (Lk. xvi. 24, Jn. xiii. 26, Rev. xix. 13). The basic meaning of the word, accordingly, has already been worn down.

Moreover the local view, according to which εἰς with βαπτίζειν indicates the goal, as with all verbs of movement, must not be made the norm for the entire linguistic use on the basis of Mk. i. 9. Certainly it does have such a secondary implication in the Galatian passage, where βαπτίζειν ἐν also stands; but generally it is weakened. Mk. i. 9 does not serve as a decisive example for the Pauline usage, for there is a contrary example in 1 Cor. x. 2, εἰς τὸν Μωϋσῆν, where the local significance would be an absurdity. Certainly, this passage is to be regarded as a

[13] *Theol. de s. Paul.* II, 265f.

[14] W. Heitmüller, *Im Namen Jesu*, 139, B. Weiss, Jülicher, Sanday-Headlam, Cornely, Gutjahr, Sickenberger, Lagrange, Huby, Gaugler on Rom. vi. 3; Wikenhauser, *Christusmystik* 71f.—H. Weinel, *Bibl. Theol.* 247, draws a sharp line of division between the formula Βαπτίζειν εἰς τὸ ὄνομα and βαπτίζειν εἰς.

[15] Jülicher, Kühl, Lietzmann, Kuss on Rom. 6. 3; Bauer, Wörterbuch col. 262, see under βαπτίζειν 2 bβ.

[16] Prat. *Théol.* II, 552f.

[17] *ThW* I, 537, 24f; cf. the whole section 537, 11–42, further *ThW*, II, 430, 39–42 and Gal-Komm on iii. 27.

[18] Ad. Maier, Zahn, Schlatter, Barrett on Rom. vi. 3; Burton, Schlier on Gal. iii. 27; J. Weiss, *Urchristentum* 499, E. Jacquier on Acts XIX. 3; J. Coppens in *DB*, Suppl. I, 897; J. Thomas, *Le Mouvement Baptiste*, 380, n. 2. Cf. also H. Bietenhard in *ThW v.* 275ff: 'Essentially the formula εἰς τὸ ὄνομα is synonymous with the simple εἰς. One may even ask whether the Hebraism εἰς τὸ ὄνομα here and there was not consciously replaced (by Paul!) by the 'more Greek' simple εἰς.'

[19] Oepke in *ThW* I, 527, 20–528, 6; Flemington, op. cit. 11f.

[20] Mk. x. 38f, Lk. xii. 50. Jesus uses the picture of the baptism of death; Lk. xi. 38, Mk. vii. 4 *v. I*, βαπτίζειν stands for the Jewish bath of cleansing. Otherwise βαπτίζειν relates to the Johannine and Christian baptism.

secondary imitation of the expression βαπτίζειν εἰς Χριστόν; but this procedure would be impossible if βαπτίζειν εἰς Χριστόν necessarily possessed a mystical significance. Besides, in 1 Cor. x. 2 the element in which the Israelites were 'baptized' is expressly named: ἐν τῇ νεφέλῃ καὶ ἐν τῇ θαλάσσῃ.

The 'baptism of Moses' is manifestly a 'sign of adherence to Moses, in order to belong to him as the leader chosen of God' (Huby). This passage, therefore, suggests that the formula βαπτίζειν εἰς should be closely linked with βαπτίζειν εἰς τὸ ὄνομα. Among the many baptisms that existed at that time, baptism is defined by means of the name of the person to whom it sets a man in a particular relationship of belonging.

Along with baptism in the name of Jesus and that of Moses we hear in Acts xix. 3–5 of baptism in the name of John. Paul asks the disciples of Apollos: εἰς τί have you been baptized? They answer: εἰς τὸ 'Ιωάννου βάπτισμα. After instruction from Paul they request to be baptized εἰς τὸ ὄνομα τοῦ κυρίου 'Ιησοῦ. In this place therefore εἰς simply expresses a relation, and in connection with baptism it means the same as εἰς τὸ ὄνομα.

> Undoubtedly εἰς τί or εἰς 'Ιωάννου βάπτισμα is not the same as εἰς τίνα or εἰς 'Ιωάννην; but the disciples of John could not answer in that way, for John did not baptize in his own name. Nevertheless it may be discerned from this manner of speaking how, in the various baptisms, it depended always on εἰς τίνα or εἰς τί or εἰς τὸ ὄνομα τινός they took place. Hence a sharp distinction between βαπτίζειν εἰς and βαπτίζειν εἰς τὸ ὄνομα would be illusory.

Finally we ought to set βαπτίζειν εἰς in parallelism with πιστεύειν εἰς; the latter suggests the direction of faith, but it does not express any mystical movement to Christ.[21] The change from εἰς to εἰς τὸ ὄνομα with πιστεύειν in Jn. iii. 18 is noteworthy. It is impossible that so great a distinction exists between the two as between juristic-real and mystical ways of speaking. The expression ἁμαρτάνειν εἰς Χριστόν (1 Cor. viii. 12) should also be compared.

After this basic clarification we must accord especial attention to Gal. iii. 27 and Rom. vi. 3. According to the Galatian passage the addressees 'put on Christ (as a garment)' in baptism. The meaning of this picture, frequent in the ancient world and a favourite of Paul's,[22] is not

[21] Cf. Blass-Debr., sections 187. 6 and 206; Moulton-Thumb 101–3; Bauer, Wörterbuch col. 1311f, see under πιστεύειν 2 aβ; Oepke in *ThW* II, 430, 19–39; further my dissertation, *Der Glaube im vierten Ev.* (Breslau, 1937), pp. 6–11.

[22] Paul adduces the same picture in Rom. xiii. 14 in the interests of an ethical appeal; in Eph. iv. 22–24, Col. iii. 9f for the stripping off the old and the putting on the new; in Rom. xiii. 12, Eph, vi. 11, 14, 1 Thess. v. 8 of the buckling on the weapons (of light); in Col. ii. 12

to be sought in the idea that the baptized outwardly became like Christ. Equally removed from Paul is the Mystery idea that the *mystes* through initiation became a second Osiris or another Mystery divinity.[23] Such assimilation in symbol to the Mystery god does not do justice to the *Pneuma*-union with Christ, as Paul understands it. Rather there are in the background certain concepts of the heavenly garment with which the elect are clothed. But here the garment represents Christ Himself, in whom the glory of heaven and of the future world is embodied.[24]

Does now ἐνεδύσασθε describe the actual course of baptism under the picture of putting on clothing, and so develop symbolically the event mentioned in ἐβαπτίσθητε, or does it only state the *effect* by means of a picture?

> The aorist appears to tell in favour of the former; but it may merely establish the result of an event; in such case 'it simply alludes to a total happening, as it has taken place, without distinguishing between the various steps in its course (*aor. constativus*)'.[25]

It would be possible to interpret the whole baptismal event as a unity under the image of 'putting on': the baptismal water is like a garment in which the baptized are plunged; it represents Christ as a *Pneuma*-sphere into which they are removed.[26] *All* (πάντες, *v.* 26, ὅσοι *v.* 27a, πάντες, *v.* 28b) are immersed into Christ and become 'a single man in Christ Jesus', without respect to national, social and sexual distinctions. But this exposition arouses misgivings. The imagery would attain its complete effect only under the presupposition that all were immersed *unitedly* into the baptismal water, but that is hardly probable. It is better therefore to adhere to the view that only the *effect* is symbolically described: through baptism 'to Christ' the believers attain so close a union with Christ that they are wholly 'clothed' with Christ and represent new men, for whom the former natural distinctions have

[23] In the worship of Isis the mystes was clothed in the garment of the divinity and gazed on by the people with reverence; Apuleius, *Metam.* XI, 24 (Turchi 209, 16–34). In the cult of Mithras a man was believed to be what his mask represented (animal symbols according to the degree of initiation). Porphyry, *de abstin.* 4. 16: καὶ γὰρ δόγμα πάντων ἐστὶν τῶν πρώτων τὴν μετεμψύχωσιν εἶναι ὃ καὶ ἐμφαίνειν ἐοίκασιν ἐν τοῖς τοῦ Μίθρα μυστηρίοις (Turchi 288, 19–22). Cf. also F. J. Dölger, *Ichthys* I, 115; Babylonian priests appear veiled in a garment like a fish; it symbolized the closest union with the divinity Ea-Oannes, the Babylonian fish god. Cf. the bas-relief of Konjica (reproduced by Dölger p. 117).

[24] Gnostic ideas are compared with this by E. Käsemann, *Leib und Leib Christi*, Tübingen 1933, 87–94; cf. Oepke, Schlier ad loc; Wikenhauser, *Christusmystik*, p. 72, n. 6.

[25] Moulton-Thumb, 177.

[26] So Wikenhauser, *Christusmystik*, p. 72.

---

of putting on various virtues; in 1 Cor. xv. 53f of being clothed in immortality at the resurrection (cf. 2. Cor. v. 2f). For other applications of the picture cf. Steinmann-Tillmann ad loc., W. Straub, *Bildersprache*, 24f.

become meaningless. While they *all* experience this, they form also 'a single man in Christ Jesus'; through Christ and in Christ they have become a new unity. Thus here also the meaning of βαπτίζειν εἰς = 'baptize to', in the sense of the statement of a goal, should be firmly held.[27]

As has already been remarked, an event characteristic of the Mystery religions is not to be considered as in mind. It would be remarkable if Paul twice described the same 'mystery' (baptism) in such different ways (Rom. vi and Gal. iii). And the liturgical exposition afforded by the (white) baptismal robe is first attested at a relatively late date.[28] It is sufficient to explain Paul's mode of expression from the nature of the pictorial language.

If the translation 'immersed into Christ' is not necessary for Gal. iii. 27, neither does it seem rightly alleged for Rom. vi. 3. They that are baptized εἰς Χριστόν are also baptized εἰς τὸν θάνατον αὐτοῦ; a 'being immersed into the death of Christ' is an idea scarcely conceivable pictorially. The 'death of Christ' is nowhere considered in the Pauline writings as a sphere, but always as the *event* that took place on Golgotha. The expression, which is formed on the analogy of βαπτίζειν εἰς Χριστόν, draws a consequence from the fact of our 'baptism to Christ': if we were subjected to Christ and bound to Him, then we are also included in the event of his death and his death has become effective in us. Thus our baptism becomes a 'baptism of death', a being buried with Him (*v.* 4), so that we are fully delivered up to death (εἰς τὸν θάνατον *v.* 4). Christ is not a 'sphere' into which we are plunged, but the personal Christ with all that happened to Him; our baptism 'to Christ' has the goal of uniting us with this Christ and with everything that happened to Him. If the *dying* with Christ is especially emphasized, that is because the Apostle is particularly concerned with our death in respect to the power of sin (*v.* 2—cf. further § 6).

In any case, in the preponderating application of βαπτίζειν with a technical sense, the pictorial interpretation of 'immerse' must be held with reserve and only applied where the context suggests it; that is not the case in Gal. iii. 27 and Rom. vi. 3. In the latter, the point of departure is the linguistically unobjectionable formula εἰς τὸ ὄνομα. It is possible to do justice to the deep theological content of Rom. vi without hearing

[27] Cf. A. Grail in *RB* 58 (1951) 503–20, especially 506f; Schlier ad loc.

[28] The custom is attested in the fourth century; it is expressly reported of Constantine the Great by Eusebius, *Vita Constantini* IV, 62 (Heikel I, 143). The putting on of new garments after baptism is a natural development, but it is not very strongly emphasized according to the liturgical testimonies that are to hand, L. Eisenhofer, *Handbuch der kathol. Liturgik* II, Freiburg 1933, p. 263. That is the more noteworthy, since the garments and wrappings that were worn at initiations into the mystery cults were regarded as particularly holy.

in βαπτίζειν εἰς Χριστόν the overtones of a mystical 'immersion' into the Christ, providing that the statements of the context (cf. especially σύμφυτοι *v.* 5) are rightly weighed.

An important principle of interpretation has now emerged. Any figure that may be present to Paul's mind at any time is to be viewed in the light of the context in which it occurs. The images he employs change, the thing signified remains.

§5. INCORPORATION INTO THE BODY OF CHRIST

In 1 Cor. xii. 13 βαπτίζειν εἰς gains a special significance: we are baptized not only εἰς Χριστόν (that is presupposed), but also 'in a single Spirit εἰς ἓν σῶμα'. The same power and effect of baptism is thus set forth as in Gal. iii. 2f: all former natural distinctions become unimportant, since the baptized attain a new existence in Christ and are brought to a higher unity. While, however, in Gal. iii. 28 it is said that all are 'one person in Christ Jesus', in 1 Cor. xii. 13 the thought of the 'one Body' emerges. Is the corresponding *v.* 12a purely a comparison, so that the baptized become a single Body, a 'Body of Christ' (*v.* 27), which may be considered as an organism similar to the natural body? Or is the 'one Body' a reality that already exists, namely the 'Body *of Christ*' (*v.* 27), and are the baptized incorporated *into* the already existing Body of Christ? Grammatically the question is to be posed thus: Has εἰς here a consecutive meaning, does it denote the result of the event, or is it the local εἰς? Whereas the former used to be generally accepted,[29] more recent investigations concerning the 'Body of Christ' have frequently led to the second view.[30] According to this, the 'Body of Christ' does not first come into existence through baptism, but it exists beforehand and the baptized are received into it. Without embarking in detail upon the difficult and much disputed questions concerning the 'Body of Christ', the latter commends itself on objective theological grounds. From that the consequence appears to follow that βαπτίζειν εἰς here has preserved the meaning of 'immerse into'. On the other hand the idea of 'plunging into' a body is somewhat unusual and is nowhere to be met in the σῶμα-doctrine of the letters to the Colossians and Ephesians. Admittedly, one can come to terms with the local colour of βαπτίζειν εἰς in our passage if allowance is made for the uniqueness of the reality of the 'Body of Christ', which is not conceivable in earthly-spacial

[29] Cf. Lietzmann, Allo, Wikenhauser, (*Kirche* 102f), Schlier (*Christus und die Kirche* 40f), etc. also H. D. Wendland, J. Héring ad loc.

[30] E. Percy, *Der Leib Christi in den paulinischen Homologoumena und Antilegomena*, Lund 1942, 15ff; S. Hanson, *The Unity of the Church in the New Testament*, Uppsala 1946, p. 70; W. G. Kümmel in the appendix to Lietzmann's commentary on the Corinthian Letters (p. 187); E. Schweizer in *ThW* VI, 415, 25ff; I. Hermann, *Kyrios und Pneuma* 79ff.

categories. Yet the possibility remains of construing the εἰς as *final*; εἰς ἓν σῶμα then denotes the goal of the baptismal event. In that case we may interpret the statement: we have all been baptized *for* a single Body, so that we belong to it and have been incorporated into it; through the *one* Spirit we have been inserted into *one* Body, namely the Body of Christ; we are not thereby necessarily bound to the pictorial idea of being 'immersed into' it.[31] This interpretation lies in the same line as the other application of βαπτίζειν εἰς (see above, §4). Whatever may be thought of that, it is not the picture but the thing signified that is of moment, namely the conception of the working of the one Spirit and the perfect unity to which the baptized are called.

The utterance has not been inspired by a common, impressive celebration of baptism.[32] Paul is concerned to hold a mirror before a church that has long been constituted, and especially before the charismatics who disturb its unity. He goes back to baptism because in it the principle of unity is recognizable, namely in the Spirit who is bestowed jointly on all.

It is not unimportant for the interpretation of baptism to determine whether the Spirit is considered as a personal Mediator of unity, or as a common element, or as an effective power. Grammatically ἐν ἑνὶ πνεύματι permits all these interpretations,[33] hence the context must be examined. In *vv.* 4–11 the bestowal of the charismata through the Spirit is described; but according to the triadic statement in *vv.* 4–6 they are regarded as a distribution of various ministries through the one Lord and as an operation of one and the same God Himself. The Spirit appears as a personal Agent (cf. especially *v.* 11 καθὼς βούλεται), and most Catholic scholars therefore think on the personal Spirit of God.[34] According to the recent investigation of I. Hermann, however, the Spirit in this section is looked on as the divine power that goes out from the Lord. 'The working of the Lord ... includes the working of the Spirit; the working of θεός however takes up into itself the working of the *Kyrios* and thereby at the same time also the working ascribed to the Spirit. To put it otherwise: the operation of the *Pneuma* is a part of the operation of the *Kyrios*, as this belongs to the inclusive working of

[31] Cf. Huby ad loc; Cerfaux, op. cit. 219f; M. Barth, op. cit. 332–7.

[32] According to 1 Cor. i. 14, 16 the baptism of individual members of the Church and of families also appears to have taken place in a domestic celebration. There are moreover no traces elsewhere in Paul of any developed, formal baptismal ritual.

[33] For the instrumental ἐν, cf. Blass-Debr. § 195; Robertson 589–91; Abel § 47d; the personal action is also expressed in this way, Blass-Debr. § 219. 1.

[34] H. Bertrams, *Das Wesen des Geistes nach der Anschauung des Apostels Paulus* (*NTlAbh* IV. 4), Münster i. W. 1913; M. Meinertz, *Theologie des NT* II, 79–83; Allo ad loc, and excursus p. 94; Wikenhauser, *Kirche* 91–93 etc.

θεός.'[35] Paul describes the distribution of the charismata, so far as the operation of the πνεῦμα is concerned, by three prepositions which here scarcely admit of distinction: διὰ τοῦ πνευματος 8a, κατὰ τὸ αὐτὸ πνεῦμα 8b, and twice ἐν τῷ πνεύματι in *v*. 9. In *v*. 11 the action of one and the same πνεῦμα is summarized, who distributes to each (the charisma apportioned to him) 'as He will'. The *Pneuma* divides the charismata, not according to the will of the believers, but according to his own will, yet corresponding to the disposition of the *Kyrios*. The Spirit effects the 'distribution of the ministries' as the Lord of his community wills to give them. The *Kyrios* works through the *Pneuma*, and He works in all charismata also, corresponding to the one and the same *Pneuma*.

After these basic statements the Apostle begins his exhortation that those who possess the charismata seek to preserve the unity and communality given through the working of the Spirit of the Lord. He does that, however, not in the form of imperatives, but through the illustrative description of a body which has many members yet which is but one (*v*. 12). By means of this picture the Corinthians should recognize how they ought to conduct themselves. But before Paul extends this comparison in all its breadth (*vv*. 14–26) he wishes to show that it is applicable to the entire community. Verse 13 adduces the basis for it (γάρ): all the baptized have been incorporated through the one Spirit into a single Body, the Body of Christ. If the above exposition is right, that the 'Body of Christ' exists beforehand, Paul oversteps the comparison in *v*. 13, in that he proceeds from the picture to the reality. For the 'Body of Christ' the activity of the *Pneuma* is of essential significance. In *v*. 13a ἐν ἑνὶ πνεύματι and εἷς ἓν σῶμα obviously correspond to each other.

In baptism the Spirit adds new members to the Body and so builds it up; He is the life-principle for the Body, and at the same time—since He himself is but one and builds up one Body—He is the principle of unity. The relation of the *Pneuma* to Christ, whose Body He animates, is not made plain in this passage, but from other statements it can be seen that the *Pneuma* proceeds from the risen Lord (cf. 1 Cor. xv. 45, 2 Cor. iii. 17), who thus continues his work through the Spirit and through Him creates his own Body, the Church.[36] The Spirit stands in closest connection with Christ and carries on his work; the idea of 'divine power' corresponds better than that of an independent personality,[37] although the trinitarian concept is thereby not excluded.

[35] I. Hermann, *Kyrios und Pneuma* 75.
[36] Wikenhauser, *Kirche* 114–21; Hermann, op. cit. 140–5.
[37] Cf. the discussion with Bertrams (op. cit.) in Hermann, op. cit. 132–9.

From this it follows that πνεῦμα is not a 'sphere' or a (symbolically conceived) 'element',[38] into which the baptized is 'immersed', rather He is the power that builds up and quickens the Body of Christ. In that all the baptized receive the divine power that flows through all, they all become one 'body' through this power (ἐν instrumental).[39]

The idea of the penetration of the baptized with the divine *Pneuma* throws light on another baptismal text. The unity of the baptized with Christ, Gal. iii. 27f, is comprehensible only on the basis that Christ Himself is *Pneuma* (2 Cor. iii. 17) and the baptized 'put on' this *Pneuma*-Christ. From this point of view the Christ κατὰ σάρκα is absolutely without significance (2 Cor. v. 16). In 1 Cor. vi. 11 also ἐν τῷ πνεύματι could be similarly understood: the process of justification and sanctification result from the life-creating power of the Spirit that proceeds from the risen Lord and that takes hold of and fills the baptized. The passage is similarly 'triadic' as 1 Cor. xii. 4–6, 2 Cor. xiii. 13, but not formally trinitarian.[40] The Pauline utterances offer a basis for the later doctrine of the Trinity but they are conceived in other categories—those of the *Heilsgeschichte*.

[38] So since Deissmann not a few exegetes, e.g. J. Weiss, Robertson-Plummer, Lietzmann. Cf. further Wikenhauser, *Christusmystik*, 26–37; E. Schweizer in *ThW* VI, 415–7.

[39] For the second expression ἓν πνεῦμα ἐποτίσθημεν see below § 13.

[40] Cf. I. Hermann, op. cit. 111.

CHAPTER THREE

Baptism as Salvation-Event

σὺν Χριστῷ

We saw that Paul took over some of his views on baptism from the primitive Church, especially the conception of cleansing from sins, appropriation for the Lord Jesus Christ and imparting of the Spirit. His own theological penetration of the dogmatic content of baptism led him to put the conception of the baptized man's belonging to Christ on a deeper foundation. That close, essential and experiential unity with Christ, which became a basic theme of his theology and a principal feature of his piety, was viewed by him as an effect of baptism. At the same time baptism became significant for his theology of the Church, because this experience of salvation made visible the unity of all in Christ and formed the foundation for the symbol of the 'Body of Christ'.

Despite all that, however, it is possible to look upon baptism in a purely external fashion, as a mere means or point of departure. The question must be faced, therefore, whether Paul also viewed its administration as significant, as something inwardly bound up with the salvation-event. Such a theological interpretation of the baptismal event, a marriage of the existing rite with the weighty thought of his theology, the Apostle did, in fact, undertake in several important passages of his letters. In them the basic idea appears that a saving event, closely bound up with Christ, is enacted in baptism. The Apostle coined a concise and characteristic formula: 'baptism is a dying and rising σὺν Χριστῷ'. It is from this point of view that we shall approach the heart of his baptismal theology. In order to grasp the Apostle's train of thought clearly we must embark on a careful investigation of the text.

Section 1. THE LOCUS CLASSICUS, Rom. vi. 1–11

§6. AN EXPOSITION OF THE MAIN ARGUMENT

In Rom. iii. 21ff Paul had set forth his fundamental theses concerning the way of deliverance for sin-laden humanity, deprived of the glory of God (*v.* 23): apart from the law and only through faith, all, alike Jews and Gentiles, are graciously justified by God on the basis of the bloody atoning death of Jesus. The Apostle had then illustrated the saving significance of faith in the person of Abraham and described the physical progenitor of the Jewish people as the 'father of us all', including the Gentiles (iv. 16f); he then celebrated him as the prototype of all those who are justified through faith (ch. 4). Although the fact of God's gracious blessing and deliverance, and the way thereto, has been clearly expounded (δικαιωθέντες οὖν v. 1), the Apostle manifestly wanted to go on and expound the glorious effects of this act of God (εἰρήνην ἔχομεν v. 1); but he cannot finally do this till he reaches ch. 8. On his way to it he touches many other themes, in his vivid way of putting things, with an overpowering fulness of thought; they are all very important for his total construction, and they bestow on his exposition in ch. 8 a real clarity, assurance and penetrating power.

First the Apostle reflects on the fact that full salvation, the δόξα τοῦ θεοῦ (v. 2), did not arrive with the basic deliverance; we are still ἐν ταῖς θλίψεσιν (v. 3). But the full glory is even now grasped in ἔλπις, which is placed on a sure foundation through the divine saving deeds that have already taken place (v. 1, 11).

Under the impress of the unique and towering form of the Mediator, the κύριος Ἰησοῦς, 'through whom we have now received the reconciliation', Paul directs his attention to the whole religious history of mankind; in it Adam and Christ appear alongside each other as the two Founders of the race (Adam is the τύπος of the 'future', second Adam, v. 14) and at the same time they stand over against each other as the great Antagonists in the drama of ruin and redemption (v. 12–21). By this means the certainty (πολλῷ μᾶλλον *v.* 17), fulness (περισσεία *v.* 17) and cosmic universal validity (εἰς πάντας ἀνθρώπους *v.* 18) of the salvation won by Christ is made plain. The powerful spectacle, wherein Paul struggles for an adequate expression of his thronging thoughts and continually makes new beginnings, leads to the assertion: where sin gained strength and fulness, the grace of God became yet richer and mightier (ὑπερεπερίσσευσεν *v.* 20).

This statement, so decisive for theodicy and the story of salvation, can be misunderstood if it is applied to personal ethics in a perverted manner: 'Let us therefore persist in sin, that grace may increase in fulness!' That is the point of departure for ch. 6.[1] The detailed arguments of our section (*vv.* 1–11 or 14) are devoted to settling this inference from Paul's theology;[2] even if it was not drawn by those to whom

[1] Some older expositors (Bisping, B. Weiss) and more recent ones (Kühl and Gutjahr) begin a new section with ch. 6. Jülicher rightly opposes that view, (p. 263).

[2] That the frequent objections (iii. 1, 3, 5, 9, 31 etc.) are not merely stylistic is shown by iii. 8, cf. Zahn, Jülicher, Lietzmann, Lagrange on vi. 1, although Cornely and Sanday-Headlam consider that the actual objections are hardly conceivable in this form.

the Letter was addressed, it undoubtedly was drawn by some. Another false deduction (*v.* 15) occupies him in the further course of the chapter.

From this it is clear that the section vi. 1–14 is motivated by an ethical-parenetic point of view, and this must be carefully observed when interpreting Paul's representations about baptism. The Christ-related baptismal teaching Paul is able to take for granted (ἢ ἀγνοεῖτε *v.* 3; πιστεύομεν *v.* 8; εἰδότες *v.* 9), but in the central passage (*vv.* 4–6) he manifestly offers his own views. His dogmatic theological conceptions are swallowed up in ethics; this ethical tendency breaks out at appropriate points (περιπατήσωμεν *v.* 4) and it even forms the culmination of his exposition (λογίζεσθε κτλ *v.* 11). In *vv.* 12–14 he draws some practical consequences (οὖν *v.* 12), but for our investigation of his baptismal thought they may be disregarded.

To try to introduce a further subdivision into the section vi. 1–11[3] would be difficult. The Apostle strives again and again to make clear his ruling fundamental thought, which finds at length a decisive expression in *v.* 11. Therein the relation of the passage to v. 12–21 becomes plain. This endeavour after an adequate literary clothing ought not to be characterized as an 'unclear progress of thought', and as little can one detect 'a certain embarrassment' caused through the descent from the lofty height of v. 12–21, where a shifting of values or interposition between 'formerly' and 'now' are unknown, to the inadequate realization of the new order in the ordinary Christian life.[4] The rapid transition from categorical dogmatic utterances to moral imperatives is everywhere manifest in Paul.[5]

Verse 1 clearly attaches to v. 20: 'What sort of conclusion then are we to draw?[6] Let us persist in sin that there may be all the more grace?' Verses 2–4 are devoted to an immediate refutation of this false deduction. Paul seeks to weaken the objection through the insistence: we *died* to sin (*v.* 2), we are *dead* for it (*v.* 11), and therefore have nothing more to do with it. The chief emphasis in these verses, relating to this dying and being dead, falls on the words:

v. 2. ἀπεθάνομεν τῇ ἁμαρτίᾳ,
v. 3. εἰς τὸν θάνατον αὐτοῦ ἐβαπτίσθημεν,
v. 4a συνετάφημεν ... εἰς τὸν θάνατον.

[3] Sickenberger: *vv.* 1–7 dying with Christ in baptism, *vv.* 8–14 living with Christ free from sin. Lagrange sees in the three verbs ἀγνοεῖτε *v.* 3, γινώσκοντες *v.* 6, λογίζεσθε *v.* 11 three steps (p. 143), but that is quite artificial.

[4] Jülicher, p. 264.

[5] Cf. Rom. vi. 12 with 14; 8, 9, 11 with 12–14; 1 Cor. vi. 9 with 11; 2 Cor. v. 18f with 20; Col. iii. 1a with 1b; Gal. v. 25a with b; cf. the excursus of P. Althaus (*NTD*) 53–55.

[6] As iii. 5; iv. 1; vii. 7; ix. 14.

Verse 4b carries the progress of thought a stage further, in that it takes up the ζήσομεν of *v.* 2 and sets the 'newness of life' (*v.* 4c) over against this 'life of sin', which really is no life at all (hence it negatives the question).

Verse 2: 'All we who died to sin, how can we possibly live in it any longer?' (That is indeed impossible!). 'The dative (*dat. incommodi*) denotes the person, thing or power to whose detriment and loss the death has happened, and in such contexts it is peculiar to Paul.'[7] The second half of the sentence does not merely bring the reverse, but through ἐν αὐτῇ it interprets the sphere of power as that of sin, from which we have escaped. Hence a question is raised that itself involves a conclusion (ζήσομεν).[8]

The Apostle has in mind here the steps in the argument offered in the succeeding verses; he means therefore the 'death' in baptism. He immediately explains himself more plainly to his readers through the attached question; its form indicates that he is alluding to something known to his readers, or that ought to be known to them.[9]

Verse 3: 'Or do you not know (You surely do know!) that all we who were baptized to Christ Jesus were baptized to His *death*?'

On βαπτίζειν εἰς see above, § 4.

The reason for the Apostle's bringing baptism into relation with the death of Jesus in this context seems to be that he is already thinking about the symbolism of the bath of baptism as he expounds it in the following verse. That would suggest the inference that this symbolism must already be known to his readers. A deliberate over-estimation of those addressed can as little be excluded as in vii. 1. There is no evidence to show that the interpretation of baptism in terms of a dying (and rising) with Christ, as expounded by Paul, was already current in the Church. The later witnesses to the view manifestly go back to this very passage of Rom. vi. The possibility remains, then, that the baptismal instruction in the primitive Church set the first sacrament in relation to the death of Jesus in a general way only (cf. 1 Cor. xv. 3),[10] while Paul, grasping more deeply the symbolism and significance of the bath

[7] Cf. Blass-Debr. § 188, Radermacher, p. 128; Moulton-Thumb calls it the dative of 'the interested person', p. 155, Cf. further Zahn. p. 294, n. 80.

[8] The future certainly does not compel the view that it is not a deliberative question, cf. Blass-Debr. § 366, 2.

[9] Ad. Maier rightly observes (p. 199) that in distinction from this formula the other οὐ θέλω ὑμᾶς ἀγνοεῖν 'introduces something new, notable or remarkable (cf. xi. 25, 1 Cor. x. 1, xii. 1 etc.).'

[10] Gewiess (op. cit. 75ff) denies a preaching of an atoning death for our sins in Acts, but he reminds us (79f) of 1 Cor. xv. 3 and Jesus' own interpretation of His death as proof that this conception was not foreign to the primitive Church. For Paul cf. also 1 Th. v. 10. Heb. vi. 1–2 does not permit any inference in this respect with regard to the primitive Apostolic teaching on baptism. Even Justin 1 *Apol.* 61. 13 (Goodspeed 71. 8), when expounding the Trinitarian baptismal formula, conjoins with the name of Jesus Christ τοῦ σταυρωθέντος ἐπὶ

of baptism, gave his own interpretation of it in *v*. 4. That is decidedly the more probable view. It would appear that behind *vv*. 3–4 stands the early kerygma, taken over by Paul, that Christ died for our sins, was *buried* and was raised (1 Cor. xv. 3f). Into this saving event that once happened to Christ we are drawn through baptism.

In any case the Apostle assumes the relation of baptism to the death of Jesus as something already known, and in what follows he does not wish to prove it, but only to illustrate it (not γάρ but οὖν *v*. 4).[11]

Verse 4: 'We were therefore buried with Him through baptism in the direction of His death ... ', i.e. so that we thus actually attained to 'death' (for sin).

> Among the exegetes uncertainty and disunity prevails as to whether εἰς τὸν θάνατον should be linked with the verb or with βαπτίσματος. The majority (A. Maier, Cornely, Gutjahr, Bardenhewer, Sickenberger, B. Weiss, Jülicher, Lietzmann, Dodd, etc.) favour the latter. Grammatically this is possible in the *Koine*, even without repetition of the article.[12] Zahn unhesitatingly attaches it to the verb, especially because of the lack of αὐτοῦ. O. Michel and O. Kuss follow suit, but Lagrange and Sanday-Headlam hesitate in their decision.
>
> The fine distinction between *v*. 3 εἰς τὸν θάνατον αὐτοῦ and *v*. 4 without this genitive should not go unobserved. Baptism immediately suggests the thought of the death of Jesus, and on this account we find the συνετάφημεν emphasized. The expression '*buried* with' expresses more clearly the complete succumbing to death. 'The event of dying, of departure from this world, was first really concluded by burial'; in the thought of the ancients, a dead man went fully into the realm of the dead only at this point.[13] At the same time, however, Paul will have also thought of the rite of immersion, in which the baptized person disappeared beneath the surface of the water as into a grave.[14] The conceptual difficulty, that death

[11] οὖν in the sense of confirmation.

[12] Radermacher p. 117, Robertson p. 74, Moulton-Thumb, p. 133; Blass-Debr. § 272 regard our passage as the single example of this order.

[13] E. Stommel, '"Begraben mit Christus" (Röm. vi. 4) und der Taufritus,' *Römische Quartalschrift* 49 (1954) pp. 1–20, here p. 7.

[14] The view supported by E. Stommel (op. cit.), that the moderate depth of the *early* Christian baptisteries shows that *primitive* Christian baptism was not administered by a complete immersion, is hardly to be maintained in view of the Jewish practice in proselyte baptism. The first testimony for baptism by infusion is Did. 7. 3.

Ποντίου Πιλάτου. When in the Apost. Constit. V, 7, 30; VI, 23, 5; VII, 43, 5 baptism 'to the death of Jesus' is attributed to the commission of Christ Himself, this commission of the divine Founder is rather a deduction from the passage in Romans. The tendency to support the once-for-allness of baptism through linking it with the once-for-all death of Jesus may be observed in VI, 15, 2.

precedes burial, has already been met by Thomas Aquinas when he writes, 'Physically a man dies first and is buried afterwards, but spiritually the grave of baptism produces the death of the sin' (*mortem peccati*, the dative would be more correct).[15]

The 'being buried with' Christ presupposes a Pauline view of baptism that must later be carefully investigated (cf. Part 2, chapter II). The σύν-sayings emerge here in immediate connection with baptism 'to Christ' and 'to His death'. Behind them stands the conception that baptism brings us into closest relation to Christ and to His dying, however the idea may be expounded. We shall at this juncture follow further Paul's train of thought.

'We were buried therefore with Him through baptism, so that we are *dead*'—in Paul that at once calls for the counterpart of *life*. For him death is never the last thing in the saving event. In accordance with the precedent of Christ the movement demands a continuation:

'In order that, as Christ rose from the dead through the Father's fulness of might,[16] we also should walk in a new life.' Καινότητι and ζωῆς each carries for itself a particular tone: καινότητι in distinction from the life in sin alluded to in *v.* 2, ζωῆς in opposition to θάνατον in *v.* 4a.

The expression περιπατεῖν, also attested elsewhere of moral behaviour, betrays the practical tendency of the Apostle, but it also presupposes in a realistic manner the 'possession of life'. To raise the question 'ontological *or* ethical' is out of place, since Paul applies all the emphasis on the opposition 'death or life'. For him being and ought belong together in the sense, 'Become what you are!' or, 'Unfold what you possess!'

The argument proceeds from Paul's ruling conception of the death and resurrection of Christ.[17] For Paul the guarantee that the baptized man rises from death to life does not reside in the fact that after immersion he emerges again from the water, but it is in the sacramental fulfilment with Christ of the historical death and resurrection of Christ. *From now on the two-sided view of death-life, dying-rising, dominates the train of thought.*

[15] Lect. 1 in Rom. vi (ed. Vivès I, 962).

[16] Cf. Col. ii. 12 τῆς ἐνεργείας τοῦ θεοῦ; if Paul in Rom. vi. 4 writes δόξης, it is not to be rectified through textual criticism (A. Pallis, *To the Romans*, Liverpool 1920, would read διὰ τῆς δεξιᾶς τοῦ πατρός) but the nuance should be kept: δόξα = majesty; cf. H. Kittel, *Die Herrlichkeit Gottes* (Beihefte z. *ZNW* 16), Giessen 1934, pp. 216f; Bauer, *Wörterbuch* col. 403, see under 1a; G. Kittel in *ThW* II, 251, 3–9. Πατρός, because the Father appoints the Son in power through the resurrection, cf. Rom. i. 4.

[17] Cf. W. Schauf, *Sarx* (NtlAbh II, 1–2), Münster 1924, pp. 43ff; P. Feine, *Ntl. Theologie* 191–4; P. Amiot, op. cit. I, 278–81.

The death and resurrection of *Christ* as the preceding event determines that which we experience in baptism. In ὥσπερ-οὕτως καί lies a comparison which, on account of the peculiar relation of Christ to the person attached to Him in baptism, also becomes a proof: corresponding to the fact that Christ did not remain in death, but was raised from the dead, we also should walk in a new life.[18]

The γάρ *v.* 5, introduces the proof that 'life' follows 'death'. The emphasis therefore rests on 'life' or 'resurrection'. This twofold progression that Christ first experienced is now applied to 'us', i.e. who believe and are baptized. In *v.* 4 the walk in a new life was the purpose and goal of 'being buried with' Christ, which was disclosed in the same event that Christ suffered (ὥσπερ-οὕτως καί). The Apostle now desires to put this on a firmer foundation, in that he seizes again on the συνε-τάφημεν and declares our *inner connection* with Christ's dying and rising (with emphasis on the rising); he thereby excludes a merely external co-ordination of the event in Christ and Christians. Hence the expression 'σύμφυτοι' (from συμ-φύω), which emphasizes the close unity.

Verse 5: 'For if we have become men united with the form of His death, so shall we also be with (that of) the resurrection.'

> The translation must be justified in the following paragraphs; here we would simply say: In contrast to the procedure adopted in the first edition of this book we connect σύμφυτοι immediately with τῷ ὁμοιώματι and therefore do not fill it out with an αὐτῷ (as in *v.*4). The second half of the verse is a compressed mode of expression for, 'So shall we also be σύμφυτοι τῷ ὁμοιώματι of the resurrection'.

As in the Adam-Christ parallels a fulness of ideas crowds in upon Paul, which he similarly wishes to bring to the light. With σύμφυτοι κτλ he harks back to συνετάφημεν (*v.* 4): through baptism we have been united in the closest fashion with the event of Christ's dying and burial, and thereby attained to death (for sin). The same line of thought is continued in συνεσταυρώθη (*v.* 6) and ἀπεθάνομεν σὺν Χριστῷ (*v.* 8).

A second thought, which is important to Paul, may be perceived in γεγόναμεν: the condition into which we have been transferred (perfect!) is an abiding one. Through our unity with Christ, entered upon in

[18] Cf. the ὥσπερ Mt. xx. 28 (instead of Mk. x. 45 καὶ γάρ!); further Jn. v. 21–26. The ὥσπερ in the Adam-Christ parallels is also significant, Rom. v. 12, 19, 21; 1 Cor. xv. 22; admittedly it expresses first a comparison, but also a correspondence and causal connection. Similarly καθώς in the relation of Jesus to His disciples has a comparative and demonstrative meaning, see Jn. vi. 57; xiii. 15, 34; xv. 12; xvii. 22; Rom. xv. 7; 1 Cor. xi. 1; 2 Cor. i. 5; x. 7; Eph. v. 2, 25.

baptism, we have *for ever* died to the power of sin. In what follows Paul accentuates this idea yet more strongly: 'that we should no more serve sin' (*v.* 6). Christ died to sin ἐφάπαξ (*v.* 10), so also we. Over against the power of sin we have become really *dead* (νεκροί, cf. *v.* 11).

The conception that most strongly emerges, however, is that as we have been united with the dying of Christ, so also we have with his resurrection. Precisely this is emphasized by Paul in *v.* 4 by means of the ἵνα-sentence: the goal of our 'becoming buried with' Christ is the new life, sacramentally bestowed, that also ought to work itself out in a new walk of life. To make this step that is expected of the Christian more plain, in accordance with the pattern event of Christ, the Apostle makes a fresh beginning. He lays all emphasis on the entry into the realm of life, the participation in the resurrection (ἀλλὰ καί[19]): if we have attained to death with Christ, we shall also *quite certainly* attain with Christ to resurrection. This idea is continued in the following verses and is explained in them. Verse 8, similarly formed through the εἰ-sentence, expressly says: 'so shall we also live with Him', and in *v.* 11 a result of the saving event is declared to be, 'living to God in Christ Jesus'.

The last thought to be developed rests on the fact that the death and resurrection of Christ must not be divided from one another. The primitive Church, and with it Paul, confessed with regard to Christ: 'He was delivered on account of our misdeeds and raised on account of our justification' (Rom. iv. 25). In the act of baptism the baptized man enters upon fellowship with Christ, and in such a manner that he gains a participation in Christ's death and resurrection—as in His death, so also in His resurrection. He attains thereby to death for sin and life for God. His fellowship with Christ is a single and unified one, but in relation to his dying and rising with Christ it maintains a double aspect: a being dead (for sin) and a being alive (for God). In order to represent this unity with Christ in His dying and rising, Paul uses the σύν-composita, which expresses a double idea: present sacramental unity with Christ and the fulfilment with Him of his once-for-all death.[20] A difficulty arises for *our* thinking how the Christ event that historically took place earlier can become effective in a present action, i.e. how we can really fulfil it *with* Christ; yet this manner of thinking was possible for Paul—how, is a matter for later investigation (see part 2, chapter II).

[19] On ἀλλὰ καί cf. Blass-Debr. § 448, 6.

[20] P. Gächter also has expounded this double aspect in his essay, 'Zur Exegese von Röm. vi. 5', in *ZKTh* 54 (1930) pp. 88–92. 'The Apostle was thinking partly on the participation of the favoured one in Christ's life, partly on his becoming like Christ' (91). Gächter thinks that in v. 5 there has been a mixture of two ideas as in Gal. v. 5 and 2 Th. ii. 10.

From this it is further to be concluded that *v.* 5b does not immediately relate to the future bodily resurrection (as Cyril of Alexandria,[21] Chrysostom, Thomas, Bisping, Bardenhewer maintained, cf. also Lietzmann); it indicates in the first place the logical consequence of the dying that has been spoken of (so Cornely, Zahn, Kühl, Jülicher, Lagrange, Sickenberger, Gaugler). Certainly the aspect is already open to the future, since we actually possess the resurrection life of Christ in us—a life which does not age but presses on to the consummation (cf. Rom. viii. 11).[22] This point of view, however, is not in the forefront at this juncture; it stands in the background like a last promise, but it is brought out by Paul *v.* 8 (συζήσομεν αὐτῷ).

It would be possible to maintain, with regard to this passage, that the Apostle, in his pictorial manner of thinking, has the emergence from the water in view (cf. Althaus); but the fact that he *deduces* the resurrection from the 'Christ-event' (*v.* 4) by no means compels us to this interpretation.

Having set our sacramental dying with the death of Jesus and our inner unity with Christ in its proper light, Paul comes back to his first thesis ἀπεθάνομεν τῇ ἁμαρτίᾳ (*v.* 2), and he expounds the significance of the saving event with profundity and clarity. He declares nothing that is really new, but repeats what has been said already in a manner that is only possible by reason of the exposition given in *vv.* 3–5.

A participle loosely links it up with what has gone before; it has no logical or deeper connection with the preceding context, but it attaches to the forceful thrust of his speech and could as well have been replaced by another main verb.[23]

Verse 6: 'From this it is perfectly clear (and this is what really matters here): our old man was crucified with Him, that the body (which was in the possession) of the power of sin might be completely destroyed, so that we are no longer in the service of the power of sin.'

From the previous discussion of the Apostle's it must have become plain to the readers that in baptism they are drawn sacramentally into the event of the death of their Lord. After these statements Paul has no need to return to the picture of immersion in baptism. *From that which happened to Christ* he is immediately able to draw conclusions as to *the saving event that happened to the baptized*, and thus more strongly

[21] PG 74, 796A. For further information on the Patristic teaching, see Schelkle, *Paulus Lehrer der Väter*, pp. 203–6.

[22] Gennadius expresses this well (Staab 365): ἡμεῖς τοῦ θανάτου κεκοινωνηκότες αὐτῷ διὰ τοῦ βαπτίσματος, κοινωνοὶ ἦμεν τῆς ἀκηράτου καὶ ἀπαλαιώτου καὶ παμμακαρίας ἐκείνης ζωῆς.

[23] Cf. Rom. xii. 9ff; Moulton-Thumb 284ff and 352ff, who also provide examples from the papyri; Blass-Debr. § 468.

to emphasize the saving significance of the sacramental action. Accordingly, he uses the expression 'crucified with', which is not at all suitable to the picture of baptism, but which admirably represents a total and unreserved dying to the power of sin.

Theologically this procedure is bold and powerful. For in truth, Christ has not 'died to the power of sin' in the same manner as we do, since He personally was never subject to it; but Paul does not shrink from this expression (*v.* 10), for on the other hand he exchanges for it the grandiose picture of us men and women, with our body of sin, being 'crucified with' Christ (see further on this § 8).

As to καταργηθῇ, many recent exegetes[24] hold that this term 'by no means affirms the destruction of the body of sin' but only that 'it is rendered powerless and ineffective' (B. Weiss). The thought of still being able to sin concurs with that view. The LXX, which employs the word only in 2 Esd. iv. 21, 23; v. 5; vi. 8, supports the meaning 'destroy'.

The context of our passage enables us to decide the issue. There we see the parallel (in chiastic form):

ὁ παλαιὸς ἡμῶν ἄνθρωπος—συνεσταυρώθη,
ἵνα καταργηθῇ— τὸ σῶμα τῆς ἁμαρτίας.

The emphasis undeniably falls on the καταργηθῇ; the powerful picture of crucifixion, of violent destruction, is chosen on its account. It is not the power of sin in person that is destroyed, but our body, in so far as it was subjected to it (cf. Lagrange ad loc). Thus is explained how it is possible for it to fall again into sin: the power of sin is still present, but the territory over which it used to hold sway, the σῶμα with its ἐπιθυμίαι (vi. 12) and its μέλη, that formerly were such adaptable instruments for sin, is no longer in subjection to it. *This* σῶμα, the σῶμα τῆς ἁμαρτίας, is destroyed. That we still remain in a θνητὸν σῶμα (vi. 13), a ψυχικὸν σῶμα (1 Cor. xv. 44) the Apostle naturally knows very well.[25]

The verse thus is intended to give powerful expression to the thought of our dying over against the power of sin; through our death that power loses its bond-servants. The logical development of this must mean that

[24] Delling in *ThW* I, 454, 22–25 defers the complete destruction to the parousia; contra Bauer, *Wörterbuch* col. 825; Schlier, *Taufe* 338.

[25] Therefore it is also wrong when Schlatter, *Gottes Gerechtigkeit* 208f, sees in this a 'renunciation of the body'. Σῶμα, which the Fathers quite wrongly understood as 'totality of sin', may well have been preferred by Paul to σάρξ, not because it suits the picture of crucifixion better, but because he has in view more particularly the bearer of the μέλη (cf. *vv.* 12–13) or the possessor of the σάρξ (σῶμα τῆς σαρκός, Col. ii. 11). Moreover the boundaries are indeterminate, cf. Käsemann, op. cit. 122f.

to be crucified with Christ has the purpose (ἵνα) of destroying the body that belongs to sin, with the result that (τοῦ with a final-consecutive infinitive) we are no longer in service to the power of sin.[26]

But Paul also desires to base more firmly and expound the positive counterpart, the ζῆν τῷ θεῷ; this he does in *vv.* 8–10. He adds to *v.* 6 another brief demonstration (γάρ) of the negative aspect, concluding with the ἀποθανεῖν τῇ ἁμαρτίᾳ, by a general statement. In the total structure *v.* 7 does not possess a great importance, but it provides a difficulty for exegesis.

Verse 7: 'For he who has died has become (even with death) free from (the power of) sin (i.e. actually absolved).'

> Even older exegetes recognized a proverbial manner of expression in the saying, without being able to prove it in any way. The passages adduced by Billerbeck[27] relate entirely to *freedom from fulfilling the commandments.* K. G. Kuhn,[28] followed by Schrenk,[29] thinks he has found a rabbinic theologoumenon that completely corresponds to our saying in Rom. vi. 7: 'All who die make atonement through their death.' If the passages are examined they yield the conclusion that death, sometimes with, sometimes without previous repentance, is looked upon as an atonement, and the guilty thereupon is regarded as declared righteous. That, however, is the interpretation of *v.* 7 in the sense of justification (Thomas, cf. Gutjahr), which the more recent exegetes (as Chrysostom long ago) rightly refuse; the saying is concerned not with freedom from the *guilt* of sin but with freedom from the *dominion* of sin. Now admittedly Paul could have used the rabbinic theologoumenon in a different sense; even so the linguistic aspect does not fit. The corresponding term in the LXX to כפר, which in the Hithp. = be atoned for,[30] is never δικαιοῦσθαι but rather ἐξιλάσκεσθαι (e.g. 1 Sam. iii. 14). The agreement therefore is only external and cannot bear closer examination.[31]
>
> We shall not go astray if, with W. Bauer,[32] we understand the

[26] The genitive of the infinitive with article is very frequent in the N.T., especially in Paul; it preponderately possesses a final meaning and only seldom a consecutive (Blass-Debr. § 400, 2 and 5). Here the latter is given (against Lagrange).

[27] III, 232 and 234 (on Rom. vii. 3).

[28] In *ZNW* 30 (1931) 305–310.

[29] In *ThW* II, 222, 30–223, 2.

[30] J. Levy-Goldschmidt, *Wörterbuch* II, 385.

[31] Schlatter's exegesis that δεδικαίωται, which approximates most closely to the popular Greek linguistic usage, signifies that what is lawful has been done to a guilty person through his punishment, does not illuminate the issue any better. Schlatter manifestly transfers to *our* death the view that Jesus' death for sin has fulfilled its demand (cf. the similar thought as to νόμος, Gal. iii. 13), but that is not contained in Rom. vi.

[32] *Wörterbuch*, col. 392, 2c.

δικαιοῦσθαι more in the sense of 'setting free'; its forensic meaning, admittedly, will then not be so strongly emphasized (contrary to many exegetes, who again thereby obscure their own expositions). It appears that Paul wishes to represent death as the looser of bonds, similarly as in vii. 3, but that in vi. 7 he takes up a picture of judgment, i.e. the picture of acquittal. A transition to this significance can be found in the loosing of vows; the LXX in Sir. xviii. 22 reproduces this by δικαιοῦσθαι—μὴ μείνῃς ἕως θανάτου δικαιωθῆναι.[33] In Rom. vi. 7 ἀπό strengthens the liberating or separative meaning.[34]

Death thus frees from the rule of the power of sin—first the death of Christ, but then also our sacramental 'death', i.e. in so far as we die with Christ, we are crucified with Him.

Death, however, both for Christ and for us, is a junction to *life*: that is a natural transition to the stronger argument of the second and positive statement: *we live for God* (the thesis which the Apostle had deduced from the Christ event and on which he had kept his eye since *v.* 4).

Verse 8: 'But if we died with Christ, we have the confidence that we also shall live with him.'

Just as the Apostle could not strongly enough emphasize the fact of our stepping out of the dominion of the power of sin, so now he seeks to represent the acquisition of life as something *sure and abiding*. Therefore πιστεύομεν affirms less the holding of an opinion or a conviction than having confidence; it has taken up into itself something of ἐλπίς (v. 1–11). The Apostle directs his gaze to the future, without denying the possession of life in the present. The particles of time, οὐκέτι (*v.* 9 twice) and ἐφάπαξ (*v.* 10), bring to the fore the certainty and irrevocability of this saving event.

The concept of *life* thus finds a varied application and one suited to the prevailing point of view. If Paul is immediately concerned with the *moral* life lived without sin for God (*v.* 2), this life is yet based on the *real* reception of life in baptism through *resurrection* 'with Christ'. It is an essentially *new* life, and its quality of otherness should show itself in a new *walk* of life (*v.* 4). As a sacramental gift of God, this life is an essential element of salvation; as such it is something abiding and ideally cannot be lost. In the συζήσομεν (*v.* 8) attention is directed to the consummation of the possession

[33] The 'simple' explanation (of Chrysostom, Theodoret, Estius) that the dead can no longer sin, is also unsatisfactory; ἀπὸ τῆς ἁμαρτίας means, as in the entire section, the power of sin, not personal sin.

[34] Blass-Debr. § 211; Abel § 46. g. 1.

of life; the final and indisputable possession of the divine life is at any rate included in the progress of Paul's thought.[35]

Verse 9: 'We know indeed that Christ, since He was raised from the dead, does not die any more (a second time more), that no death has power over Him.'

Θάνατος, *without article*, does not denote here the well known cosmic power of ruin, to which Christ was never subject in the same sense as sinful humanity (v. 12); rather it signifies the physical power of existence to which Christ was subjected through his incarnation (Gal. iv. 4) and obedience to God (Rom. v. 19). But after His death on the cross this power of existence has no more power over Him, it can no more lay claim to Him (οὐκέτι κυριεύει).

Paul is urgent to set forth *our* ultimate dying for the power of sin and *our* irrevocable and assured life for God; he does it yet more starkly in the case of Christ, whose experience we share only in a mystery. The twofold οὐκέτι is not enough for him, he must state it yet again *positively*, and this he does by means of the word that has become the standing term for the one-for-allness and ultimate validity of the redemptive act of Christ: ἐφάπαξ.[36] One must listen carefully to the manner in which the following sentence heads up to this word and gathers all its emphasis up in it; the Apostle, making a fresh start, stresses the other aspect, the absolute and abiding life.

Verse 10: 'For the death that He died, He died to the detriment of the power of sin, *once for all*; but (the life) that He lives, He lives to God.'

The little relative sentences with ὅ are to be interpreted as inner accusative-objects; New Testament Greek is as fond of them as profane Greek.[37] The datives in themselves have no other meaning than in *v.* 2. Since the statement is formulated with respect to us (*v.* 11), no further consequences from it should be drawn for the relation between Christ and the power of sin (on this cf. 2. Cor. v. 21). The dogmatic difficulty, that Christ could not have been 'accountable' to sin, misled Chrysostom,[38] and other Greek

[35] Cf. Sanday-Headlam, Barrett. H. Windisch pays particular attention to the statements about 'life', *Taufe und Sünde*, 167–76. He considers that in *v.* 5 there is an intimation of future resurrection of the dead (173) but contrariwise he relates *v.* 8 to the present life (174). The reverse is perhaps more likely in view of the drift of Paul's thought. Nevertheless Windisch's remark on *v.* 11 is excellent: 'Paul looks on this life in accordance with the continuing fact of its existence' (175).

[36] Cf. Stählin in *ThW* I, 382f. The conception in the Letter to the Hebrews bears out his theological evaluation (Heb. vii. 27; ix. 12; x. 10; cf. ix. 28).

[37] Blass-Debr, § 153, Robertson ('cognate accusative') 477–9. Linguistically the affinity is strongest in Gal. ii. 20, ὃ δὲ νῦν ζῶ κτλ.

[38] Hom. XI in Rom. (Montf. IX. 532B).

Fathers in dependence on him, to the false interpretation, 'He died on account of our sins'. For that reason more recent Catholic exegetes stress that Christ *voluntarily* subjected himself to the rule of the power of sin.

The direct continuation of the thought would run: 'So you also (in baptism) died once for all to the detriment of the power of sin and live (irrevocably) for God.'[39] But Paul gives a different turn to the conclusion, which is at the same time the conclusion and climax of the whole meditation.

Verse 11: 'So consider yourselves also as dead for the power of sin but living for God in (the fellowship with) Christ Jesus.'

Λογίζεσθαι is originally proper to the language of the merchant: 'to place to someone's account'—so it is frequently attested in the papyri.[40] In this passage the technical usage is considerably worn down; it signifies here 'to estimate someone, look on someone as'.[41]

The Apostle desires to apply to the Christian now the sharply pointed and seemingly absolute statement of *v.* 10, without weakening it at all. The *fact* that they have died to the power of sin and live to God is represented in the same weighty manner as in the case of Christ: they have died once for all to the power of sin and now live to God alone; cf. the crass antithesis μέν—δέ and the emphasized contrasts νεκρούς—ζῶντας. But conformably with the main concern of the whole section, he immediately springs from the fact to the *application*: that which has happened to them should also have its effect in their personal living. The inference of *v.* 1 is therefore quite impossible.

Νεκρούς shows that the Apostle now no longer thinks about the sacramental dying (ἀποθανεῖν). The effect of this once-for-all act lasts on and makes the recipients perpetually 'dead' for the power of sin. That is the fruit of his exposition of the ἐφάπαξ.

Admittedly no special emphasis lies on the expression ἐν Χριστῷ Ἰησοῦ (B. Weiss), but in fact the whole exposition reaches its peak point here. The Christian has become entwined in a living fellowship with Christ, and in accordance with this he has to consider himself dead for the power of sin and living for God. Now if the Apostle speaks no longer of the sacramental event but of the abiding condition, the ἐν Χριστῷ takes the place of the σὺν Χριστῷ.

Thus the Apostle's progressive argument, carried through with a powerful dynamic and tension, attains to a point of rest. In its course he

[39] On this dative cf. K. H. Rengstorf, *Mischna Jebamot*, Giessen 1929, 89–92.
[40] Bauer, *Wörterbuch* vol. 940f; F. Preisigke, *Wörterbuch* II, 28.
[41] Cf. Bauer, *Wörterbuch*, col. 941, see under 1b at the end.

built up his answer to the objection of *v.* 1, assuredly not out of any embarrassment with the object dealt with at such length! He did not take lightly the danger to which his basic thesis was exposed, but in his reply he developed a well founded and positive representation of the individual way of salvation, in close adherence to the great Christ event, till at length the sharply opposed thesis and antithesis confronted one another: *dead* for the power of sin, *living* for God in Christ Jesus (*v.* 11). The moral application had to issue from this as the practical result (cf. the parenesis of *vv.* 12–14). On this account the argument time and again did not receive a final formulation but was diverted prematurely into ethics. Basically, however, the characteristic elements of his theology are not denied.

§7. ROM. vi. 5a. Σύμφυτοι τῷ ὁμοιώματι τοῦ θανάτου αὐτοῦ

Verse 5 plays a significant role in the question whether Rom. vi. 1–11 is to be interpreted after the fashion of the Hellenistic mysteries. For does it not describe a deeply mysterious event that can only be interpreted on the analogy of the initiatory rites of the Mysteries? Do we not see here the beginning of a Christian 'Mystery cult'? And does not the term ὁμοίωμα signify an abstraction which the great Alexandrines, in dependence on the Platonic philosophy for this mode of thought, developed fully and productively?

O. Casel, who believes that he has newly uncovered this 'Christian Mystery' view, and vigorously defends it, appeals to Rom. vi and translates *v.* 5 as follows: 'For if we were planted in the likeness of his death, so shall we also participate in the resurrection.'[42] In adhering to this interpretation he renews the evaluation of this passage given by Cyril of Jerusalem in his 'Mystagogical Catechesis' to the newly baptized (II. 5ff). Simon Stricker gives the same translation and a detailed exegetical representation of it.[43] Moreover Protestant scholars like H. Windisch, J. Weiss, A. Jülicher, H. Lietzmann, R. Bultmann also incline to an interpretation along the line of the Mysteries.[44] On the Catholic

[42] Kultmysterium 31.

[43] In his essay, Der Mysteriengedanke des hl. Paulus nach Röm vi. 2–11; in *Liturgisches Leben* I (1934) pp. 285–96. H. Keller offers a highly individual interpretation in an essay 'Kirche als Kultgemeinschaft' in *Ben Mon* 16 (1934), pp. 28–31. Admittedly he does not go all the way with Casels (p. 29, n. 1) but he likewise stresses the *realism* in the concept of the ὁμοίωμα. 'Baptism as a counterpart to the redemptive death of Christ is itself crucifixion, a death of the baptized on the cross. As an image of the death of Christ it possesses the capacity to accomplish this same death, i.e. the saving death, in every man' (29). The chief idea of the essay, that the *Church* appears as the 'chief bearer of the event, in which the imitation of Christ is realized', (31) is hardly Pauline.

[44] H. Windisch, *Taufe und Sünde* 169, calls baptism in the Pauline interpretation a 'mysterious δρώμενον'; similarly J. Weiss, *Urchristentum* 500f; Jülicher in *Schriften des NT* II³-1917, 264f; Lietzmann in the *Handbuch z. NT* VIII ⁴1933, 67f; Bultmann, *Theol.* 138ff, 293 (for B. there is no doubt about this).

side the Mystery teaching of O. Casel has been developed further, especially by V. Warnach.[45] Here, however, there has been an increasing tendency to move away from a dependence on the Hellenistic Mystery religions to the idea of cultic representation, as it shows itself in the Old Testament and in late Judaism, especially in the passover feast. In this way it is believed that a Christian 'cult-mystery' can be established, for which Paul with his exposition in Rom. vi is the chief witness. The expression ὁμοίωμα forms an especial point of contact; it is considered to be comprehensible only as a cultic 'image', i.e. as a cultic symbol in the sense of Casel's. It is therefore necessary for us first of all to make a careful investigation into the linguistic evidence. First we must clarify the grammatical construction and then examine the meaning of the individual terms.

I. *The Grammatical Construction*

Attempts have been made to link up the separate elements of the sentence in various ways.

1. The connection of σύμφυτοι with the genitives τοῦ θανάτου and τῆς ἀναστάσεως has found least agreement; the dative then appears as an added dative of conformity, more closely defining the expression.[46] Blass-Debrunner also argue for the possibility of linking σύμφυτοι with the genitives, but they consider that it is more natural to join the term to the preceding word.[47] Actually ὁμοίωμα in the other passages, Rom. i. 23; v. 14; viii. 3; Phil. ii. 7; Rev. ix. 7 always has a genitive with it, so this unity cannot be torn apart. The advantage of this construction would be that it would not be necessary to insert ὁμοιώματι again before ἀναστάσεως; but it must be set aside on the ground already mentioned.

2. Casel, Stricker and Warnach, as Chrysostom before them, do not make the second genitive ἀναστάσεως depend on ὁμοιώματι, nor do they make it depend on σύμφυτοι but immediately on ἐσόμεθα. Stricker explains this as a 'genitive of belonging'.[48] Warnach defends the interpretation, making appeal to 1 Th. v. 5, 8 (ἡμεῖς δὲ ἡμέρας ὄντες);[49] we belong to the resurrection as to a new aeon.[50] But in all the passages where Paul speaks of the ἀνάστασις, this expression never denotes a

[45] V. Warnach, 'Taufe und Heilsgeschehen nach Röm. vi', *ALW* III, 2 (1954) 284–366; also 'Die Tauflehre des Römerbriefes in der neueren theologischen Diskussion', in *ALW* V, 2 (1958) 274–332.
[46] Schwarzmann, op. cit. 35–48; also Schlier at first (in *EvTh* (1938), 337), but he adopted in *ThLZ* 1947, col. 324 the translation, 'grown together with the "likeness" of his death'.
[47] § 194, 2 appendix.
[48] Op. cit. 292.
[49] In *ALW* III, 2, 312f.
[50] In *ALW* V, 2, 307ff.

sphere (of rule) but always the event of resurrection, whether it be of Christ or of Christians. With most expositors, therefore, we must assume in *v.* 5b an ellipse of (σύμφυτοι) τῷ ὁμοιώματι. The sentences before and after are already closely bound to each other because of *v.* 4; probably they are also linguistically formed in a similar way. If an αὐτοῦ is lacking with τῆς ἀναστάσεως, the resurrection of Christ is nevertheless in view, as in *v.* 4; the αὐτοῦ has thus fallen out because of the brevity. However, in *v.* 4 an αὐτοῦ is purposely lacking after τὸν θάνατον; the general manner of expression calls attention to the fact that we also attain (with Christ) the resurrection.

3. The connection of the words in *v.* 5a remains the chief problem. In more recent exegesis not a few expositors[51] insert an αὐτῷ, on the analogy of *v.* 4, and interpret ὁμοιώματι as instrumental.

Hesitation with regard to the ellipse on the grounds of grammar are unnecessary for the everyday speech of that time.[52] The objection that the αὐτῷ that is suggested for insertion is too far removed overlooks the consonance in the beginnings of the sentences of *vv.* 4 and 5 (each having a compound with σύν) which makes the repetition of the αὐτῷ superfluous. Besides, σύμφυτοι γεγόναμεν is not simply a verbal form (perhaps for συμπεφύκαμεν); it is a verbal adjective+verb, hence the ellipse appears more natural ('We have become (persons) grown together'). The dative may be omitted with such verbs compounded with σύν, so far as the meaning is clear; cf. συναποθανεῖν καὶ συζῆν (supply 'with Paul') 2 Cor. vii. 3; συναπεθάνομεν-συζήσομεν (supply 'with Christ') 2 Tim. ii. 11; συμβασιλεύσομεν (the same) 2 Tim. ii. 12.

Nevertheless misgivings do arise with regard to this interpretation. The simplest and most natural procedure is to connect σύμφυτοι immediately with τῷ ὁμοιώματι, and so to take the dative as sociative, not instrumental. In so far as that gives even a tolerable meaning, this construction is to be preferred to supplying an αὐτῷ (cf. O. Michel ad loc). Connections with σύν mostly have the dative with them; with the instrumental meaning one would rather expect ἐν (τῷ) ὁμοιώματι (cf. Blass-Debr. § 195).

4. In the most recent exegesis, therefore, the view has become more and more widespread that τῷ ὁμοιώματι κτλ should be linked directly with σύφυτοι.[53] Doubts about it arise solely on objective grounds: How

[51] A. Maier, B. Weiss, Jülicher, Kühl, Gutjahr, Bardenhewer, Sickenberger, Leenhardt, Bauer (*Wörterb.* 1124); cf. also Cornely, Sanday-Headlam, Dodd, Nygren, Lagrange, M. Barth, op. cit. 239f.

[52] Cf. Blass-Debr. § 481; Radermacher 217; Robertson 1201f, also Sanday-Headlam ad loc.

[53] So already the older exegetes, so far as one can discover; in more recent times Zahn, Lietzmann, Schlatter, Althaus, Gaugler, O. Michel, Kuss; Casel, Warnach, J. Schneider (in *ThW* V, 191f.), etc. Cf. also C. K. Barrett.

is one to conceive a 'growing together with the ὁμοίωμα of his death'? This difficulty can be removed only by a closer investigation of the terms σύμφυτος and ὁμοίωμα.

II. Σύμφυτοι

The term σύμφυτος was not uniformly rendered, even by the older commentators.

1. Frequently the meaning was weakened. Origen repeatedly reproduces it by σύμμορφος (*conformis*), once by *consors*.[54] Cyril of Alexandria translates the expression by σύμμορφοί τε καὶ ταυτοειδεῖς,[55] Oecumenius by συμμέτοχοι.[56] That these interpretations do not do justice to the root φυ- needs no more than mention.

2. The interpretation that took it in the sense of συμφυτεύειν was particularly influential. It provided an image that could be used and found a support in the translation of the Vulgate: *complantati*. The original significance of συμφυτεύειν = 'to plant together with' appears to have guided Chrysostom: just as the body of Christ, buried in the earth, brought forth as its fruit the salvation of the world, so our body, buried in baptism, matures the fruit of righteousness, holiness, becoming the children of God, and innumerable other blessings.[57] He thereby really does think of a planting (φυτεία) and he endeavours to show the likeness (ὁμοιότης) between our planting and Christ's. Rufinus has preserved a very similar exposition of our passage by Origen: *Velut plantam alicuius arboris mortem Christi ostendit, cui nos complantatos vult esse, ut ex succo radicis eius radix quoque nostra suscipiens producat ramos iustitiae et fructus afferat vitae*.[58] Theodore of Mopsuestia also adduces the comparison with a plant that dies and rises to new life.[59]

3. This picture of planting was then especially related to the saying of Christ that he is the Vine, and our connection with him was understood as an ingrafting (Rom. xi), consequently as a growing with him. This exposition was dominant from Cyril of Jerusalem;[60] it was adopted by Thomas,[61] Cornelius a Lapide, Calmet, and extends to more recent times (Klee 1830) even into the present.[62]

4. Recent exegetes rightly derive the term from συμφύειν, i.e. 'grow together'. In classic Greek σύμφυτος also gains the technical meaning of

[54] σύμμορφος (conformis): in Joa. I, 9 (GCS IV, 15, 12 Preuschen); II, 33 (IV, 91, 5 Preuschen); in Luc. hom. 17 (IX, 115, 8 Bauer).
[55] PG 74, 793C.
[56] PG 118, 432.
[57] In Rom. hom XI (Mont IX, 530 DE).
[58] In Rom. vi. 5 (PG 14, 1043 C).
[59] Catena (Staab 121, 24ff); on the contrary Diodor, according to the Catena, used the picture of growing together. Cf. further Schelkle, *Paulus Lehrer der Väter* 211f.
[60] *Myst. Cat.* II, 7 (Quasten 86).
[61] In Rom. VI, lect. 1 (ed. Vives I, 92b).
[62] Schneider, *Leidensmystik* p. 46; Schwarzmann, op. cit. 28–32; Barth op. cit. 236 and 238.

inborn, proper, natural,[63] yet without giving up the root meaning 'grow together'; this is the only possible meaning in our passage. The contexts in which the verb συμφύειν, as also the verbal adjective σύμφυτος, stand are instructive. For σύμφυτος Passow offers the excellent example from Theophrastus: σύμφυτον πᾶν τὸ ζῶν τῷ ζῶντι,[64] by which an organic connection is intimated. But the application of the term can also be extended to the inorganic sphere.[65] The expression was commonly employed in medical language for the growing together of broken bones,[66] in philosophy for the inner affinity of body and soul,[67] and for the sexual union.[68] The verb occurs in only a few passages in the New Testament: in Lk. viii. 7 it is said that the thorns grew so thickly together with the good seed (they *overgrew* it) that they choked it. In sum, we may say that the term expresses a close unity and intertwining without being limited to any definite area of application.[69]

5. Gächter asserts that σύμφυτος can be slightly bent so as to signify 'grow in'.[70] He takes as his starting point the exposition of our passage by Chrysostom and appeals for support to two passages in Methodius. Gächter admits that Chrysostom's interpretation is false, but Chrysostom, unlike Gächter, probably attributed to the σύν less the meaning of 'in' than 'together with' or 'alongside' (see under 2).

Methodius says in the 'Banquet' (IV. 5—Bonwetsch p. 51, 2), 'The virgins thirst for the heavenly place, which is a σύμφυτος.' Gächter's interpretation of this in the sense of 'native soil of the plants' is hardly right. Methodius means that the heavenly place 'belongs to' the virgins.[71] The picture of implanting is not present.

The second passage, De resurr. I, 55, 4 (Bonwetsch p. 314, 14–17) speaks of Adam's fall, which did not take place before the ἐνσωμάτωσις of the soul, ἀλλὰ μετὰ τὴν εἰς τὸ σῶμα σύμφυσιν τῆς ψυχῆς γίγνεται τὸ παράπτωμα. That likewise does not mean, 'after the implanting of the soul in the body' (as one puts a plant into the earth), but 'after the uniting (the growing together) of the soul

[63] F. Passow, *Handwörterbuch* II, 2, pp. 1653f; for the papyri Preisigke gives the meaning, 'standing in full cultivation, not neglected'. The word thus possesses a certain polarity of meaning, yet in Rom. vi. 5 the fundamental meaning must serve as the starting point.

[64] See under σύμφυτος p. 1654.

[65] Aristoteles, *Meteor.* 4. 1 (ed. Bekker I, 376b, 15f): θερμότης καὶ ψυχρότης ὁρίζουσαι καὶ συμφύουσαι καὶ μεταβάλλουσαι τὰ ὁμογενῆ καὶ τὰ μὴ ὁμογενῆ.

[66] Aristoteles, *Hist. anim.* 2. 6; 2. 8; 4. 4 (ed. Bekker I, 745b, 6f; 747a, 12; 773a, 14f).

[67] Plato, *Phaedr.* 246D (ed. Bekker I, 40, 16f).

[68] Plato, *Conv.* 191A and 192E (ed. Bekker IV, 405, 4f; 408, 9f); Aristoteles, *Pol.* 2. 4 (ed. Bekker II, 126ab, 13).

[69] Cf. O. Kuss, 'Zu Röm. vi. 5a', *ThGl* 41 (1951) 430–7; M. M. Bourke, *A Study of the Metaphor of the Olive Tree in Rom.* xi, Washington 1947, 112–24.

[70] Op. cit. 88.

[71] Passow, see under 1, Liddell-Scott, see under 1, 2 and 4.

with the body'; for the author continues: 'ὅτι τὸ συναμφότερον ὁ ἄνθρωπος'. That corresponds with other sayings of Greek philosophy.

We must agree with Gächter, therefore, that συμφύειν means 'grow together', only the nuance of '*im*planting' or 'growing *in*' must be refused. That idea is represented in the New Testament (Jas. i. 21) and in the writings of the Apostolic Fathers (Barn. i. 2; ix. 9; Justin II. *Apol.* 6. 3; 8. 1; 13. 5) by its own expression ἔμφυτος. Justin in II. *Apol.* 8. 1 speaks of the ἔμφυτον πάντι γένει ἀνθρώπων σπέρμα τοῦ λόγου and in 13. 5 of the ἐνοῦσα ἔμφυτος τοῦ λόγου σπορά. Here it is plainly discernible that the Greek was well aware of the distinction which the prepositions σύν and ἐν expressed in these compounds. That is important, for the figure of implanting and of ingrafting (for which Paul uses ἐγκεντρίζειν in Rom. xi. 17, 19, 23, 24) must clearly be refused in our context. In using σύμφυτοι Paul does not have in mind the bath of immersion, into which we sink or are implanted, but a growing together, a close union.

But what does it signify that we have become united with τῷ ὁμοιώματι of the death of Christ?

III. 'Ομοίωμα

To a considerable extent the interpretation of our verse depends on the understanding of the term ὁμοίωμα. Should it be translated by 'copy', 'likeness', or 'form'? Casel and his followers translate ὁμοίωμα in our passage by 'likeness' (*Gleichbild*) and understand it in a definite sense, which perhaps should be reproduced in the words of Casel himself:

> 'In the knowledge of faith we behold in the sacramental image (*Bild*) the original (*Urbild*) itself, i.e. the saving work of Christ. We behold it in faith and in gnosis, i.e. we touch it, appropriate it to ourselves, become conformed to it through the participation, and thereby transformed after the image of the Crucified and Risen One. ... Sacrament and saving deed are not two separate things but one, whereby the image is so completely filled with the reality that it can rightly be described as present.'[72]

Von Warnach stresses that this 'likeness' (*Gleichbild*) is 'as genuine symbol a formative appearance *and* at the same time a reality (content) that appears'.[73] J. Schneider provides an orientation on the various interpretations of ὁμοίωμα in our passage. He enumerates four solutions:

[72] *GGM* 116. [73] In *ALW* III, 2 p. 310.

ὁμοίωμα relates to (a) baptism, (b) our death in baptism, (c) the present death of Christ in the sacrament, in the sense of O. Casel, (d) the same in the sense of H. Schlier. He himself comes to the conclusion, 'This sacramentally present death of Christ and this sacramentally present resurrection are the ὁμοίωμα of his historical death and his historical resurrection.'[74]

A fresh comparison of ὁμοίωμα in our passage with the linguistic usage elsewhere is perhaps not superfluous.

'Ομοίωμα stands in the following passages of the New Testament: Rom. i. 23; v. 14; vi. 5; viii. 3; Phil. ii. 7; Rev. ix. 7.

1. Rom. i. 23 and Rev. ix. 7 are more easily cognizable and hark back to the Old Testament foundation, or more precisely to the LXX. Here the term occurs 44 times, therefore relatively frequently. That is not surprising when we learn that it appears as a designation for (a) an *idol, image*, so Deut. iv. 16–25; 1 Sam. vi. 5; Ps. cv. 20 and specially *image* in 2Kings xvi. 10; 2 Chron. iv. 3. 'Image', in contrast to 'idol' in a material or solid sense, represents a certain transition to the second meaning, (b) = *form*. Thus the appearance of God in the burning bush is reproduced in Deut. iv. 12 by ὁμοίωμα, and in the prophetic visions of Ezekiel the term occurs for the visionary forms (Ez. i. 5, 16, 26; viii. 2 etc.).

In all the LXX passages ὁμοίωμα relates to something visible; it is understandable therefore that the lexicons of Moulton-Milligan (following Souter) and Liddell-Scott[75] stress the concrete element in ὁμοίωμα, while for the abstract the term ὁμοιότης is available.

A certain vacillation in linguistic usage, however, is already perceptible in the LXX. The Hebrew דְּמוּת is often translated by ὁμοίωμα: 2 Kings xvi. 10; 2 Chron. iv. 3; Is. xl. 18; Ez. i. 5, 16, 22, 26; ii. 1; viii. 2; x. 1, 10, 21, 22; xxiii. 15; yet it is often rendered by ὁμοίωσις: Gen. i. 26; Ps. lvii. 5 (LXX); Ez. i. 10; Dan. x. 16. כִּדְמוּת in Ps. lviii. 5 (Heb.) is a simple comparative particle = 'as';[76] the LXX translates it by καθ' ὁμοίωσιν. In profane Greek ὁμοίωσις (literally = making like) is already felt to be more strongly abstract and = 'resemblance'.[77]

2. The possibility must therefore be reckoned with that ὁμοίωμα can have a reduced, more abstract meaning ('*similarity*'). Such a usage finds some support in extra-Biblical testimonies. Preisigke adduces an expression ἐξ ὁμοιώματος = 'in accordance with a similar case',[78]

[74] In *ThW* V, 191–5 (citation p. 195, 1ff).
[75] Moulton-Milligan V, 499; Liddell-Scott 1225b (but also give the meaning 'likeness').
[76] Gesenius-Buhl, *Handwörterbuch über das AT* 148, see under 1.
[77] Passow II. 1, 466; Bauer, *Wörterbuch* col. 1125.
[78] *Wörterbuch* II, 177; also Liddell-Scott.

which represents a quite reduced sense. The inscription cited by Moulton-Milligan V. 449 could also possess a similar abstract meaning: καὶ νῦν τοῖς αὐτοῖς παραγγέλλω μηδὲν ἐξ ὁμοιώμα[τος ἐπι]γράφειν ἀλ[λ]αχῆι. It is evidently a command not to write up anything in a like fashion elsewhere.

We meet such worn down expressions above all in the Apostolic Fathers. Ignatius of Antioch writes to the Trallians ix, 2 οὗ (scil. Χριστοῦ) καὶ κατὰ τὸ ὁμοίωμα ἡμᾶς τοὺς πιστεύοντας αὐτῷ οὕτως ἐγερεῖ ὁ πατήρ.[79] The similarity or resemblance does not relate to the resurrection *body* but to the *fact* of the resurrection, since it is previously emphasized with respect to Christ: ἀληθῶς ἠγέρθη ἀπὸ νεκρῶν. The 'Shepherd of Hermas' employs ὁμοιώματα for abstract instead of concrete things (m. IV, 1, 1; similarly IV. 1. 9). W. Bauer (Wörterbuch col. 1124, 1) would understand our passage in the light of this usage: 'If we have grown together (namely αὐτῷ, with him) in the likeness of his death (= through the like death as his)'. This interpretation must be associated with those that fill out σύμφυτοι with an αὐτῷ.[80] It is yet possible to appeal to Rom. v. 14, where the abstract meaning of ὁμοίωμα gives a good sense. But whoever joins σύμφυτοι immediately with τῷ ὁμοιώματι (cf. above under 1) must understand ὁμοίωμα as something concrete.

3. What significance does ὁμοίωμα receive in the other passages of the New Testament?

Rom. i. 23 depends for its wording (especially through ἐν ὁμοιώματι) on Ps. cv. 20 (LXX). The appearance of ὁμοίωμα along with εἰκών is remarkable.[81] Both expressions can signify the same thing, but here they are distinguished: ὁμοίωμα is a *copy* of a *form* (εἰκών), namely of a perishable man or of beasts.

The second Old Testament meaning (see above 1b) = 'form' is not only plain in Rev. ix. 7 but it also appears in Rom. viii. 3 and Phil. ii. 7. The theological-dogmatic exposition of these much discussed passages is not our task here.[82] That outer form in distinction from inner being is meant in the latter two places is clear from the text: in Rom. viii. 3 the Son of God is sent in the form of the σὰρξ ἁμαρτίας, but according to his being he has nothing to do with these ruinous powers. The 'form of

[79] *Funk*, *Patres Apostolici*, Tübingen 1901, reads ὃς καὶ κτλ. That relates itself to ὁ πατήρ. The change to οὗ is suggested by Zahn.

[80] So especially M. Barth, op. cit. 240f.

[81] Lietzmann explains it as a pleonasm; Kühl imports a foreign Platonic interpretation (ὁμοίωμα = a conceptual prototype; εἰκών = a material, visible copy); Lagrange rightly alludes to the influence of Deut. iv. 16 LXX. See further G. Kittel in *ThW* II, 393, 32ff.

[82] The problem is especially dealt with by J. Weiss, *Urchristentum* 376ff; cf. J. Schneider in *ThW* V, 195–7.

man' in Phil. ii. 7 affirms that Christ Jesus, according to his being, was more than this.[83] It is important to notice that ὁμοίωμα in this application attains the same significance as μορφή, εἶδος or σχῆμα, as M. Dibelius on Phil. ii. 6f observes. These terms are so little defined that the incapacity of man to see the 'form' of God is portrayed in Deut. iv. 12 with ὁμοίωμα (but Symmachus μορφή), in Wisd. xviii. 1 with μορφή, in Jn. v. 37 with εἶδος.[84]

From Phil. ii. 7 itself the close relationship between ὁμοίωμα and σχῆμα is plain. This observation is confirmed by Phil. iii. 21; Christ will transform (μετασχηματίσει) the body of our humiliation so that it may become *of the like form* (σύμμορφον) to the body of His glory. This shows therefore that ὁμοίωμα can mean simply 'form'. The idea of 'copy' can recede into the background.

Rom. v. 14 is instructive because it shows that this ὁμοίωμα-concept can also be applied to an *event*. Accordingly it need not always concern a perceptible form; an event can also have a 'form'. Men who lived between the sin of Adam and the Lawgiver from Sinai did not sin ἐπὶ τῷ ὁμοιώματι of Adam's transgression, i.e. not through transgressing a formal prohibition. The expression is to be understood either as modal ('in a copy of the transgression of Adam'—but note the definite article!) or with the meaning of κατὰ with the accusative ('corresponding to').[85] So also the death of Christ in Rom. vi. 5 has a 'form', with which we are bound in baptism. Perhaps also the cross that gave to this death its *signum* may be especially in mind (cf. *v.* 6 συνεσταυρώθη).

4. Lastly the question must be raised whether there is any relationship between the Pauline ὁμοίωμα-concept and the Greek philosophical (especially the Platonic) concept of image. All the other passages in Paul's Letters can be explained from the Biblical-Old Testament linguistic usage. The various expressions in Phil. ii. 6f are fully explained by Septuagintal forms of speech. Paul assuredly is not guided by a Platonizing εἰκών-concept in Rom. vi. 5.

On the other hand the application of ὁμοίωμα in the literature influenced by Plato is instructive. Philo does not use the term ὁμοίωμα at all (cf. Leisegang, in the indices), but on the contrary τύπος is very frequent; next to ἰδέα, χαρακτήρ, and εἶδος, it has become for him the most appropriate expression for the Platonic teaching of ideas. For 'similarity' he uses (18 times) ὁμοιότης. Later ὁμοίωμα also appears in

[83] Cf. Tillmann (Bonn [4]1931), otherwise Lohmeyer (in H. A. W. Meyer's *Kommentar*, [8]Göttingen 1928) ad loc.

[84] *Handbuch zum NT*, Tübingen [3]1927, p. 74.

[85] Zahn ad loc (p. 269, n. 42) reminds us of the Heb. על in the sense of κατὰ with the accusative.

association with the Platonic teaching of ideas. Clement of Alexandria, Strom. VIII, 23, 1 (Stählin III, 94, 5–8), similarly writes that the ὀνόματα are σύμβολα τῶν νοημάτων, τὰ νοήματα ὁμοιώματα καὶ ἐκτυπώματα τῶν ὑποκειμένων. The conceptual pair 'pattern' and 'copy' appear clearly in the prayer to the Λόγος: Δὸς δὲ ἡμῖν τοῖς σοῖς ἑπομένοις παραγγέλμασιν τὸ ὁμοίωμα πληρῶσαι τῆς εἰκόνος (Paed. III, 101, 1; Stählin I, 291, 1–2). In Strom. VII, 52, 3 (Stählin III, 39, 9–11) σύμβολον and ὁμοίωμα are used synonymously.

Cyril of Jerusalem also appears to have been influenced by this speech; he has undoubtedly taken over ὁμοίωμα from Rom. vi. 5, but he interprets it in a Platonic sense, as he betrays through the concept of the μίμησις. Thus in the Myst. cat. II, 5: he says ἐν εἰκόνι ἡ μίμησις, ἐν ἀληθείᾳ δὲ ἡ σωτηρία, and II, 6: ἐν μιμήσει ἔχει τὴν κοινωνίαν (Quasten 85, 9f and 86, 11). Nevertheless in his view baptism is not simply the ὁμοίωμα; rather *in* baptism something happens that has a similarity to the event that took place in Christ's case, cf. III. 2: ὑμεῖς δὲ κατὰ τὸ βάπτισμα ἐν ὁμοιώματι καὶ συσταυρωθῆναι καὶ συνταφῆναι καὶ συναναστῆναι αὐτῷ καταξιοῦσθε (Quasten 89, 3–6).

The result of this linguistic investigation may be summarized somewhat as follows: The Pauline ὁμοίωμα-concept has its roots in Old Testament-Jewish thinking and suggests for Rom. vi. 5 the two translations 'copy' or 'form'. Both of these have to do with something concrete, with a concrete occurrence. If 'copy' be preferred, the difficult question arises as to exactly of what it consists: the rite of baptism, in which the death of Christ is sacramentally realized through the rite, or our 'dying with' (him), in so far as it is bound up with the death of Christ. If, however, ὁμοίωμα is simply represented by 'form', the possibility also remains of considering the death of Christ itself as a 'form' with which we are bound through baptism, even as we then also attain (or ought to attain) a share in the 'form' of His resurrection. Precisely this last viewpoint, which ought not to be overlooked when filling out *v.* 5b, suggests that ὁμοίωμα should not be interpreted as a 'cult symbol', for then it could not be considered apart from the perceptible rite; but Paul has at most understood the submersion beneath the water in a symbolic manner (as a 'being buried with Christ', *v.* 4) but not the emergence from it. The argument adheres absolutely to the dying and rising of Christ which we experience with Him in baptism. From then on we are transplanted into a perpetual fellowship of death and life with Christ, which works itself out on the ethical, mystical and eschatological planes. Thus we remain continually united with the 'form' of Christ's death (σύμφυτοι γεγόναμεν).

§8. ROM. vi. 6. Συνεσταυρώθη—THE CONTENT OF THE FIGURATIVE CONCEPTION

I. Συνεσταυρώθη

When the reader of the Letter to the Romans has before his eyes the picture portrayed in vi. 4 of immersion-baptism, into the waters of which the baptized sinks as in a grave, the expression συνεσταυρώθη comes the more surprisingly to him. For this expression reminds him of what happened to Christ; by no stretch of the imagination can it be said to have been determined by the rite. Perhaps it is less the figure of baptism by immersion that has been responsible for συνετάφημεν than the thought of the complete entry of Christ into death, or of our utter dying with Christ, since it is the grave that first seals death. Accordingly, the rite and its symbolic content certainly do not stand in the foreground; that is obvious from συνεσταυρώθη. On the other hand the aorist, no less than the other aorists, ἐβαπτίσθημεν (*v.* 3 twice) and συνετάφημεν (*v.* 4), can hardly allude to anything else than the event of baptism. We remain therefore in the temporal beginning constituted by the reception of baptism, where we experience a 'crucifixion with' another. 'Our old man' was 'crucified with (Christ)': Paul seizes on this expression in order to make plain beyond a doubt the 'destruction'[86] of the 'body of sin' that it carried in itself.

The expression ὁ παλαιὸς ἄνθρωπος in the other passages where it occurs (Eph. iv. 22; Col. iii. 9) has a moral aspect. The 'old sinful man', who is 'corrupt according to its deceitful desires', must be overcome with moral effort, must be 'laid aside' (Eph. iv. 22). Here it is seen that the Pauline ethic depends on the new life in Christ. The sinful sphere, which the Christian has in principle left behind him in baptism (Rom. vi. 6), must be *personally* overcome by Him in his mortal body in a continual moral battle (Eph. iv. 22; Col. iii. 9). In Eph. iv. 24 and Col. iii. 10 the 'new man' appears as a contrast to the 'old sinful man', hence the thought as little remains fast in negatives here as it does in Rom. vi (cf. ἐν καινότητι ζωῆς *v.* 4).

The verb σταυροῦν signifies fastening to the wood of the cross and the violent putting to death thereby effected (cf. Gal. v. 24), or, in the passive, the dying on the cross (Gal. vi. 14). The emphasis does not lie on the pain (cf. Bisping) but on the killing and destroying. This, however, is exactly what the Apostle wished to say about the πάλαιος

[86] Schlatter, *Gerechtigkeit Gottes* 207, thinks of the 'judicial purpose' of the death of Jesus. 'He who had to die on the cross is entirely deprived of rights, utterly disgraced. The old man is absolutely condemned'. This point of view is suitable only for the death on the cross (cf. Gal. iii. 13). Baptism is not concerned with a juridical deprivation of rights, but with a substantive deprivation of power.

ἄνθρωπος in baptism, namely that 'he', who was a servant of sin, and so far as he was this, in baptism died in an instant, in order to give place to a 'new man'.

Yet it is not the ordinary picture of crucifixion that serves as an illustration here, but the cross of *Christ*. The baptized is transferred into the closest communion (σύν) with his crucified Lord. The connections that are thereby yielded between the unique Christ event and the saving event in baptism must later be systematically investigated. But one thing is important at this point: the liturgical symbol has retreated completely into the background; its place is taken by the thing itself, the salvation-event that we experience with Christ in baptism.

II. *The Content of the Figurative Conception of Baptism*

After this clarification we can go on to the question as to how far the picture of immersion in and emergence from the water dominates our section and what significance it possesses for the sacramental thinking of Paul.

Hitherto many exegetes have held to the view that immersion signifies to the Apostle dying with Christ and emergence resurrection with Christ. The Apostolic Constitutions, a rather late collection, concerned chiefly with canon law and liturgy, declares with all brevity: ἡ κατάδυσις τὸ συναποθανεῖν, ἡ ἀνάδυσις τὸ συναναστῆναι (III, 17, 3). The meaning of baptism as a dying and rising with Christ is therefore inferred from the symbolic representation of immersion and emergence. It is exactly in the symbolic action that the understanding of the salvation-event there enacted is found. One then feels justified in looking around for similar happenings and ideas in the religious world of that time.

Of the history of this exposition we can give but a few glimpses here. In the *Letter of Barnabas* (XI, 11) and in the *Shepherd of Hermas* (s. IX, 16, 3–7) we find the idea of καταβαίνειν and ἀναβαίνειν, but without the characteristic Pauline connection with the συν-Χριστῷ idea. Hence it is improbable that Rom. vi was in mind in these passages. The Authors rather reproduce the impressive picture of descending into the baptismal waters and ascending out of them again as an occasion to describe the passage from the spiritual death of sins (i.e. the individual personal sins) to living for God and bearing fruit:

Barn XI, 11	Herm. s. IX, 16, 4
ἡμεῖς μὲν καταβαίνομεν εἰς τὸ ὕδωρ γέμοντες ἁμαρτιῶν καὶ ῥύπου καὶ ἀναβαίνομεν καρποφοροῦντες κτλ.	εἰς τὸ ὕδωρ οὖν καταβαίνουσιν νεκροί, καὶ ἀναβαίνουσιν ζῶντες.

Justin in his (I) *Apology* (ch. 61) depicts baptism above all by means of the concept of regeneration and 'illumination' (φωτισμός 61. 12, cf. Dial 122). It is remarkable that Tertullian, in his writing *De baptismo*, does not refer to Rom. vi; discussions on the element of the water take up a great deal of his space, and in face of contemporary objections he seeks to establish the necessity and saving efficacy of baptism. It is true that the African *rhetor* explains the individual rites, but for the rest he is an Apologist. Although he has occasion in ch. 5 to mention heathen rites of initiation that bear a similarity to baptism, any discussion of the Christian sacrament in terms of 'mysteries' remains far from him.

A more positive estimate of the passage in Romans begins with Origen. With him the dogmatic and ascetic point of view completely overshadows the liturgical. He ponders the question whether perhaps Abraham, Isaac and Jacob were buried and raised with Christ.[87] He further evaluates our passage in connection with Gal. vi. 14 and 2 Cor. iv. 10 among others.[88]

From the point of view of the liturgical symbol the *Constitutions*, as has already been mentioned, are strongly interested in our passage,[89] as also the great catechists Cyril of Jerusalem and Gregory of Nyssa.[90] After their time this interpretation is a firm element of all expositions. John Chrysostom expresses his liturgical-symbolic interpretation more clearly in his exposition of Jn. iii. 5 than in his commentary on Romans: Θεῖα τελεῖται ἐν αὐτῷ (scil. ὕδατι) σύμβολα: τάφος καὶ νέκρωσις καὶ ἀνάστασις καὶ ζωή, καὶ ταῦτα ὁμοῦ γίνεται πάντα.[91]

In the west a quick glance should be given to Ambrose. It is remarkable that in one of his most important liturgical-dogmatic writings, *De mysteriis*, he makes no reference to our passage. His expositions move in the multiform world of the allegorical and symbolic. He considers the water as a bath, in which our flesh is plunged and all fleshly sin is washed away; as a grave, in which every transgression is buried; and as the wood of the cross on which Jesus was transfixed;[92] but Paul's central thought of being buried *with Christ* is not mentioned by him. It is true that in the second important liturgical work, *De sacramentis*,[93] the idea is echoed that in baptism 'the living man dies and rises again alive', and

[87] Commentary on John XX, 12 (Preuschen 342, 18–20).

[88] *Contra Cels.* II, 69 (Koetschau 190, 9–20); Comm. on John I, 25 (Preuschen 33, 31–34, 5).

[89] Especially III, 17, 1–3; cf. V, 16, 7; VII, 43, 5 (Funk pp. 211f; 285; 450).

[90] Cyril of Jer., *Cat.* III, 12 (PG 33, 441f); *Myst. cat.* II, 4–7 (Quasten 83–86); III, 2 (Quasten 89, 1–6); Gregory of Nyssa, *Orat. catech.* 35, 2 (PG 45, 89f).

[91] In Joa. ev. hom. 25, 2 (Montf. VIII, 146C).

[92] *De myst.* III, 11 (ed Quasten in *Flor. Patr.* VII, 118, 17–19).

[93] Its genuineness is today successfully defended, cf. Quasten op. cit. 137f, above all in dependence on G. Morin in *JLW* 8 (1928) 86–106, and O. Faller in *ZKTh* 53 (1929) 41–65. Cf. recently O. Faller in *ZKTh* 64 (1940) 1–14; 81–101.

that baptism is therefore a grave,[94] but this is in immediate connection with Gen. iii. 19. Mention of dying and rising with Christ first appears in the next chapter,[95] and baptism 'in the death of Jesus' then receives a long but peculiar exposition: through it we are affixed with nails to the cross of Christ in order that the devil might not be able to draw us away again.[96] The ethical tendency becomes even plainer in the commentary given on Ps. lxi. 63.[97] So also in the moralistic-ascetic writing *De fuga saeculi*,[98] the mystery meaning is not present that Stricker seeks to find in it.[99] The bent of the great Milanese teacher of the Church is more towards allegorical interpretation and moral application.

This short survey[100] shows how varied the viewpoint can be under the heading 'dying and rising': dogmatic, ascetic, mystic, liturgical, allegorical.

We must therefore gather the precise figurative and theological view in Rom. vi from the text itself. What is the picture that hovers before Paul in Rom. vi, and how far does it extend?

> Zahn and Schweitzer[101] refuse all symbolism for Rom. vi, Zahn giving as his reason that Paul would otherwise have firmly adhered to the picture of submersion and emergence and would not immediately have returned again in *vv.* 5–11 to the conception of dying. Actually συνετάφημεν, as we saw, does not unconditionally demand the idea of the bath of immersion; yet it is a plausible assumption that this picture was before the eyes of Paul and his readers. Baptism is visualized as a 'baptism of death' through submersion, since the baptized disappears as into a grave.

Most exegetes strongly emphasize the figurative element of our verses. H. Gunkel[102] and Lietzmann would even find an allusion to death, and that through drowning. In Egypt, as Herodotus II, 90 attests, anyone who was drowned in the Nile was considered to be deified and was reverently embalmed and buried; the term *esietus* for the 'immersed' is to be met even in Tertullian;[103] but all trace of such a thought is lacking in Paul. The dying in this passage is not characterized by sinking in

[94] *De sacr.* II, 6, 19 (Quasten 149, 19–27). [95] II, 7, 20 (Quasten 149, 32f).

[96] II, 7, 23 (Quasten 150, 10–21). [97] CSEL 64, 396, 16 Petschenig.

[98] *Mortuus quidem semel est, sed moritur unicuique, qui baptizatur in morte Christi, ut consepeliamur cum eo et resurgamus cum eo et in novitate vitae illius ambulemus* (CSEL 32, 206, 5–8 Schenkl).

[99] Op. cit. 295.

[100] On the exegesis of the Fathers see further Schelkle, *Paulus Lehrer der Väter* 197–206; J. Daniélou, 'Die Symbolik des Taufritus', *Liturgie und Mönchtum* 3 (1949) 45–73.

[101] Op. cit. 255.

[102] *Zum religionsgeschichtlichen Verständnis des NT* (FRLANT 1), Göttingen [2]1910, p. 83.

[103] So reads Reifferscheid-Wissowa (in CSEL 20, 205, 22). On this cf. F. J. Dölger in *AC* 1 (1929) 174–83; Oepke in *ThW* I, 530, 38–531, 18.

water but by συσταυρωθῆναι (*v.* 6). Similarly the opinion of Sanday-Headlam,[104] who see the dying symbolized in the immersion and the being buried in the submersion, finds no support in the text. It offers only the one word συνετάφημεν, and that means figuratively: we have disappeared beneath the surface of the water, as the dead disappear in the grave.

The idea that the emergence signifies resurrection may in itself be close at hand. Conceivably the Apostle does not exclude it, but nowhere does he say anything about it in the text of Rom. 6. Verse 4 is so framed that Paul:

(4a) starts from the figure (ταφή) and salvation event (σὺν Χριστῷ) in baptism,
(4b) advances from the *death* to speak of the historic fact of the *resurrection* of Christ, and
(4c) draws conclusions from the resurrection of *Christ* as to the 'newness of life' *for us also* (καὶ ἡμεῖς).

Zahn rightly says of *v.* 5: 'While therefore the connection of the baptized with the death of Christ seems from the first to be given in the relation of baptism to that death (*vv.* 3–4), the conviction that the baptized are united with the resurrection of Christ is expressed as a conclusion from their union with the death of Christ (*v.* 5). The Christian reader himself supplies from *v.* 4 the minor premiss for the major premiss of the syllogism (*v.* 5a): "Christ's death is not to be envisaged without resurrection", or, "(Christ's death) is the introduction to it".' Verse 6 definitely excludes the figurative application of the parallel submersion-burial. Similarly *vv.* 8–10 do not suggest a return to this image or to the double one of submersion and coming up. If the Apostle was arguing from the liturgical-ritual action, then *v.* 8 would have had to run differently. Instead of 'dying' we would have expected 'being buried', instead of 'living with (Him)' 'rising with (Him)'. Paul draws his argument from *the salvation event* of the death and resurrection of Christ, as *vv.* 4 and 5 show. That the same consideration dominates Paul's thinking can be perceived even from iv. 25: 'He was delivered up (to death) on account of our sins and was raised on account of our justification.' *The opposition 'death and life' in Rom. vi has not been taken from the figurative nature of baptism, but from the reality of the death and resurrection of Christ.*

For Paul, then, the sacramental symbol is only a point of departure for his theological statements in Rom. vi. That this is a quite different

[104] Pp. 153f.

approach from that of a man dominated by liturgy, or from that of a 'mystagogue', can be confirmed by a comparison with Cyril of Jerusalem. The bishop of Jerusalem has read far more out of the event from which Paul derives his figurative συνετάφημεν, to say nothing of the fact that he mentions numerous other rites administered both before and after the real act of baptism. For him the point of comparison does not lie simply in the event, but also in the locality. In *Myst. cat.* II, 4 he tells the newly baptized that they were led to the sacred baptismal basin (κολυμβήθρα, lit. = pool) ὡς ὁ Χριστὸς ἀπὸ τοῦ σταυροῦ ἐπὶ τὸ προκείμενον μνῆμα.[105] Therein lies a quite different application of the symbolism. The *place* gains a sacred significance, just as the Jordan, whose waters the Lord Himself sanctified through his baptism, plays a great part in the iconography and liturgical terminology of baptism.[106] Further, in virtue of the double significance of submersion and emergence, the bishop of the fourth Christian century sees a double meaning symbolized in the baptismal water also; the clear standing water becomes to him a 'grave' and 'mother', because the ascending up (out of the water) to light, the resurrection to life, is a new birth: καὶ τὸ σωτήριον ἐκεῖνο ὕδωρ καὶ τάφος ὑμῖν ἐγένετο καὶ μήτηρ.[107] Accordingly, the effect of it is not simply cessation from sin (for Paul = dying to the mischief wrought by the power of sin), but also becoming the children of God.[108]

Lietzmann is not unjustified in speaking of the 'baptism of death': the union with death, the becoming buried, is the primary element in the Pauline view in Rom. vi.[109] Dying to the ruin wrought by the power of sin, with the goal of walking in a new life for God, is something different from the 'new birth' of the mystery religions. The numerous examples which A. Dieterich reproduces in his 'Mithrasliturgie'[110] admittedly also have their goal in a fresh quickening, but Dieterich himself associates these with the 'varied kinds of rejuvenating magic', with which the Greek as well as German popular beliefs were acquainted.[111]

> The *mustes* goes through many torments, like the sufferings of death, and finally attains to a wonderful light and to pure places and meadows. He is 'together with holy and pure men and from

[105] Quasten 83, 14f.

[106] Cf. H. Leclerq in DAL II, 1 (1910) col. 359ff, 382ff. The passage of the Israelites through Jordan also contributed much to the symbolism of the Jordan, cf. F. J. Dölger in *AC* 2 (1930) 63–79; P. Lundberg, *La Typologie baptismale*, 146–166; J. Daniélou, *Sacramentum Futuri*, Paris 1950, 233–245.

[107] Ibid. (Quasten 84, 15–16).

[108] *Myst. cat.* II, 6 (Quasten 86, 8–9).

[109] That is recognized in most recent works.

[110] Pp. 162f.

[111] Op. cit. 159.

that place (above) he contemplates the unconsecrated band of the living, who are still unclean and walk beneath him in much filth and dust, and throng together, and who still remain in the fear of death because of (their) evil, because they do not believe on the blessings that are to be found there (above)'.

In these Mysteries, the chief thing is and remains the ascending up to a new and 'higher' existence, or as Dieterich himself[112] expresses it in words from Hippolytus: ἡ γένεσις ἡ πνευματική, ἡ ἐπουράνιος, ἡ ἄνω.[113]

It is not only Paul's representation in Rom. vi that stands in contradiction to this, for we recall his stress on the ethical tendency of the sacramental dying, issuing in a life obedient to God in this world under the sway of sin; nor is it only the universality of baptism that separates the Christian rite from the arrogant pride of these initiates in their mysteries: the whole conception of the mystery event itself is different. The Apostle is concerned about the sacramental 'being buried', but there the concern is to experience a painful mortification; for Paul a 'rising with Christ' is *opened up*, there a transference to a higher condition of the soul happens in the mysterious experience itself; with Paul the 'mystery' remains essentially a baptism to death, not to be separated from water and submersion, but there a 'birth' takes place, a quickening through renewal and an elevation of the powers of the soul.

W. Tr. Hahn carries out a comparison of baptism with the Phrygian *taurobolium*, and he concludes with respect to the rite: 'whereas the outward course of the action in baptism matters little to Paul, so that he nowhere stays to discuss the matter ... for one who describes the Phrygian Mystery the whole weight falls on the dramatic accomplishment of the action. Each individual act has its own symbolic significance. Naturalistic-animistic ideas, like the transmission of new life into the soul of the dead through the blood, or the necessity for a renewal of the initiation, are undeniable. If a certain symbolism does attach to the Christian baptismal action, in Paul's estimate no importance attaches to it.'[114]

Admittedly the problem of the relation between early Christian and pagan Mystery ideas is thereby only postponed. The question arises whether the cults of dying and rising gods offer an analogy to the event from the point of view of concept and content. This problem must be dealt with later (§ 20). Here it is enough to repudiate the symbolic parallelism.

[112] Op. cit. 164. [113] Refut. *v*. 8, 41 (Wendland 96, 19). [114] Op. cit. p. 13.

In itself the possibility ought not to be dismissed out of hand that the origin of the image contained in βαπτίζεσθαι is to be assigned to the metaphorical language of the Old Testament. To the latter the 'new birth' in the Hellenistic sense is foreign; but it does know the figure of overflowing waters and of sinking in the flood, especially in illustrating distress and sorrow, cf. Ps. xvii. 16; xxxi. 6; xxxix. 2; xli. 8; lxviii. 2, 16; cxxiii. 4 (LXX); Job. xxii. 11; Jon. ii. 5; Is. xliii. 2. It is true that the *verbal* significance of βαπτίζειν gives no support for this in the Old Testament-Jewish sphere;[115] but Jesus himself uses the figure (Mk. x. 38; Lk. xii. 50),[116] and that is significant. The idea that these sayings could not have been formulated in this manner except in a milieu of Hellenistic speech,[117] needs to be accepted only by one who attributes to Jesus an imperfect mastery of his own language. That Paul directly makes use of a tradition of such sayings of Jesus in Rom. vi. 4 is not very likely, since he does not consider death as baptism but conversely baptism as death.[118] But he could have drawn from the same treasury of images that brought together the affliction of death and the flood of waters.

This hypothesis, however, does not possess great probability. The picture of a man drowning is something different from that of the grave. Moreover Paul does not start out from suffering and death and seek a picture for it, but he interprets subsequently the proceedings of baptism that are already given him. Since the thought of Jesus' death and resurrection dominates his whole theology, it is most plausible to attribute to him this interpretation of baptism as a being buried with Christ. If it be borne in mind that in Gal. iii. 27 he describes baptism as 'putting on Christ', in Col. ii. 11 as 'the circumcision of Christ', in Tit. iii. 5 as 'regeneration', it will be recognized that we have to do with picture language here, not with the terminology of the Mysteries. Moreover Paul, as a genuine Jew and a man of the ancient world, had a gift and predilection for plastic imagery; yet he did not use this ability for unbridled fantasy but disciplined it and put it in the service of his proclamation of the salvation of Jesus the Christ. He also sought to show that in the baptismal event we meet the crucified and risen Lord and are most closely bound with Him.

115 Cf. Oepke in *ThW* I, 532–4.

116 The connection with the saying about the cup Mk. x. 38 points yet more strongly to the Old Testament background, cf. Ps. lxxiv. 9; Is. li. 17–22; Lam. iv. 21; Ezk. xxiii. 31–33. Cf. Billerbeck I, 836–8; further O. Kuss, Zur Frage einer vorpaulinischen Todestaufe: *MüThZ* 4 (1953) 1–17.

117 Oepke in *ThW* I, 536, 24–33.

118 Contra J. Coppens in DB Suppl. I, col. 888; O. Cullmann, *Die Tauflehre des NT*, 12ff; Flemington, op. cit. 31f, 72f.

Section 2. OTHER TEXTS

§9. GAL. ii. 19 (cf. v. 24; vi. 14)

The saying about 'being crucified with' Christ in Rom. vi. 6 provides a link with the Letter to the Galatians. Since this Letter stands both temporally and essentially nearer Romans than the Prison Epistles, in which are found the most closely related passage to Rom. vi, namely Col. ii. 12, as well as certain other points of contact, the Galatians passages will be examined first.

In Gal. ii. 19 the Apostle speaks of his being liberated from the dominion of the Mosaic *nomos*, in which he did not experience justification and salvation (cf. *v.* 16), and of his entry into the sphere of the divine life. That the event of baptism was bound up with this decisive turning point in his life is plain (Acts. ix. 18; xxii. 16); but Paul does not expressly mention his baptism here (as also elsewhere). Does he, notwithstanding, have it in mind? The perfect συνεσταύρωμαι does not direct attention to a definite and determinable point of time, as the aorist συνεσταυρώθη does in Rom. vi. 6; but ἀπέθανον stands in front of it, and the contrast ἀπέθανον-ζήσω reminds us of the opposition of death and life in Rom. vi. Since there is a correspondence there, 'on the part of Christ' and 'on the part of the baptized', the comparison between Rom. vi. 10 and Gal. ii. 19a is justified:

Rom. vi. 10.	Gal. ii. 19a.
(Χριστὸς) ἀπέθανεν ...	(ἐγὼ) ἀπέθανον
ζῇ τῷ θεῷ	ἵνα θεῷ ζήσω

Paul has died over against the *nomos* (treated as personified), as the baptized in Rom. vi dies over against the power of sin (cf. Schlier ad loc). But he amplifies it with the addition 'through the law'. It can hardly be that in this short phrase the Apostle introduces a different *nomos*, perchance that of 'the Spirit and Life' (Rom. viii. 2);[119] if it were so, a similar explanatory attribute would most certainly be necessary. That Paul has died to the hapless Jewish *nomos* precisely *through* this same *nomos*, gives the sentence its terseness and sharpness.

That this strict tyrant gradually drove him (διά causative) to escape his clutches through death would be a simple explanation;[120] but it founders on the fact that Paul 'thinks concretely and objectively' (Oepke ad loc), and that ἀπέθανον contains no action on Paul's part—he knows only too well that all his endeavours to shake off the yoke of the *nomos*

[119] So Lagrange ad loc; cf. on the contrary διὰ νόμου Χριστοῦ Gal. vi. 2.
[120] On this cf. Augustine, Expos. 17 in Gal. (PL 35, 2115), further Zahn and Burton ad loc.

would have been fruitless. No, he has been drawn into an event in which the *nomos* itself was dethroned and robbed of its sovereignty.

This inclusive event comes to light in the following clause: 'I have been crucified with Christ.' Paul's dying has been included in the death of Christ on the cross, who in our stead took on Himself the curse of the law (Gal. iii. 13). The curse of the law has unloaded itself on Christ and therewith exhausted itself. The evil tyrant no more has authority over those whom Christ represented at that time. They have withdrawn from the sphere of his rule and are 'dead' in respect of him. But who are they, for whose benefit this accursed death of Christ that frees from the *nomos* takes place? In principle all men, factually, however, only those who believe in Christ (ii. 16; iii. 14). To the latter Paul belongs; he also has died to the *nomos*, because he has been crucified with Christ.

When did this 'dying' of Paul take place? The συνεσταύρωμαι gives no exact information about it, for the perfect expresses the continuous power of this event. The goal and the immediate consequence of the freeing from the *nomos* was life for God (θεῷ ζήσω), and this is realized and continues in close personal fellowship with Christ (*v.* 20). Here also, as in Rom. vi, the *death* (over against the power of ruin) is not to be thought of apart from the simultaneous resurrection to *life* (in Christ for God). Because, however, Paul's attention directs itself at once to this present salvation, so passionately apprehended by him, the point at which this event began is no longer discernible in συνεσταύρωμαι; we are referred back to ἀπέθανον. This aorist does not signify that Paul died 'simultaneously' with Christ on the cross, but rather that he was bound up with the once-for-all crucifixion of Christ through baptism.[121] From now on the Apostle, 'crucified with (the Christ)', is most closely associated with the Χριστὸς ἐσταυρωμένος, iii. 1; his personal entry into this union with his Lord took place when the step of *faith* was taken (ἐπιστεύσαμεν ii. 16), just as for those he was addressing the reception of the Spirit (mediated through faith and baptism) marked the initial stage (ἐναρξάμενοι πνεύματι) of their salvation and signified the remaking of their existence. Paul thus 'dies' to the *nomos* when he becomes a Christian, because he then enters into a union with Christ, who 'through the law died to the law', and from that time he has 'been crucified', because in baptism he became 'crucified with' Christ. The hour of his birth in faith (Damascus) and his baptism—they both belong inseparably together for him[122]—had drawn him into the event that

[121] Cf. W. Tr. Hahn, op. cit. 66.

[122] J. Schneider, *Passionsmystik* p. 34, n. 2, sets 'conversion' and baptism sharply over against each other, but he thereby denies their inner connection, in which both alike stand under the viewpoint of the attainment of salvation.

once took place on Golgotha for our salvation. The death of Christ now becomes effective for his deliverance; baptism brings him into the saving union with the cross of Christ.

A comparison with the related passage Rom. vii. 4–6 is instructive. According to this statement also believers in Christ have been made dead for the *nomos* (ἐθανατώθητε[123]), and in truth 'through the body of Christ'. If this expression immediately awakens a recollection of the hour of salvation on Golgotha (in which this actually and in principle happened for all), the continuation shows that the Apostle had in view their 'being put to death' in baptism. For in the next two verses (γάρ) he confirms this dying over against the *nomos*, with the goal of belonging to the Risen One (and of living for God), in such a manner as to leave no doubt concerning the point of time of their personal change from death to life.

Verse 4	Verse 6
	(κατηργήθημεν) ·
ἐθανατώθητε τῷ νόμῳ	ἀπὸ τοῦ νόμου ἀποθανόντες
εἰς ... τῷ ἐκ νεκρῶν ἐγερθέντι	ὥστε ... ἐν καινότητι πνεύματος

The ἀποθανόντες of *v.* 6 is temporarily settled by νυνί; this denotes the Christian period of their life in contrast to their earlier pagan (ὅτε *v.* 5) life. The 'dying away' from the powers of ruin that hold men captive thus occurs at the turning point between the two, i.e. in baptism. This passage relates also to the efficacy of Christ's death and resurrection, in that it applies the effects and consequences (ἵνα, εἰς τό ... ὥστε) of the Christ event to the baptized. Without formally speaking of dying and rising with Christ, it makes the inner connection plain (especially in *v.* 4) between the salvation-event in baptism and the great Christ event. Of the rite of immersion and emergence we hear nothing; no metaphorical expression of any sort alludes to it. The kerygma of the death and resurrection of Christ alone guides the movement of thought—a confirmation of the results we gained from Rom. vi. Moreover the Apostle, when writing Rom. vii, will still have had vividly in his consciousness the flow of thought in Rom. vi. But now, back to Galatians!

In Gal. ii. 19b, as in Rom. vi. 6, the Apostle might also have said συνεσταυρώθην. But he overleaps this stage of the appropriation of salvation, because in the present context he is concerned with the continuing *life* for God in the fellowship of Christ. In the argument

[123] According to Schlatter, *Gottes Gerechtigkeit* 226, θανατοῦσθαι· as contrasted with ἀποθνῄσκειν means 'to be put in the condition of a dead man'.

with Peter he battles that the freedom from the law that has been won should completely interpenetrate the Christian way of life (*v.* 14b). Because Christ has become the centre of his life in place of his own ego (*v.* 20a), his 'life in the flesh', i.e., his outward behaviour, continues to be determined and led solely by faith in his Lord, to whose love he knows himself most deeply indebted (*v.* 20b).

The perfect συνεσταύρωμαι Gal. ii. 19b makes it obvious that Paul not only considers entry into the fellowship of Christ as a becoming crucified with Christ, hence that he can bring the act of baptism into closest connection with the event of Golgotha; he also looks on the Christian existence itself as an abiding union with the *Christus crucifixus*. At this point we find ourselves related to the sacramental event at a further stage. The statement in Gal. ii. 19, first uttered in the interests of Paul's teaching on justification, at the same time leads to personal mysticism. The restrained ardour of the Apostle, fighting for 'his Gospel', is plainly perceptible. The Christ, whom he proclaims as Redeemer from the forced labour of the *nomos*, has also become his personal Saviour, has personally loved him, and given himself to the death on the cross personally for him.[124] Hence συνεσταύρωμαι possesses here a mystic warmth.

This mysticism of the cross is brought in a peculiar manner to ultimate expression in vi. 14. The Jewish enthusiasts for the law, who themselves do not keep the law, do but hide their human arrogance and ambition behind their zealotic demand for circumcision (*v.* 13). But Paul will not boast at all, except in the cross of Jesus Christ, through whom the world is 'crucified' to him and he to the world (*v.* 14). It does not exist any more for him, nor he for it. He is καινὴ κτίσις (*v.* 15). That is the last consequence drawn from the συνεσταύρωμαι, the radical application of it to his own ego. But here also, as in ii. 19, it becomes plain through the following sentence that this 'mysticism of death' is at the same time a 'mysticism of life'. Through death (to the power of sin, Rom. vi. 6, the *nomos*, Gal. ii. 19, the 'world', vi. 14) Paul has attained with Christ to life 'for God', a life that is completely new, fashioned after Christ because united with Christ.

Accordingly, for this 'being crucified with' (Christ) three stages are recognizable:

(1) The crucifixion of Christ, which in principle takes place 'for all' (ὑπὲρ ἡμῶν Gal. iii. 13);

[124] This is the one passage in which Paul speaks of himself personally as object of the love and sacrifice of Christ.

(2) The 'crucifixion with' (Christ) of the Christian at the time of his personally becoming a Christian, i.e. at his baptism (ἀπέθανον Gal. ii. 19a);

(3) The Christian's 'state of having been crucified with' Christ, in his continuous fellowship with the Lord (συνεσταύρωμαι Gal. ii. 19b; cf. vi. 14).

But that has not exhausted the possibilities which for Paul are opened up in this area of thought. The Letter to the Galatians, which above all is occupied with the cross of Jesus (v. 11; vi. 12), makes yet another contribution in v. 24. The remarkable feature that immediately catches the eye here is the active συσταυροῦν, for hitherto we have met the verb only in the passive. Concern for ascetic repression of the inclinations of the flesh is not in mind;[125] the aorist points to a definite event: becoming a Christian, or baptism. This is not represented thereby as 'an act of will of the baptized' (Oepke ad loc); for in the other texts, so far as the operation of salvation is concerned, it is always considered as the work of God. The 'crucifying of the flesh' is the free moral act of a man, which he accomplishes at his conversion to Christ (cf. Steinmann-Tillmann ad loc), the human act responding to the divine work of grace in baptism.

Συσταυροῦν is thus evaluated as an *ethical* act. Because the Christian *became* crucified with Christ in baptism, he *ought* also at the same time to crucify his flesh with its sinful passions and desires. In the ethical application the same concept of 'evil desires', which the power of sin uses as its aides, emerged in Rom. vi. 12 as in Gal. v. 24. The ethical character of the verse in Galatians, formulated as an affirmative proposition, is due to the context. By the expression 'those who belong to Christ', the Apostle understands Christians who unreservedly deserve this name and have adopted the exhortation added in *v.* 25 as the basis of their Christian life. Perhaps it is not accidental that here also after the crucifying—though admittedly not in any inner connection with it—Paul speaks of *life* (in the Spirit). In any case the thought of crucifying also becomes a moral motive.

The watchword συσταυρωθῆναι has led us away somewhat from the theme of baptism, but it has opened up the vista to wider connections. We recognized that Gal. ii. 19 looks back to the point of time when a man becomes a Christian. For Paul the 'becoming crucified with' Christ then took place personally. He died with Christ 'through the *nomos* to the *nomos*', in order to live for God. From then on he sees the

[125] Chrysostom, Theophylact, Cornelius a Lapide, Estius, etc.

law of 'being crucified with Christ', in order to live in Christ for God alone, as extended to his very being, indeed as effective in his entire existence.

§10. COL. ii. 11–13; iii. 1–4

The idea that in baptism a saving event σὺν Χριστῷ takes place is expounded by Paul not only in the classic passage, Rom. vi. 1–11, but also with all clarity in Col. ii. 12. A comparison of the two passages offers a good method of arriving at a better understanding of the sacramental view of dying and rising with Christ. Is the same figurative representation of baptism present as in Rom. vi, and does it appear as a grave in which the old sinful man disappears? Or does the submergence and emergence become a symbol for the death and resurrection with Christ? If ἐν ᾧ in *v.* 12 is referred to the immediately preceding βαπτίσματι and not to the further removed Χριστόν (*v.* 8), then the emergence from the baptismal water is formally equated with the resurrection. We would then find expressed the interpretation of the symbolic occurrence that we refused for Rom. vi.

> Both interpretations are represented, even though the more recent exegetes who treat the passage in its context in the main relate ἐν ᾧ to Christ. The connection with βαπτίσματι is favoured by Estius, Natalis, Bisping, Haupt, Abbott, Oepke,[126] Prat.[127] Haupt is led to this close association with βαπτίσματι through the coordinating of συνταφέντες and συνηγέρθητε; but it is open to question whether this coordination, which doubtless is linguistically present, does not remain preserved in the other interpretation also.

Since the construction of the period offers good hope of assisting in its clarification, it is here distinctly sketched:

v. 10 a	καὶ ἐστὲ ἐν αὐτῷ	πεπληρωμένοι
b		ὅς ἐστιν ἡ κεφαλὴ πάσης ἀρχῆς καὶ ἐξουσίας,
11 a	ἐν ᾧ	καὶ περιετμήθητε περιτομῇ ἀχειροποιήτῳ
b		ἐν τῇ ἀπεκδύσει τοῦ σώματος τῆς σαρκός,
c		ἐν τῇ περιτομῇ τοῦ Χριστοῦ
12 a		συνταφέντες αὐτῷ ἐν τῷ βαπτίσματι
b	ἐν ᾧ	καὶ συνηγέρθητε
		διὰ τῆς πίστεως τῆς ἐνεργείας τοῦ θεοῦ
		τοῦ ἐγείραντος αὐτὸν ἐκ νεκρῶν

[126] In *ThW* I, 543, 34f. [127] Op. cit. II, 311, n. 1.

In the construction so outlined the structural line ἐν αὐτῷ (10a)—ἐν ᾧ (11a)—ἐν ᾧ (12b) is striking. We might have expected *v.* 12 to begin with ἐν ᾧ. The verse division has manifestly been influenced by the contrast συνταφέντες-συνηγέρθητε. But an analysis of *v.* 11 shows that *v.* 12a essentially belongs to its preceding context.

The nature of the 'spiritual[128] circumcision' (*v.* 11a) is indicated by the immediately following expressions with ἐν:

1. ἐν τῇ ἀπεκδύσει κτλ = 'in stripping off the body of flesh'. The setting aside of the 'body of flesh' is illustrated by making use of the figure of Jewish circumcision, in which a small part of flesh is 'taken off', cf. Rom. vi. 6 the 'destruction of the body of sin'. That no doubt should remain that Christian 'circumcision' is meant Paul adds:

2. ἐν τῇ περιτομῇ τοῦ Χριστοῦ = 'in the circumcision of Christ'. The latter is a 'Christ-genitive'; it characterizes the circumcision as spiritual in distinction to fleshly, such as is possible only 'in Christ'.[129] But now the Apostle desires to leave this Jewish figure and to speak plainly in his own language:

3. συνταφέντες ἀυτῷ ἐν τῷ βαπτίσματι = 'buried with him in *baptism*'. Here the Christian term appears. The συνταφέντες, also attached grammatically to περιετμήθητε, offers an analogy to this image, whereby the ἀπέκδυσις is the *tertium comparationis:* the being buried signifies a total disappearance, a total stripping off the old body.[130]

Hence *vv.* 11a–12a form inclusively, with respect to language and symbolism alike, *a perfectly complete whole.* Paul draws out a comparison, with increasing clarity as he proceeds, between Jewish circumcision and Christian baptism, and the latter appears as the ideal fulfilment of the ancient rite. In this context the Apostle is concerned to show that this has become possible 'in Christ' and in Him alone.

With *v.* 12b a new line of thought on the significance of Christ begins. Certainly it has been influenced, and perhaps even occasioned, by the still resounding συνταφέντες. Just as in Rom. vi, the Apostle cannot remain standing at death. The grave immediately wakens in him

[128] ἀχειροποιήτῳ lit., 'not made with hands', denotes the contrast with the spacial-temporal world of experience, cf. Mk. xiv. 58; Acts. vii. 48; 2 Cor. v. 1. Lohmeyer, *Kol.* (p. 108, n. 4) translates it 'invisible'; that may be an element in the concept, but it is not the decisive one—baptism is visible!

[129] It is not an obj. gen., as v. Soden thinks (*Handkomm. z. NT.* Freiburg 1891), 'the circumcision relating to death', cf. Col. i. 22; Rom. viii. 3; nor is it a subj. gen., a 'circumcision which Christ himself performs' (Chrysostom, Theophylact, cf. Meinertz); but a gen. of quality (so most recent scholars) in the sense of a 'Christ-genitive', cf. O. Schmitz, *Christusgemeinschaft* 153–5.

[130] The ἀπέκδυσις in baptism cannot be explained by the idea that occurs later, that the demonic forces and powers were 'stripped off' through the cross of Christ, as Käsemann, *Leib und Leib Christi* 139f. Verse 15 stands at too great a remove for this.

the thought of the resurrection. As Christ rose from the dead, all we who were buried with Him are also raised with Him, 'because of faith in the power of God,[131] who raised Him from the dead'. That Paul in writing συνηγέρθητε is still thinking of baptism is not to be doubted; but he no longer speaks of baptism as the mediating cause, but of faith, and that has a good reason. For faith rivets together the death and resurrection of Jesus into an inseparable event, and understands both as the one salvation-event, faith, namely, in the God who, by His unlimited might and majesty, can call the dead to life (cf. Rom. iv. 17), and most powerfully revealed this might and majesty in the raising of His Son (Eph. i. 19f; cf. the heaping up of expressions for 'might' δύναμις, ἐνέργεια, κράτος, ἰσχύς, as well as the emphasis on abundance τὸ ὑπερβάλλον μέγεθος). What faith affirms for Christ, that it affirms also for those who have been buried σὺν Χριστῷ in the water of baptism: they have risen in and with Christ. Thus it is seen in this passage also, that Paul argues from *faith*, i.e. from the confession that Christ has died, was buried and has been raised, not from the rite and its symbolism.[132]

The antithesis συνταφέντες-συνηγέρθητε produces an after effect in the following verse in νεκρούς-συνεζωοποίησεν. But νεκρούς, denoting a condition, calls attention to a modification in the thought, even as the fact that God now appears as subject makes it evident that a change of standpoint has taken place. Haupt characterizes this well: 'Previously *baptism* was represented as a dying with Christ, here the *former life* is apprehended as a condition of death' (ad loc). But does not συνεζωοποίησεν again mean baptism? Essentially yes, but formally no. Paul is obviously thinking of the point of time at which one becomes a Christian, and which factually is manifested in baptism; but he is not concerned about the means but the effect; those who formerly were 'dead' have now become the 'living'. One thing only he stresses again in this Christological context: it was a saving event σὺν Χριστῷ. This verse accordingly is a confirmation that the dogmatic interest outweighs the liturgical.

With regard to the view of baptism in this passage, if *v.* 13 is brought into relief by *v.* 12, it is nevertheless not right to set the aorist συνεζωοποίησεν temporarily and essentially on a plane with χαρισάμενος and the following aorist participles. J. Cools[133] draws

[131] Obj. not subj. gen. (Rendtorff translates: Through the faith that derives from the working of God). Knabenbauer rightly alludes to Rom. x. 9.

[132] Cf. also Lohmeyer: 'Their sequence (i.e. of the two ἐν ᾧ sentences, *vv.* 11 and 12) has been determined by the content of the confession: He has died, has been buried and raised' (*Kol.* p. 108).

[133] Op. cit. 302f.

from this the inference that 'making alive with Christ' relates to the historical, once-for-all event. A sacramental resurrection of *Christians* lies fully in the range of the Apostle's thought, namely in so far as the resurrection of Christ has already occurred (Rom. vi. 4) and the baptized are closely united with it (Rom. vi. 5 σύμφυτοι). The expression συνεζωοποίησεν belongs to this view. Resurrection signifies life. In Col. ii. 13 Paul speaks of his readers earlier walking in sin and of their subsequent reception into the sphere of Christ's life, represented as God's deed of power and grace. But no short section is introduced before χαρισάμενος, which linguistically could be recognized by association with the participle and *change from the 2nd to 1st pers. plur.* (ὑμᾶς to ἡμῖν). The aorist participle χαρισάμενος therefore relates to a former time ('after that') and leads back from the level of personal appropriation of salvation on the part of the addressees to that of the universal saving act of God.

A comparison of Col. ii. 12 with Paul's view of baptism in Rom. vi. 4ff yields the following results:

1. The baptismal teaching of the Apostle in Rom. vi is completely confirmed by the condensed, yet clearly comprehensible thought of *v*. 12. Baptism is relation to the death of Jesus. According to its rite, the bath of baptism operates like a grave. When this grave closes over the head of the baptized, the old man of sin and flesh disappears. But *faith* knows: Christ has been raised to a new and glorified life, and because the baptized is bound σὺν Χριστῷ, he too does not remain in death, but is raised up by the same power of God the Father to a new life in God. Verse 12 may be regarded as a good summary of the thought of Rom. vi.

2. Paul's view of baptism receives fresh illumination by the comparison with circumcision. In both cases something is 'stripped off'; in the Jewish rite, in a physically real manner, a little piece of flesh; in Christian baptism, in a sacramentally real manner, the 'body of flesh'. The conformity of the pictures of circumcision and of the grave shows that the double aspect of submersion and emergence is not present to the Apostle's mind. Baptism is a symbol of these things because it is a baptism of death, and it is a 'sacrament of life' only because it unites with Christ who rose from death.[134]

[134] Lohmeyer's construction is very refined. He finds death in the figure of circumcision, burial in baptism, and resurrection in faith (p. 108). Admittedly L. relates the 'circumcision of Christ' to Christ's death, as many before him (von Soden, cf. also Haupt). Nevertheless the participle συνταφέντες *v*. 12a closely adheres to *v*. 11 and demands that this verse be interpreted as referring to baptism, even as the unambiguous statement of *v*. 12a.

3. The employment in Col. ii of various expressions for entry into the fellowship of life with Christ shows that for Paul the conception of dying and rising with Christ is but one possibility among various others of describing this appropriation of salvation. He can also represent baptism as 'the circumcision of Christ', in which everything sinful is stripped off and a man is consecrated to God. Instead of the double expression 'dying and rising with Christ', he can use the expression 'being made alive with Christ'. At all times the decisive thing is the result: the attainment of fellowship with Christ Jesus (Rom. vi. 11).

Along with these agreements the differences between Rom. vi and Col. ii should be observed:[135]

1. In Rom. vi 'rising with' (Christ) as a factor of salvation is only silently presupposed, since the Apostle immediately proceeds to the ethical appeal to 'walk in a new life'. In Col. ii, on the contrary, 'resurrection with' (Christ) is expressly mentioned; it has already (sacramentally) taken place (aorist).

2. In Col. ii. 12 *faith* is the means that unites death and resurrection, whereas in Rom. vi faith is not so much as mentioned.

These differences are to be explained by the differing situations presupposed in the Letters and the practical tendency which the Apostle from time to time pursues. In Rom. vi the Apostle was motivated by an endeavour to draw from the sacramental salvation event of dying and rising with Christ the ethical consequence: thus you have died to the power of sin and you live for God. Col. ii is dominated by a stronger dogmatic interest. There was a threat that Christ be dethroned by the Gnostic false teachers from his unique position as Mediator of salvation in favour of the στοιχεῖα τοῦ κόσμου (*v.* 8).[136] Against this the Apostle shows the Colossians that in Christ, and in Him alone, they *have* attained to full salvation and that they must hold firmly to this *faith*.

The close connection between sacrament and ethics, however, is not dissolved in Col. ii, only Paul first gives the application to the moral attitude in iii. 1: 'If you, therefore, have risen with Christ, seek that which is above....' The moral tendency here, once more corresponding to the situation of the Letter, takes a somewhat different direction from that in Rom. vi. The prevailing viewpoint is not that the Colossians should die to the power of sin, but that they, who have died to the στοιχεῖα τοῦ κόσμου (ii. 20), should no longer allow themselves to be led astray by the false teachers and return to the service of the στοιχεῖα (*vv.* 16–23). Everything that the false teachers prescribe in connection

[135] Cf. W. Tr. Hahn, op. cit. 38–42.
[136] Cf. J. Gewiess, *Christus und das Heil nach dem Kol.*, Diss. Breslau 1932, especially 1ff, 31f.

with this 'worship of angels' (*v.* 18), e.g. abstention from foods and drinks, feasts and festival days (*vv.* 16, 21), is but a shadow of the future realities that Christ has brought (*v.* 17); it belongs to the corruptible and not to the incorruptible heavenly kingdom, and is a part of the human and not the divine order (*v.* 22). To all these things the Colossians have died with Christ; but they have also risen with Him to the real salvation. In accordance with the new being that is theirs, they no longer belong to the lower world of men but to the heavenly world of God (iii. 1f); they have been called from corruptibility to the incorruptible divine δόξα, which they bear in themselves even now in a veiled fashion, but which will be unveiled at the appearing of Christ (iii. 4). These soteriological statements, however, are again diverted into the channel of ethics. For Paul, as in Rom. vi, knows the perpetual susceptibility of the baptized to temptation.

Col. iii. 1–4 is instructive above all for its σὺν-Χριστῷ-utterances. In *v.* 1 συνηγέρθητε τῷ Χριστῷ relates to the appropriation of salvation, cf. ii. 12. Yet here also the Apostle does not have before his eyes the *symbolism* of dying and rising in the baptismal rite; for the dying is mentioned *after* the rising (*v.* 3). The occasion was provided by the sharply stated antithesis τὰ ἄνω-μὴ τὰ ἐπὶ τῆς γῆς (*v.* 2).

In *v.* 3 σὺν Χριστῷ is employed under a different point of view: 'For you have died, and your life has been hidden σὺν Χριστῷ in God.' The perfect κέκρυπται suggests a condition, and so does not refer again to the entry to salvation. By 'life' is meant here the true, deeper life of Christians in contrast to the simple transitory life in the world, life as an element of the divine salvation in contrast to life adjudged as mere existence. The contrast 'below'-'above' still shimmers in the background from *v.* 2. According to their existence believers in Christ are still on the earth, but Christ is already 'above' with God, 'enthroned at the right hand of God' (*v.* 1b). The life that is an element of salvation, that we have attained through being raised with Christ (resurrection indeed signifies life), cannot have its full effect in us as it has in Christ, for we are still on earth. As we still walk in the 'body of humiliation' (cf. Phil. iii. 21), it cannot yet be revealed in its glory; in its δόξα it is still hidden σὺν Χριστῷ in God. Because of the spacial element in the conception that has been described, this σύν includes a local meaning: with, along with, in the presence of Christ. Since it deals with a condition that is already given, this statement cannot be regarded as eschatological; it could be termed *transcendental.* Paul uses σὺν Χριστῷ with the same meaning in Phil. i. 23: in the presence of Christ, the Lord now exalted to the right hand of God.

Verse 4 finally brings σὺν Χριστῷ in an eschatological context: 'When Christ, our life (at the parousia), appears, then you also will become visible *together with him* in divine glory.' Actually, one might have expected after *v.* 3: then your (previous hidden) life will become visible, and that in glory. But the ardour of Paul's piety towards Christ ever and again hinders him from all schematic formulations. He has joined 'our life' with Christ; therefore our life is not only *with* Christ, but He *is* our life—it is 'an expression of deepest Christ-mysticism' (Meinertz).[137] Accordingly the Apostle must continue in a different manner: 'Then you also will appear σὺν Χριστῷ', and that outwardly visible, as bearers of the life of God that shines in its glory.

So the line runs from sacramental saving event to eschatology: although we still find ourselves on earth, we are nevertheless already united with Christ, who is enthroned at the right hand of God, and through Him and with Him (σὺν αὐτῷ) we belong to the heavenly world. But the parousia will bring the unveiling of our glory, again 'with Christ'. The *sacramental* saving event σὺν Χριστῷ is not yet a final, perfect good. The true salvation, as Christ Himself has attained it, is still veiled for those who are united with Him. But as it is already transcendentally present in the time between, it will be given them at the end of this age, and in truth again σὺν Χριστῷ. Thus for Paul sacrament and eschatology, present and eschatological utterances belong together in the theology of salvation. That which holds these view-points together, different in themselves though they be, is the formula σὺν Χριστῷ. Initial salvation and final salvation alike come from God σὺν Χριστῷ.

§11. EPH. ii. 4–6

The centre of gravity of Paul's theological statements on baptism in Rom. vi. 1–11 and Col. ii. 12f lies in the fact that it is an event of salvation σὺν Χριστῷ. In Eph. ii. 6 a new compound with σύν appears, joining the others we have already discussed: συνεκάθισεν (ἡμᾶς) ἐν τοῖς ἐπουρανίοις ἐν Χριστῷ Ἰησοῦ. The idea of our ascending a throne in heaven with Christ goes far beyond anything that Paul has hitherto suggested in his characteristic utterances about baptism.

Is the author[138] speaking about baptism at all in Eph. ii. 4–6? Any doubt on that disappears when we observe the context and recognize the close relationship of the passage with Col. ii. 13. Precisely as in

[137] This expression appears again in Ignatius of Antioch, Eph. iii. 2; vii. 2; Smyr. iv. 1; Magn. i. 2.

[138] On the Pauline authorship of Ephesians, cf. above p. 5, n. 9.

Colossians, only in far greater detail (*vv.* 1–3), he contrasts the walk in sin under the sway of demons, that characterized the readers in earlier days (πότε *v.* 2), with their present condition of salvation made possible by the freely bestowed kindness of God (*v.* 4). The sudden change is denoted by the three expressions with σύν, which extol the emancipation from the sphere of the divine wrath as the mighty act of divine love and pity (the subject is θεός), and at the same time link this salvation event most closely 'with Christ'. This can take place only in baptism (cf. Eph. iv. 4; v. 26). The agreement between Eph. ii. 5 and Col. ii. 13 is almost verbal:

Col. ii. 13	Eph. ii. 5
καὶ ὑμᾶς νεκροὺς ὄντας	καὶ ὄντας ἡμᾶς νεκροὺς
τοῖς παραπτώμασιν ...	τοῖς παραπτώμασιν
συνεζωοποίησεν (ὑμᾶς) σὺν αὐτῷ	συνεζωοποίησεν τῷ Χριστῷ

It is only as object that the first person plural takes the place of the second, and in Col. ii. 13 the omission (marked by the points) is filled out by an amplification on the uncircumcision of the flesh. However one may explain this remarkable agreement,[139] the similarity in any case is so great that only the same salvation event can be meant, and according to the Colossians passage it is undoubtedly baptism.

> Certain of the Fathers like Chrysostom, Theophylact, Ephraem, Oecumenius, interpreted the 'us' not in an individual manner but as a unity (the Church), and they maintained: as Jesus rose from the dead and received in heaven his seat of honour and glory, in principle salvation was also apportioned to us, since Jesus was the new Head of humanity. This explanation, which is right in itself but in the context insufficiently takes account of baptism, was adopted time and again. Cools expresses himself similarly as in Col. ii. 13, that we (as individuals) *at that time* were already raised with Christ and removed into heaven.[140]

The special and characteristic element appears first in *v.* 6. One is immediately struck by the fact that after συνεζωοποίησεν *v.* 5, which obviously can only look back to the resurrection of Christ, συνήγειρεν follows yet again in a peculiar manner. On that account many have rightly separated *v.* 6 from *v.* 5. Not a few exegetes consider that both aorists in *v.* 6 contain a prevision of our future resurrection and

[139] Meinertz, *Einl.* 137, attributes the priority to Col; J. Schmid, *Eph-Brief* 392ff, and Michaelis, *Einl.* 198f, emphasize the close relationship only in general terms. A detailed discussion is found in Percy, *Die Probleme* 360–433.

[140] Op. cit. 303.

exaltation, and have been determined by Paul's vivid experience of deliverance and strong consciousness of faith.[141]

But should the 'raised with' (Christ) have a different significance here from its occurrence in Col. ii. 12, where without doubt it looks back to the sacramental event?

An answer to this question can only be gained by an exegesis that sets out from the presuppositions of Ephesians. The key to it is offered in a comparison of Eph. ii. 6 with i. 20.

i. 20.	ii. 6
ἐγείρας αὐτὸν (= Χρ.) ἐκ νεκρῶν	καὶ συνήγειρεν
καὶ καθίσας ἐν δεξιᾷ αὐτοῦ	καὶ συνεκάθισεν
ἐν τοῖς ἐπουρανίοις	ἐν τοῖς ἐπουρανίοις
	ἐν Χριστῷ Ἰησοῦ

Unmistakably, the same thing that was earlier said of Christ is now transferred to us who are Christians (cf. Haupt ad loc), only with this difference, that God made our resurrection and assumption of a throne come to pass 'with *Christ*'. At this point we touch a specific group of ideas in Ephesians not found in Colossians in this pronounced form, namely the 'ascension to heaven of the Redeemer': by it He is exalted above all demonic powers in the air (ii. 2) and lower realms of heaven (vi. 12) to God, who granted Him the place of honour at his right hand and laid at his feet the entire demonic hierarchy (i. 21).[142] This triumphal procession to the highest heaven is biblically supported in iv. 8ff by a citation from Ps. lxviii. 19. By this means, as also by the clarity of the Christological confession, this view is preserved from any Gnostic misinterpretation, even though Gnostic ideas perhaps provided the material. These characteristic conceptions of Ephesians, which we have barely touched on here, have mingled in ii. 6 with the baptismal statements that have been our concern. With a bold look the author has grasped the tremendous potentialities of our 'becoming alive with Christ'. If we (in baptism) have really attained to life 'with Christ', we also have a part in the triumph of the Risen Lord and in his heavenly ascent to the throne. The statements about Christ are then actually transferred to us, though always with the significant addition σὺν αὐτῷ.

If awareness of this conception of Ephesians is sharpened, the differences between it and Col. ii. 12f are recognized at once:

[141] This interpretation enjoyed the favour of Theophylact (PG 124, 1053 B), Jerome (PL. 26, 468), Thomas Aquinas (lect. II in Eph. II sub II, ed. Vives II, 245: *nunc per spem, et tandem in futuro in re*), Estius (ed. Sausen IV, 171). Cf. further von Henle, Belser, Dibelius ad loc.

[142] On this cf. Schlier, *Christus und die Kirche* 1–18; Bultmann, *Theol.* 175.

1. In Col. ii baptism is described *before* the parallel of *v.* 13, in connection with the figure of circumcision, as a being buried with Christ (*v.* 12); this is completely lacking in Eph. ii.

2. The συνηγέρθητε in Col. ii. 12, as in Rom. vi, is connected with this being buried; in Eph. ii this two stage event is reproduced by a *single* expression συνεζωοποίησεν (in Col. ii. 13 the same expression also provides a summary and application to the addressees); but συνήγειρεν in *v.* 6 forms a unity with the following συνεκάθισεν.

3. Our installation in heaven is especially characterized by ἐν Χριστῷ Ἰησοῦ. Granted it is also said in Col. ii. 12 that we have been jointly raised 'in Christ' (ἐν ᾧ), that is intended above all to emphasize the significance of Christ over against the assertions of the false teachers (cf. ii. 8). In Ephesians this point of view disappears; the addition in Eph. ii. 6 ἐν Χριστῷ Ἰησοῦ could be important for the investiture in heaven of Christians with Christ.

> The formula 'in Christ (Jesus)' in Ephesians is difficult to interpret, and doubtless should not be interpreted in the same way in all places;[143] but whether, in contrast to the chief Pauline Letters, it has mainly an instrumental sense (as J. A. Allen thinks) is questionable. When one considers the cardinal conception of the 'Body of Christ', it seems more plausible to think in terms of our existence 'in Christ', our incorporation in the 'Body of Christ'. H. Schlier is surely right: 'It is not rhetorical plerophoria that occasions the Apostle to add to σὺν Χριστῷ the expression ἐν Χριστῷ, but rather exactness of expression. While the dead have become united with Christ and made alive in baptism, and while they have been raised from death (in union with Christ in baptism) and have been set in heaven, they have exchanged their previous existence, out of which they came, for a new one, i.e. for existence in Christ. And conversely: while they came in baptism into the life "in Christ", they were also raised together with Him and exalted into heaven' (ad loc p. 111).

The baptized therefore are already in this present time 'raised with Christ and installed in heaven', though the full wealth of the divine grace can be revealed only in the future (cf. *v.* 7). Hence the closing statements of *v.* 6, with all their emphasis on present salvation, are to a certain extent also 'proleptic'. A similar saying is to be found in Eph. i. 3. The 'blessing with all spiritual blessing', which was bestowed on us in

143 Cf. J. A. Allen, The 'in Christ' Formula in Ephesians, in *NTS* 5 (1958/59) 54–62.

heaven[144] 'in Christ', is an expression for the fulness of salvation; but we do not yet fully participate in this. Rather we have received the 'pledge of our inheritance' (i. 14), the promised Holy Spirit; but with Him we possess a real foundation and guarantee of the full heavenly inheritance which will be ours in the future. If this position of hope, occupied by the Christian, reminds us of uncontested Pauline passages like Rom. v. 2ff; viii. 24; xv. 13; Gal. v. 5, a 'proleptic' aorist as in Eph. i. 3; ii. 6 is also found in Rom. viii. 30. The chain of thought which, as in Eph. i. 4f, begins with the eternal decree of God, leads on over the individual steps of the way of salvation to the future transfiguration (ἐδόξασεν); that exists in hope, but it has not yet become effective reality.[145] One may still ask whether the ἐν Χριστῷ 'Ιησοῦ at the end of Eph. ii. 6 approximates to the realistic local view: it is in Christ as our *Head*, the Head of the Body, i.e. the Church (i. 22f), that we have our place in heaven. This idea, possibly suited to a Gnostic outlook,[146] but wholly translated into the Christian, should be carefully weighed, for the Christ who is enthroned in heaven is already designated in i. 22f as the κεφαλή of the Church; she is his σῶμα, the πλήρωμα of Him who 'fills the "all" in all (things)'.[147] On the other hand Christ, as the κεφαλή of the ἄνθρωπος conceived in cosmic proportions, preserves his position of authority over the Church, directing it in all things and promoting the growth of the Body (iv. 16, cf. v. 22–33).[148] Since the Church belongs to Christ it attains even now a presence in heaven, and its members on earth can be regarded as those who 'in Christ' already belong to heaven. This exposition of the concept of the Body of Christ—apart from the Gnostic background—is not new.[149] The close relationship

[144] ἐν τοῖς ἐπουρανίοις occurs only in Eph. i. 3, 20; ii. 6; iii. 10; vi. 10; and is a formal expression for ἐν τοῖς οὐρανοῖς, cf. the excursus of Dibelius-Greeven on i. 3 (p. 58); Schlier, *Eph.* 45–48.

[145] In Rom. viii. 30 it is to be observed that the chain of thought is developed from the viewpoint of *God*, for whom the realization of his purposes is perceptible with a glance. But in Eph. ii. 6 also God is the subject of the statements: here also his gracious deliverance must be exhibited to the last consequence: He works on us, with and in Christ, the same thing as He works on Christ.

[146] Cf. Schlier, *Christus und die Kirche* 37–48 (nevertheless he is cautious in applying the idea to Eph. ii. 6, cf. pp. 1f); Käsemann, *Leib u. Leib Christi* 142f. Bultmann *Theol.* 307, would understand the formula ἐν Χριστῷ as primarily eschatological, it denotes being incorporated in the σῶμα Χριστοῦ through baptism. For criticism of the view cf. Wikenhauser, *Kirche* 232–40; (in denial) F. Mussner, *Christus, das All und die Kirche*, Trier 1955, 91–94.

[147] The idea of the πλήρωμα cannot be discussed here; cf. the commentaries, Wikenhauser, *Kirche* 187–91; J. Gewiess, 'Die Begriffe πληροῦν und πλήρωμα im Kolosser- und Epheserbrief', in: *Vom Wort des Lebens* (Festschrift für M. Meinertz), Münster i. W. 1951, 128–41; A. Feuillet, 'L'Eglise plérôme du Christ d'après Eph. i. 23'; *Nouvelle Revue Theol.* 88 (1956) 449–72; 593–610; G. Delling in *ThW* VI, 290f; 300–4.

[148] Cf. Wikenhauser, *Kirche* 190 and 200.

[149] Cf. Knabenbauer ad loc: *intime cum eo iuncti tamquam membra capiti adnexa in Christo resuscitato et in gloria collocato etiam nos iam sumus resuscitati et in caelo adscripti*; further Abbott Huby ad loc.

of life 'in Christ' to the 'Body of Christ' may also be deduced from iii. 6: the Gentiles should become 'fellow heirs, fellow members of the Body (σύσσωμα) and fellow sharers of the promise ἐν Χριστῷ Ἰησοῦ'. Hence this thought also presumably stands behind ii. 6. Yet over against the spatial conceptual figures of Gnosticism, it must be affirmed that the typical Pauline manner of thinking in terms of salvation *history* has not disappeared in Ephesians. It determines the train of thought even in Eph. ii. 4–7. The salvation event that God's love and pity set in motion, and in which individual Christians gain a share in baptism, finds its perfection only in the coming aeon (ἐν τοῖς αἰῶσιν τοῖς ἐπερχομένοις, *v.* 7).[150] Till then Christians must approve themselves by 'good works', which God has already 'prepared beforehand that they should walk in them' (*v.* 10), and for which they possess the power because they 'have been created in Christ Jesus'. In contrast to Gnosticism, hope for the consummation of salvation, the 'day of redemption' that is yet to be (iv. 30), remains preserved despite all 'realized eschatology'.

One thing has become obvious in this attempt to understand the passage from within the area of thought occupied in Ephesians: the liturgical act of baptism, with its ritual symbolic content, does not give Paul any kind of impulse for his formulations of the doctrine of baptism. The considerations that motivate him are great Christological ideas, which are here bound up with bold conceptions, cosmic in breadth and that belong to the history of salvation. Ultimately it is the *fact* of the gracious deliverance that most deeply impresses Paul (cf. the parenthesis in *v.* 5). That the redemption has taken place historically διὰ Ἰησοῦ Χριστοῦ (i. 5): that the individual appropriates it to himself σὺν Χριστῷ in faith and baptism, and then is really ἐν Χριστῷ: these are but various aspects and stages of the way of salvation that God in his pity has opened up to man.

§12. DISPUTED PASSAGES

Tr. Schmidt considers that all passages that speak of dying and rising with Christ, as of a once-for-all act that took place in the past, are to be related to baptism.[151] J. Schneider contests this viewpoint: in his judgment we must abide by the view that where Paul refers to fellowship with Christ in his passion, he has baptism in mind only if he expressly mentions it.[152] Whereas the first named writer proceeds from the

[150] The plural, as the singular, (cf. i. 21), stands for the well known late Jewish conception of the coming aeon, cf. H. Sasse in *ThW* I, 206, 20–22. H. Schlier, on the contrary, holds that the 'aeons' are regarded as personal beings, Eph. ad loc; cf. H. Greeven in the new edition of the commentary by Dibelius ad loc.

[151] *Leib Christi* 213.

[152] *Passionsmystik* 84.

conception of the Church, and baptism is important to him as its foundation, his opponent is concerned with Paul's 'Passion-mysticism' and therefore interprets Paul's language above all in the light of his personal experience and his mysticism.[153] It is certainly not irrelevant whether such disputed utterances belong primarily to mysticism or to the sacramental world, and whether personal piety or the confession that binds the fellowship is the chief issue in them.

Since the relation to baptism is uncertain we would ask: Is there by chance a surer criterion for these passages, by which we may learn whether Paul speaks of 'mystic' non-sacramental union? It could possibly be maintained, with Gal. vi. 16 in mind, that a continuance in *death* (without mention of resurrection) is characteristic of the 'mysticism of suffering'. But that is by no means true. That the Christian with his Lord attains to resurrection through the cross is an element also in the Pauline 'mysticism'; indeed it imparts to it its peculiar characteristic. In the 'mysticism', too, the goal is resurrection and transfiguration, cf. 2 Cor. iv. 11; Phil. iii. 10f; Rom. viii. 17; 2 Tim. ii. 11f. Life with Christ and the impartation of his power ought not to be reserved for heaven or for the parousia; it is known even now along with suffering on earth, cf. 2 Cor. vi. 9f; xiii. 4.

Such 'mystical' utterances thus exhibit a certain harmony with the sacramental texts. And yet there is a real criterion. It lies in the fact that the mystic way with Christ essentially begins in *suffering*, whereas baptism speaks only of dying with Christ, of being crucified with Him, of being buried with Him. The *mystical* dying with Christ consists factually in *sufferings*, which the Christian takes on himself for the sake of Jesus (2 Cor. iv. 11) and in conformity with Him (Phil. iii. 10). Therefore where the context speaks of suffering, we have to do with 'mystical', not sacramental statements.

Accordingly, Phil. iii. 10f may be regarded as a classic passage for the 'mysticism of suffering'. Here growth into conformity with Christ is the result of actual suffering.[154] It is not a simple, external approximation to the likeness of Christ, 'in that one also suffers and dies' and experiences sufferings 'which correspond to the inner laws of fellowship

[153] W. E. Wilson, in his article in *Exp. Times* 42 (1931) 562–5, has attempted to base the entire range of thought about 'dying and rising with Christ' on the personal experience of Paul. In so doing he absolutizes the viewpoint of mysticism in suffering, which is only one possibility alongside others. The foundation at all times remains the 'Christ event', the death and resurrection of Christ. The matter will be dealt with more fully in the systematic section.

[154] Paul does not have in view death as an impending martyrdom as Lohmeyer ad loc, and G. Heinzelmann (*NTD* ad loc) believe. If the present participle does not permit a precise temporal determination, it is nevertheless very possible that 'signs of death', viz. suffering, is meant, as in 2 Cor. iv. 10f; cf. Gal. vi. 17. The imprisoned Apostle does not count on a martyr's death with certainty, cf. Phil. i. 24f.

with Christ';[155] σύν suggests being inwardly united with the sufferings of Jesus, so the sufferings of the Apostle can be viewed as 'sufferings of Christ' (cf. 2. Cor. i. 5).[156]

Rom. viii. 17 is also to be numbered with these passages. The viewpoint in this chapter is determined by the conception of sonship to God and the participation in glory that results from it. But, as with Christ, the path to that lies through suffering: 'If we suffer with Him we shall also be glorified with Him'. This saying makes it certain that Paul did not look on the mystic way, through suffering to glory with Christ, as purely personal or as an Apostolic vocation, which could perhaps be inferred on the basis of 2 Cor. iv. 12 and Col. i. 24f. It is rather the general way of salvation for the Christian. Every Christian should become like his Lord and united with Him, not alone sacramentally but also in personal suffering and endurance with Him.

2 Tim. ii. 11f also is integrated through its context in this frame of the Pauline Christ-mysticism. Externally *v.* 11 strongly reminds us of Rom. vi. 8: 'For if we have died with Him, we shall also live with Him.' But the continuation in *v.* 12 shows that there is no thought of a sacramental dying: 'If we endure, we shall also rule with him.' That is the endurance, the constancy in hardship and suffering, which the 'worthy soldier of Christ Jesus' must exhibit (*vv.* 3–5, 9–10). He that patiently persists, even when treated as a common criminal for Christ's sake (*v.* 9), will, so surely as he goes with his Lord into shame and humiliation, also reign with Him.

Other passages sometimes adduced in connection with baptism are not to be explained by Christ-mysticism, but by the contrast between 'formerly' and 'now' created by conversion. We have repeatedly drawn attention to the transition from the earlier period of spiritual ruin into the present condition of salvation ἐν Χριστῷ, which in fact was always bound up with baptism, yet this does not need formally to be examined. Since the contrast was very strongly felt, as death and life, loss and gain (cf. Phil. iii. 7f), these expressions remind us of the oppositions that are to be met with in the context of baptism. Obviously all this lies for Paul along the same line that was drawn for him personally through the Damascus experience.

As an example, Col. i. 13, is to be understood in the framework of ruin and redemption. God has 'rescued us from the power of darkness and transferred us into the kingdom of his beloved Son'. He has fitted us for a 'share in the lot of the saints in light', i.e. for the heavenly realm

[155] W. Michaelis ad loc; he expressly excludes the idea of a later mystic experience.
[156] Cf. E. Loymeyer, Σὺν Χριστῷ 250f; further on Phil. iii. 10; O. Schmitz, op. cit. 196f.

of the divine light. Before becoming Christians the believers were excluded from it. They belonged to the kingdom of darkness, over which the demonic powers held sway (Eph. vi. 12). Therefore Eph. v. 8 can actually run: 'You were *darkness* once, but now you are *light* in the Lord.' The parenesis attached to this, however, is clearly baptismal parenesis, as the fragment of an old baptismal hymn in *v.* 14 confirms.[157] The primitive Church thus thought of the step that was taken in baptism, from the sphere of ruin into the realm of salvation, in terms of the contrast of light and darkness, and in this respect the Christians possibly were not uninfluenced by similar ideas in Qumran. The decisive mark in their case, however, is that they know themselves set under the saving sovereignty of their heavenly Lord.[158] When Col. i. 13 states, God has 'translated us into the kingdom of his dear Son', the same thing is really meant as in Eph. ii. 5f. In fact, therefore, the passage has an inner relation to baptism. This decisive turn the Christians owe to the merciful God, the Father of their Lord Jesus—more than that Col. i. 13 does not say. In the *further development* of this view, under the influence of the conception of light and its eloquent symbolism, baptism, wherein this step into the sphere of divine light was accomplished, was described in the post-Apostolic age as φωτισμός.[159]

Paul uses the expression in 2 Cor. iv. 4, 6 for the illumination which the *Gospel* brought or signified for the whole inner man. The description, with its rich contrasts, clearly shows that he still understands it in a purely metaphorical way. The verb φωτίζειν occurs more frequently, somewhat as in 2 Cor. iv. 6, of the confession of faith (Eph. i. 18, iii. 9), or of the action of Christ, who by his appearing in flesh brought life and incorruptibility to light through the Gospel (2. Tim. i. 10), and who by his second coming will make manifest 'that which is hidden in the darkness', namely the secret intention of men (1 Cor. iv. 5). With Paul, therefore, the expression has no firm relation to baptism. It is different in Heb. vi. 4 and x. 32; the Christian's standing in salvation is impressively described with the four expressions of vi. 4f, and among them is included ἅπαξ φωτισθέντας; this state of salvation has its foundation in baptism, and according to vi. 1f an elementary baptismal instruction was bound up with it. Moreover

[157] Cf. R. Schnackenburg, "'Er hat uns mitauferweckt", Zur Tauflehre des Epheserbriefes', *Liturgisches Jahrbuch* 2 (1952) 159–83; B. Noack, Das Zitat in Eph. v. 14, *StTh* 5 (1951) 52–64.

[158] Cf. R. Schnackenburg, *Gottes Herrschaft und Reich*, Freiburg i Br. 1959, 209ff; a comparison with the Qumran texts is also found there.

[159] Justin I *Apol.* 61. 12; cf. the verb φωτίζειν in I *Apol.* 61. 12, 13; 65. 1; *Dial.* 39. 2; 122. 1, 3, 4, 5; 123. 2. The original figurative meaning is still everywhere perceptible.

ἅπαξ points to the once-for-all event of baptism (cf. the contrast to this in x. 2!), which opens to those cleansed for ever the 'new and living way' into the sanctuary (cf. x. 19–22). The expression is briefly alluded to in x. 32. Thus it is on the way to acquiring a fixed linguistic usage, even if it does not yet possess the same signification as in Justin. The verb is more strongly figurative that the substantive φωτισμός, which first appears in Justin.[160]

The baptismal *confession* could well be in mind in Rom. x. 9f, since the passage possesses an almost liturgical style. The formula, 'Jesus is Kurios' (cf. Phil. ii. 11; 1 Cor. xii. 3), the terms 'believe' and 'confess', the assurance of being 'saved' (cf. Mk. xvi. 16; Acts xvi. 31)—all this echoes baptismal terminology. The address in the second person could also recall the oldest form of the baptismal ritual, which probably included question and answer (cf. the Western text of Acts viii. 37).[161] In that case Paul makes allusions to the liturgical practice of the primitive Church in Rom. x. 9f, but no more than this; for in the context he is concerned with the saving power of faith (*vv.* 6–8, 11). The expression, 'he who calls on the name of the Lord' (cf. *vv.* 12f), is also employed in the context of baptism (Acts xxii. 16), but in our passage it means generally one who confesses Jesus Christ (cf. Acts ix. 14, 21; 1 Cor. i. 2). In any case the Apostle's reminiscence of baptism in *vv.* 9f shows that he was capable of linking without further ado primitive Christian baptism with his teaching on justification by faith (cf. § 18).

If we do not feel at liberty to extend the passages which relate to baptism as widely as many scholars would like, a rich material nevertheless remains. From it the conclusion follows that in the Pauline theology baptism forms a hard core that must not be wished away.

[160] Cf. the commentaries of A. Nairne (Cambridge 1921), J. Bonsirven (Paris 1943), O. Michel (Göttingen 1949), C. Spicq (Paris 1953) ad loc.

[161] Cf. O. Cullmann, *Die ersten christlichen Glaubensbekenntnisse*, Zürich ²1949, 14–16; .N. D. Kelly, *Early Christian Creeds*, 40–49.

CHAPTER FOUR

Uncertain and Derived Baptismal Statements

§13. πνεῦμα-SAYINGS AND BAPTISM

THAT baptism and the reception of the Spirit are associated is not to be doubted, according to 1 Cor. vi. 11; xii. 13. The life ἐν Χριστῷ that is begun through baptism is at the same time a life ἐν πνεύματι (cf. Rom. viii. 9ff),[1] since the fellowship of the baptized with Christ is possible only through the Spirit. But for us the question arises whether, in Paul's view, this reception of the Spirit is bound up with baptism, or whether there is for him a specific sacrament appointed essentially for the impartation of the Spirit. Are there perchance characteristic expressions and rites that point to the existence of a special sacrament of the Spirit, such as that which the later Church called 'confirmation', or can we reckon all the relevant πνεῦμα-texts along with the baptismal sayings?

First a negative observation should be made: the rite of laying on of hands, which is essential to confirmation, does not receive mention in this sense in the Pauline Letters. It is first mentioned in the Pastoral Epistles as a sign of transference of ministry and consecration to Paul's disciples and fellow-workers (1 Tim. iv. 14; 2 Tim. i. 6) and also to others (1 Tim. v. 22). If Paul in the baptismal texts does not allude to the laying on of hands, which for him also probably formed the conclusion of the baptismal ritual (Acts. xix. 6), it may be presumed that for him other images employed in connection with the Spirit spoke a more compelling language. We think especially of 1 Cor. xii. 13b: 'We all have been imbued with one Spirit (ἐποτίσθημεν).' This expression, which is attached to the 'baptism for (or in) a single Body', already discussed by us, has been accorded three basic interpretations: it has been related to baptism, to the Supper and to confirmation.

1. The relation to baptism is favoured by the majority of recent Protestants, such as Bachmann, Robertson-Plummer, J. Weiss, Lietzmann, and among Catholics by Ad. Maier and Allo. A major argument urged in its support, that the picture of drinking the Spirit into oneself corresponds to that of being plunged (or submerged) in the Spirit (*v*. 12a),

[1] Cf. Deissmann, *Die ntl. Formel 'In Christo Jesu'* 85ff; Prat, *Theol* II, 479; Wikenhauser, *Christusmystik*, 29f. 50.

we have already rejected (see above, § 5). But in itself the figure of 'being given to drink' applies very well to baptism. Yet it must be asked whether the relation to the cup in the Supper does not lie closer to hand.

2. Without doubt the number of those who refer this expression to the Lord's Supper is not inconsiderable: Cyril of Alexandria,[2] Thomas Aquinas,[3] Estius, Cornelius a Lapide, Nat. Alexander; among recent Catholics Reinhard,[4] Cerfaux,[5] P. Benoit;[6] on the Protestant side the Reformers, and of recent scholars Schlatter, Käsemann,[7] H. D. Wendland. They appeal chiefly to 1 Cor. x. 2–4, where baptism and the Supper are set in close juxtaposition.

Against this view we must draw attention to the aorist ἐποτίσθημεν; it conjures in the mind a definite act, but not a repeated reception, such as is presupposed in the Supper. Moreover the feeding with the manna should not be struck out of the narrative of the desert wanderings, and the representation of the eucharist only by the picture of drinking is, to say the least, unusual.

3. The majority of more recent Catholic exegetes give their vote for confirmation here: Bisping, Belser, Cornely, Prat,[8] Gutjahr, Sickenberger, Huby. Prat considers that the following supply compelling grounds for this view: (a) the verb in the aorist suggests a rite that is past, analogous and parallel to that of baptism; (b) baptism itself cannot be in mind, since it has just been named; (c) the verse describes the formation of the Body of Christ; after incorporation in Christ the Holy Spirit draws near to infuse a new life into the freshly baptized and to complete the incorporation; (d) the picture already used in the Old Testament of the outpouring of the Spirit tells in favour of this.

It would also be possible, however, to connect these viewpoints with baptism; the introduction of *v.* 12b with καί does not require a change of topic, it may simply bring a (new) figure.

If we wish to penetrate more deeply into this question, we can only do so through a clarification of the significance of the figure. Most exegetes, especially those who interpret the expression of the Supper, understand ποτίζειν as 'make to drink'; and this meaning is extraordinarily well attested, especially with regard to the watering of cattle.[9]

> Grammatically the passive, 'we have been caused to drink', used with the accusative is wholly without objection;[10] the textual variant

[2] PG 74, 889 AB. [3] Lect. 3 in 1 Cor. xii (ed. Vivés, p. 401b).
[4] *Das Wirken des Hl. Geistes im Menschen nach den Briefen des Apostels Paulus*, Freiburg 1918, p. 28.
[5] *La Théol. de l'Église*, 183, 207. [6] In *RB* 63 (1956) 15. [7] *Leib und Leib Christi* 176.
[8] *Théol.* II, 316f. [9] Cf. the concordance of Hatch-Redpath under ποτιίζειν (II, 1197f).
[10] Blass-Debr. § 159; Bauer *Wörterbuch*, col. 1380, 1.

εἰς ἓν πνεῦμα therefore is to be recognized as a later correction, while the variant ἓν πόμα ἐποτίσθημεν (Clem. Alex.) betrays an offence at the metaphor of 'drinking of the Spirit', or has in view a stronger application to the Lord's Supper.

The idea of drinking the Spirit can hardly be anchored in the Old Testament. When mention is made of drinking in the messianic era, it is *water* of salvation that is drunk (Is. xii. 3; lv. 1; Jer. ii. 13; with ποτίζω Sir. xv. 3). The Spirit, on the contrary, is associated with the idea of outpouring from on high or of overflowing (Is. xxxii. 15; Joel iii. 1f; Zech. xii. 10). Now ποτίειζν can receive this significance also, cf. e.g. Ezk. xvii. 7; xxxii. 6 (in the passive). Is. xxix. 10 is particularly important, because ποτίζειν here represents the Hebrew נָסַךְ = 'pour out', the favourite verb used in connection with the Spirit. This figure is also to be met in the Qumran texts in reference to the Holy Spirit. Probably through the influence of Ezk. xxxvi. 25ff, one eschatological passage declares: God 'will wholly remove the perverted spirit from the midst of their flesh and cleanse them from all wicked deeds through holy spirit. He will sprinkle over them spirit of truth like cleansing water' (1 QS IV, 20f). Accordingly, it is not the picture of giving to drink that is basic here but that of watering. In the New Testament this meaning of ποτίζειν is found in 1 Cor. iii. 6–8, and the linguistic usage is extremely rich in the papyri.[11]

It would be possible to find an example to the contrary in Jn. vii. 37–39. In association with the custom of drawing water at the Feast of Tabernacles Jesus calls on men to come to Him and drink (*v.* 37). The Evangelist interprets the water figuratively of the Spirit, which believers should receive (*v.* 39). One can also see from iv. 10, 14 how the Evangelist applies the metaphor of water for the Spirit yet more strongly (cf. the close connection between both in Jn. iii. 5). But it is not permissible to argue from the usage of this late Evangelist for that of Paul.

In 1 Cor. xii. 13b therefore it is possible that the idea is presented: we have been deluged, drenched, permeated with the πνεῦμα. After the affirmation, 'We have all been baptized in a single Spirit for (or in) a single Body', the Apostle deepens the baptismal experience, 'and all have been drenched over and over (through the overflowing) of the one Spirit'. For the sacramental theology of Paul a further illustration is

[11] Cf. Preisigke, *Wörterbuch* II, 346.

given that he is more strongly impressed by the reality than the rite, but that he likes to reproduce this reality in figures, in this case by a picture that is already well known to him from the prophetic language of the Old Testament.

From this standpoint a glance should be taken at two passages which are cited as providing a hint of 'confirmation' *alongside baptism* in Paul's teaching. J. Coppens regards Gal. iv. 4–6 as one of the most articulate of the Pauline texts.[12] The Apostle is said to describe here the grace bestowed in initiation and to distinguish between our reception as children and the sending of the Holy Spirit as two successive stages; this last recalls the outpouring of the divine Spirit at Pentecost. Nevertheless, while the two effects of salvation, sonship and possession of the Spirit, are certainly distinguishable, it is hardly possible to conclude with confidence that they form two separate sacraments, for in 1 Cor. vi. 11, too, baptism and the impartation of the Spirit appear in intimate association. Paul by no means speaks expressly of receiving sacraments in Gal. iv, despite his earlier mention of baptism (iii. 27). In iv. 4–6 he desires to represent the overwhelming and gracious fulfilment of the promise that has been bestowed on Abraham and his 'children in faith'. The statement in Tit. iii. 5f, which Coppens adduces as the second Pauline proof passage,[13] is of a similar complexity, owing to its being dominated by the reality of salvation. Here, however, baptism as the 'bath of regeneration' alone has a secure position. The expression 'renewal through the Holy Spirit', together with *v.* 6, probably affirms without figurative language what the author felt he had intimated with insufficient clarity by the expression 'regeneration'. In all these texts the Apostle has in mind above anything else the reality of salvation, i.e. the outpouring of the Spirit which takes place in Christian 'initiation'.

A better clue than the rite of laying on of hands for the sacramental outpouring of the Spirit is provided by the concept of 'sealing' current in the early Church. Belser, following many older exegetes, confidently believed that he could identify this with confirmation,[14] and recently Allo and Coppens have given their assent to this interpretation.[15] But the investigations of F. J. Dölger[16] and W. Heitmüller,[17] containing a

[12] *L'imposition des mains et les rites complexes dans le NT et dans l'Église ancienne*, Paris 1925, 258f; Confirmation in *DB* Suppl. I, 143.
[13] *L'imposition des mains* 259f; Confirm. 143.
[14] On Eph. i. 13; earlier Cornelius a Lapide ad loc.
[15] Allo on 2 Cor. i. 22 'at least very probable'; Heb. vi. 2 is clearer; Coppens, Confirm. 145f.
[16] Σφραγίς 149–71. He offers also a review of the development of its investigation.
[17] Σφραγίς, in the Festschrift for G. Heinrici (Unters. z. NT 6), Leipzig 1914, 40–59; J. Quasten in *AC*, supplementary volume I (1939) 226ff.

wealth of material on the subject, have shown that σφραγίς very early became a designation of *baptism*, cf. 2 Clem. vii. 6; viii. 6; Herm. 5 VIII, 6, 3; IX, 16, 3. 4. 5. 7; 17, 4. It is to be admitted that this expression is as little a technical term for baptism in the New Testament as the other later name φωτισμός.

The question as to the origin of this designation for baptism in the early Church, whether it was derived from Judaism (circumcision, cf. Rom. iv. 11) or from the language of the Mysteries, has been widely discussed by the experts; for us it is not urgent, since it is not yet demonstrable that it is a fixed terminological mode of expression in Paul.

Did the Apostle have baptism in mind when he used the figure of the seal? Of the Pauline sources that fall to be considered, viz. 2 Cor. i. 22; Eph. i. 13; iv. 30, it would seem a commendable procedure to begin with the Ephesian passages, since the contexts in which they are set are less problematic. The possibility should not be overlooked that a later and perhaps different view from that in 2 Cor. i. 22 is set before us here.

The context of Eph. i. 13–14 is related to the call of the recipients of the Letter (καὶ ὑμεῖς *v.* 13) to eternal salvation. The way of their deliverance is described in stages:

1. ἀκούσαντες τὸν λόγον τῆς ἀληθείας κτλ,
2. καὶ πιστεύσαντες,
3. ἐσφραγίσθητε τῷ πνεύματι κτλ.

The viewpoint of the writer is the sure fact of redemption at the end, which has not yet been realized for the readers (in its full meaning). But it is *guaranteed* through the 'sealing with the promised[18] Holy Spirit'. The Holy Spirit is not simply a phenomenon belonging to the future; it was bestowed on the Ephesians even in the present as 'earnest money' for the future full inheritance.

'Αρραβών is a Semitic loan-word from the language of law and commerce. It can contain various nuances: 'pledge' (that which is given as security for another thing or action); 'payment on account' (of a debt); 'first payment' (that makes a contract valid). But it always denotes an action through which the person concerned is obliged to further action in relation to the receiver.[19]

On this account the figure of sealing should not be understood externally, as if it only dealt with 'stamping' (an object). Bauer rightly

[18] Cf. Lk. xxiv. 49; Acts i. 4; ii. 33; Gal. iii. 14.
[19] Cf. Behm in *ThW* I, 474 and Bauer, *Wörterbuch*, cols. 216f.

remarks: 'In σφραγίζω there manifestly lies more than merely "provide with a sign of recognition"; it also includes "equip with the power of heaven", as Jn. vi. 27 plainly signifies'.[20] Since, according to this last named passage, the Son of Man who has descended from heaven (cf. iii. 13, 31; vi. 62) bears on himself the seal of the Spirit (cf. i. 33; iii. 34), so in a reverse manner the Spirit in Eph. i. 13 is the 'seal' for the ascent to God.

F. J. Dölger, taking the cue from later testimonies, would bring the seal in yet closer relation to *Christ*. He calls attention to εἰκὼν τοῦ θεοῦ Col. i. 15 and χαρακτὴρ τῆς ὑποστάσεως αὐτοῦ Heb. i. 3; for him they both belong to the same circle of ideas as the seal, and he says: 'If Christ was the die-stamp, the seal, it was natural to go on to say that the soul, fashioned after his likeness in baptism, is sealed with the Logos, with the Spirit of Christ. In view of Paul's theology this order of thinking must already have lain in the Apostle's circle of vision.'[21] The Christological terminology of Hebrews is strongly influenced by the Hellenistic-Jewish Diaspora (Philo), and εἰκὼν τοῦ θεοῦ of Col. i. 15 serves to do battle with the Colossian false teaching.[22] These Christological expressions therefore are special coinage for particular contexts; they must be separated from the 'sealing with the Spirit' in Paul, even though factually there are contacts between them and they were later united.

As there is no question of a technical meaning of σφραγίζειν for baptism in Eph. i. 13, it appears to be a figurative mode of speech for the reality of the Spirit, and it immediately gives place to the other metaphorical term of 'earnest money'. Both figures complement each other excellently; the one expresses rather the outward stamp that provides protection, the other stresses more the reality of the content.

The same figurative significance and the same onward look to the 'day of redemption' that we see in Eph. i. 13 lies at the root of Eph. iv. 30.[23] The personal character of the divine *Pneuma* shines through the expression more clearly here than in Eph. i. 13, where ὅς is merely in agreement with ἀρραβών:[24] 'Do not grieve the Holy Spirit of God' (*v.* 30a). It has a contact with Is. lxiii. 10: 'They were disobedient and provoked His holy Spirit to anger.' In the post-exilic era Israel was on

[20] Bauer, *Wörterbuch* col. 1576, 2b.
[21] Op. cit. 113.
[22] On Hebrews see the commentaries by H. Windisch (Tübingen ²1931, pp. 11f), O. Michel (Göttingen 1949) and C. Spicq (Paris 1953); on Colossians especially M. Dibelius-H. Greeven (Tübingen 1953) ad loc and the excursus pp. 14–17.
[23] The ἐν (ᾧ) is to be understood as instrumental(Blass-Debr. §§ 195, 219).
[24] Blass-Debr. § 132, I.

the way more definitely to hypostatizing the Spirit of God.[25] With Paul the reality of the Spirit undergoes a concretion, which inevitably aided the development of the special sacrament of the Spirit. But the thought of any rivalry with the fellowship with Christ grounded in baptism is completely excluded, for the Spirit is always πνεῦμα Χριστοῦ (Rom. viii. 9; 2 Cor. iii. 17; Phil. i. 19).

If the connection of Spirit and sealing is recognized to be purely figurative, it is easier to give a decision on 2 Cor. i. 21f. Here it is briefly stated that God 'has sealed us'; that it happened through the Spirit confirms the figure of 'earnest money', which is attached here as in Eph. i. 13f. Before these two metaphors the Apostle uses yet a third, that of *anointing*. This could again make us think of the special sacrament for the bestowal of the Spirit, bearing in mind the later practice of confirmation, especially as it was administered in the eastern Church. First, however, a cardinal question of interpretation arises from the context of the passage: do *vv.* 21–22 relate to Christians generally or only to the preachers of the Gospel?

Among the later exegetes the majority think in terms of all Christians, chiefly because of the similar statements in Eph. i. 13f: Ad. Maier, Belser, Bousset, Plummer, Windisch, Lietzmann, Schlatter, Allo, Bauer, Bultmann.[26] But the other view has its advocates: Bachmann, Cornely, Gutjahr, Sickenberger, Amiot,[27] cf. Héring.[28]

In the whole first chapter the ἡμεῖς signifies Paul with the preachers of the word of God, especially Silvanus and Timothy (*v.* 19). In *v.* 21 Paul expressly includes the addressees (ἡμᾶς σὺν ὑμῖν) in the statement ὁ δὲ βεβαίων κτλ, but he does not repeat this σὺν ὑμῖν with ἡμᾶς in connection with the three following aorists. The tendency of the passage is to corroborate the personal asseverations of Paul, that his resolutions were genuine and without frivolous and premature planning (*v.* 17). To this end Paul appeals to the Christ whom he preached, in whom there is neither fluctuation, nor uncertainty, but rather a plain 'Yes' (*vv.* 19f). As to *vv.* 21f there are two possibilities. Either the Apostle desires to say, 'God makes us preachers also steadfast', or he directs his gaze to the Church: through their 'Amen' (*v.* 20) they received and confirmed the proclamation of Christ by the preachers. In the second case Paul would

[25] Cf. P. Heinrich, *Theologie des Alten Testamentes*, Bonn 1940, 92; W. Eichrodt, *Theologie des Alten Testaments*, II, Leipzig 1935, 27–30; J. Bonsirven, *Judaïsme* I, 212ff.

[26] Bauer, *Wörterbuch*, col. 1469, see under χρίω 4; Bultmann, *Theol.* 136.

[27] Op. cit. I, 286.

[28] J. Héring, *La Seconde Epître de s. Paul aux Corinthiens*, Neuchâtel-Paris, ad loc.

be reminded of the 'sealing' by the Holy Spirit, with which their Christian existence began.

In an instructive article W. C. van Unnik has shown that, in fact, this saying of Amen by the Church to Christ, who fulfilled the promises and who himself became the 'Amen' (cf. *vv*. 19f), is the key to the whole section.[29] In this way the preachers and the Church were united through their Yes to Christ, but all were led together through the working of God. 'The God who is steadfast and makes men steadfast has united them in the common life-in-Christ through the gift of the Spirit.'[30]

By this means the Apostle reaches back to the foundational experience of salvation that all Christians have: God has led even them to faith and the reception of the Spirit. So understood the passage stands in close connection with Eph. i. 13.[31] But what does the 'anointing' signify in this context? The figure—for it cannot be more than that[32]—is applied in 1 Jn. ii. 20, 27, under the metaphor τὸ χρίσμα = anointing oil, to the Holy Spirit whom all Christians have received and who now instructs them in all things.[33] In 2 Cor. i. 21 the symbol is not used with so pregnant a meaning. As a figure for the attainment of salvation we find 'anointing' even in Joseph and Aseneth, along with the symbols of 'bread of life' and 'drink of immortality'; Aseneth is 'anointed with the oil of incorruptibility' (χρίσματ' ἀφθαρσίας).[34] Yet the expression in 2 Cor. i. 21 affirms more than this. Here the phrase καὶ χρίσας ἡμᾶς is added by way of explanation to ὁ δὲ βεβαίων ... εἰς Χριστόν and possibly contains a word-play on Χριστόν (cf. Gutjahr ad loc): inasmuch as God 'anointed' them, He confirmed them to the 'Anointed' (= Christ); He has united them with this Anointed One through a similar anointing as that which Christ received. Actually the conception of 'anointing' is applied to Christ in Lk. iv. 18; Acts iv. 27; x. 38; Heb. i. 9; it is his messianic equipment with the Spirit. Through participating in the Spirit bestowed on the Christ, the Christians themselves have been 'anointed' by God.[35] Thus a transition is provided to what follows: the Christian's 'anointing of the Spirit' can also be considered as 'sealing'

[29] W. C. van Unnik, 'Reisepläne und Amen-Sagen', *Studia Paulina in honorem J. de Zwaan*, Haarlem 1953, 215–34.

[30] van Unnik, op. cit. 231.

[31] Cf. also I. de la Potterie in *Bibl.* 40 (1959) 14–30, especially 24.

[32] Reitzenstein, *Vorgesch. d. christl. Taufe* 184, accepts the view that as early as the time of Paul baptism was probably linked with an anointing—this lacks any support. Cf. B. Welte, *Die postbaptismale Salbung*, Freiburg i. Br. 1939; H. Elfers in *ThGl* 34 (1942) 334–41.

[33] Cf. R. Schnackenburg, *Die Johannesbriefe*, Freiburg i. Br. 1953 ad loc.

[34] Joseph and Aseneth 8; 15; (Batiffol pp. 49, 61, 64).

[35] Lampe, *The Seal of the Spirit*, p. 52: 'Through their participation in the Anointed they receive a share in his anointing, the gift of the Holy Spirit, the sign that the Messianic age has already dawned'. It is thus more than 'anointing through faith', as I. de la Potterie holds.

and as receiving the 'earnest of the Spirit' (*v*. 22). We have here, then, three figures for the 'reception of the Spirit', without the necessity of their being apportioned out to various acts or sacraments.[36] The reception of the Spirit as such, the gracious deliverance by God, and his confirming us in the way of salvation, are the things to be emphasized.

Through this discussion we have gained a glimpse into the origins of sacramental conceptions. In the beginning the actuality of the Spirit of God rules the thinking of the Apostle, whether the Spirit be mediated through the sacraments or, as in special cases (Acts ii. 10), imparted without sacraments, and he endeavours to give verbal expression to this overpowering reality by figures of many kinds. Gradually these figures become fixed coinage and at last technical terms for those external signs and events (sacraments) through which the Spirit is normally dispensed to all believers. Herein lies the easiest explanation of the difficulty, that one will seek in vain in the Pauline Letters to discover a peculiar sacrament of the Spirit alongside baptism: the actuality and fulness of the Spirit of God, whose 'outpouring' is most closely connected with baptism, dominates the Apostle's field of vision.

§14. AN OLD TESTAMENT PRESAGE OF BAPTISM. 1 Cor. x. 1ff.

In 1 Cor. x. 1–5 Paul apprehends certain events of Israel's history in a typological manner and interprets them as 'baptism' and 'spiritual food and spiritual drink'; they are significant for the understanding of Christian baptism and of the Lord's Supper, in so far as they reveal a definite idea of the New Testament sacraments.

Paul speaks in *v*. 6 of τύποι, but he does not describe baptism and the 'spiritual' nourishment as such by this term; it indicates a whole series of happenings, including the conduct of the Israelites. Here, therefore, τύποι denotes *events* (ταῦτα), whereas in Rom. v. 14 a person (Adam) appears as τύπος. Undoubtedly behind the comparison with the generation of the wilderness stands the idea that the ἐκκλησία is the true, eschatological Israel;[37] according to *v*. 11 the 'ends of the aeons' have come upon the Christians, i.e. they live at the end of this world order. It is characteristic of Paul's typological exposition, however, that he does not search out all the possible prefigurations in the Old Testament, as

[36] Belser and Allo interpret the 'anointing' as baptism, the 'sealing' and 'earnest' of confirmation, as many Anglicans do, cf. G. Dix, *The Theology of Confirmation in relation to Baptism*, Westminster 1946; L. S. Thornton, *Confirmation: its place in the Baptismal Mystery*, Westminster 1954. Against this cf. Lampe, op. cit. 3–7 and often; the same in *JThSt* (n.s.) 6 (1955) 110–16. On the controversy in the Anglican Church cf. E. Roth, 'Neue englische Literatur zum Taufproblem', *ThLZ* 76 (1951) cols, 709–16; J. Crehan, 'Ten Years' Work on Baptism and Confirmation', *Theological Studies* 17 (1956) 494–515.

[37] L. Goppelt, *Typos. Die typologische Deutung des Alten Testaments im Neuen*, Gütersloh 1939, 169–83, especially 173–6.

this soon took place in the ancient Church in a marked fashion;[38] he selects a few Christologically and ecclesiologically significant figures (Adam, Abraham, Moses) and events to illuminate his proclamation of Christ and to gain fruitful applications for the Churches. This mode of interpreting the Old Testament Scriptures is especially continued in Hebrews and in 1 Clement.[39] Moreover Paul does not seek for all kinds of precedents and patterns for baptism as the later Church, which in fact developed a rich 'typology of baptism'.[40] He sets out rather, by means of a pictorial midrashic kind of 'parenesis', to warn his readers against drawing false consequences from the means offered them for the attaining of salvation. Verses 1–5 are but the exordium to the earnest message which he preaches to them in *vv.* 6–11. The attitude of the Corinthians must be corrected by this backward look into Israelite history, remembering that it is the history of the Old Testament people of God. On the other hand, such a comparison would not be possible unless something common existed between baptism and the Lord's Supper and the events of the wilderness wanderings.

The significance ascribed by Paul to the 'baptism' in the Red Sea must be gathered from the events themselves and their effects, as he described them. Most exegetes consider the *tertium comparationis* between 'baptism to Moses' and Christian baptism to be the 'enveloping' of the Israelites by the cloud and the sea. (They are actually preserved from any contact with the water, i.e. from drowning). That is believed to be a suitable correspondence to baptism by immersion (Rom. vi), for in it the water completely surrounds the baptized person. This interpretation can be verified by the Tannaitic midrash Mekhilta. It is to be presumed that Paul was acquainted with the views on the Exodus story developed therein. In fact in this midrash we find the exposition that the Israelites were 'under the cloud' and were enveloped 'by the sea'. The passages in which the pillar of cloud was mentioned (in the Old Testament) were added together and the conclusion drawn that there were seven or thirteen different clouds, of which one went before the Israelites, while the others completely enveloped them from all four sides and from beneath as well as from above.[41] The midrash similarly interprets the

[38] Cf. Barn. vii. 3. (Isaac as a pattern of Christ); further vii. 7, 10, 11; viii. 1 etc.; Hermas v. IV 2, 5; 3, 6; s. II, 2. Cf. further J. Daniélou, *Sacramentum Futuri*, Paris 1950; G. W. H. Lampe—K. J. Woollcombe, *Essays on Typology*, London 1957.

[39] Heb. i. 4–ii. 4; iii. 7–iv. 13; x. 19–31; xi–xii (on this see Goppelt, *Typos* 205–215); 1 Clem. iv: 9–12; 17–18; 45; 55. 1 Clem uses for this the expression ὑπόδειγμα (v. 1; xlvi. 1; lxiii. 1).

[40] P. Lundberg, *La typologie baptismale*, especially pp. 10–29. Besides the passage through the Red Sea the following among others play a part: the Flood, the passage over the Jordan, the offering of Elijah, the healing of Naaman.

[41] Mekh. on Ex. xiii. 19 and xiii. 21 (translated by Winter-Wünsche, Leipzig 1909, pp. 77 and 79).

dividing of the waters as a kind of archway through water, and indeed it postulates one for each of the twelve tribes.[42] The upper and lower waters were also 'parted'.[43] So the Israelites really did go '*through* the sea' and were surrounded on all sides by water.[44]

It is plain through the expression εἰς τὸν Μωϋσῆν that Paul has brought this into relation with the Christian standpoint. This particular phrase has not been traced in Jewish-Rabbinic sources; manifestly it is an imitation of εἰς Χριστόν (Gal. iii. 27; Rom. vi. 3). The fact that Paul did not relate to Christ the baptism 'under the cloud', in the passage through the Red Sea (as later he did the rock, x. 4), but to Moses, is significant. It confirms that this Old Testament event is for Paul only a τύπος, brought forward and delineated from the point of view of the New Testament and the Christian Faith. The 'baptism of Moses' is certainly a 'baptism', but it is not baptism to the name of Jesus, with all its effects (cf. 1 Cor. vi. 11). It is possible that on this account Moses becomes in a certain sense a type of Christ, a 'Leader to salvation'. The Rabbis set forth the theologumenon, 'As was the first Redeemer, so will the last Redeemer be'.[45] But this comparison is not introduced into our pericope. The passage through the Red Sea is considered as an event that united the Israelites with Moses their Deliverer because it is viewed from the later standpoint of Christian baptism. Paul has employed the Moses typology more thoroughly in another place, viz. in the 'midrash' of 2 Cor. iii. 7–18; the comparison, however, does not relate to Christ but to the Christian Church and its possession of *doxa*.

Nevertheless, if the passage through the Red Sea is to be viewed as more than a mere figure for Christian baptism, namely as a typological event, then manifestly it becomes such under the category of the '*means of salvation*'. The great miracle that the Israelites experienced in utter distress, in a situation wherein their entire existence was at stake, was an act of divine grace, an act of divine deliverance. Christian baptism is nothing less than that. Only the threatening destruction is not physical ruin but eternal perdition. The controlling conception that makes this comparison possible is that of 'means of redemption'. We thereby gain

[42] Mekh. on Ex. xiv. 16: 'And you, lift high your staff!' Ten miracles happened for the Israelites at the sea: the sea was divided and became like a kind of archway, as it is said (Hab. iii. 14), "Thou didst pierce with his staves the head of his arrogant ones, they raged to scatter me". It was divided into *twelve* parts, as it says (Ex. xiv. 16), "Lower your hand over the sea and cleave it" ' (Winter-Wünsche 96f).

[43] Mekh. on Ex. xiv. 21 (Winter-Wünsche 100).

[44] Lundberg interprets differently, op. cit. 135–45: the Red Sea reminds Paul of the realm of the dead; the dominant point of view is the eschatological salvation.

[45] Midr. Qoh. on i. 9; Midr. Ruth ii. 14 etc., see Billerbeck I, 86f. The comparison is carried through in many individual features; it was probably current in the time of Christ and significant for messianic thought, cf. J. Jeremias in *ThW* IV, 864–7; on Paul 833f.

a valuable outlook on Paul's teaching on baptism, and it is capable of yielding the point of departure for a general presentation of his baptismal and sacramental theology (see below, § 16).

The Apostle does not see in this 'means of deliverance' a magical happening with infallible effects. His chief thesis in 1 Cor. x. 1ff is that the recipients can go astray despite their deliverance. He obviously contends *against* a false sacramental concept current among the Corinthians, according to which such miracles and signs *guarantee* eternal salvation. If this danger has always been present in the popular view, it was particularly great at that time through the Mystery religions. Similar sacramental views, divorced from ethics, are characteristic of Gnosticism right up to Manichaeism.[46] For Paul the gift of God must not be separated from the moral responsibility of man. The indissoluble connection between indicative and imperative pervades all the soteriological utterances of his Letters; the ethical 'being dead' for sin was also the chief tendency in Rom. vi. In like manner it may be observed in 1 Cor. x. 1–5 how he vindicates the ethical viewpoint over against the interpretation that was found in Corinth.

In 1 Cor. x. 1–5 Paul adduces a factual proof as an *argumentum ad hominem: all* the Israelites of that time received these 'means of salvation', i.e. they all had the *same* baptism and the *same* spiritual food and the *same* spiritual drink; 'yet God found no pleasure in most of them', and he caused them to perish in the desert (*v.* 5). Therefore—this is the unexpressed consequence—these means of salvation *alone* and *as such* do not guarantee the good pleasure of God and his redemption. There must also be added moral verification in a corresponding life, that they 'receive not the grace of God in vain' (2 Cor. vi. 1).

Nevertheless, the effect of baptism is not thereby made dependent simply on the recipients. It is and remains an act of God's grace; but it demands for its answer the moral confirmation of man. Verses 8–10 exemplify the judgments of God: often they break in immediately upon, and in any case they stand in causal connection with, shameful deeds committed by men who have received the benefactions of the love of God. That Paul attributes special blessing to the personal activity of the recipient (*opus operanti*) in this 'Old Testament baptism' cannot be deduced from the text. Admittedly the middle ἐβαπτίσαντο is remarkable,[47] but it can hardly be maintained that Paul is thereby desirous of emphasizing effort or performance of deeds. At most in the

[46] Cf. W. Bousset, *Hauptprobleme der Gnosis* (FRLANT H.10), Göttingen 1907, 276f; Lietzmann, 1 Cor. 46f.

[47] Some important textual authorities (ACDG, Irenaeus and others) read ἐβαπτίσθησαν against B P46, the Antiochian recension and Origen; the former is adopted by Merk (^{6}1948),

opening verses of ch. 10 an echo of ix. 24 could be present, but only in the sense that Paul takes up the contrast πάντες-εἷς (x. 5, meaning 'few') and generally underscores the necessity of personal moral effort. It is not *in* the reception of the sacrament itself that personal endeavour has to be made—the sacrament stands wholly under the viewpoint of the divine action; Paul demands that moral proof be forthcoming *after* the enjoyment of the divine benefit as its *fruit*.

Thus this parenthetic mention of Christian baptism strengthens the view of the Apostle presented in the other texts. The strong emphasis he lays on the inner connection between the foundational Christian means of salvation and moral demand is intensified by his refusal of a magical interpretation of the great act of divine grace.

§15. BAPTISM FOR THE DEAD. 1 Cor. xv. 29

This enigmatically brief passage has occupied exegetes throughout the centuries and called forth numerous attempts at its explanation (more than forty!).[48] To this day agreement has not been reached. Nevertheless, recent investigations have shed more light on it, and above all they have shaken the long prevailing idea of a 'vicarious baptism'. A magical custom, according to which living people get baptized for dead, would contradict not only the Apostle's opposition to a magical interpretation of the sacrament (a tendency we have just affirmed of 1 Cor. x. 1–13), but also everything else that we know about baptism in the primitive Church. Paul must either have tacitly suffered the custom or adduced it as an *argumentum ad hominem* without approving of it. This, however, in a writing wherein he warns against a false estimate of the sacraments, is not probable. The question arises whether other exegetical solutions may not offer themselves. It is to this consideration alone that we enter upon an investigation of the passage here.

1. *The Context*

In the construction of the great resurrection chapter, 1 Cor. xv. *v.* 29 appears as an interruption, as most recent exegetes affirm. After stating

[48] They may be examined in the monograph of B. M. Foschini, *Those who are baptized for the dead*, 1 Cor. xv. 29, Worcester, Mass, 1951.

Allo (ad loc), Bover (Madrid 1950), the latter by Vogels ([3]1949, Nestle ([24]1960), Kilpatrick (London [2]1958). Blass-Debr. also speak in favour of the former (§ 317). Nevertheless an alteration from ἐβαπτίσθησαν to ἐβαπτίσαντο is scarcely thinkable in view of the primitive Christian linguistic usage attested elsewhere, but the reverse is possible; cf. the more recent commentaries, especially J. Weiss and Lietzmann. Jewish baptism is well characterized by the middle, for baptism was self-administered among the Jews (cf. 2 Kings v. 14); the Israelites themselves stepped into the sea, cf. Ex. xiv. 22 and Mekh. on the passage (the action of the Benjamites, who were the first to step into sea, is emphasized in a laudatory manner, cf. Billerbeck III, 286f).

the testimony of faith concerning the resurrection of Christ, a testimony guaranteed both by the original Apostles and by Paul, and which was accepted by the Corinthians (*vv.* 1–11), the Apostle had argued from this foundation: there *is* therefore in principle a resurrection; at least it is already proved for Christ. But alongside that an *argumentum ad hominem* is built up for the general resurrection of Christians: if the possibility and the actuality of the resurrection is in principle proved, why then do you stumble at believing in the (general) resurrection of the dead, which is nevertheless the crown and perfection of your faith and hope? This is particularly plain in *v.* 19: 'If it is in this (earthly) life only that we set our hope on Christ, then we are more to be pitied than all (other) men.' But in *v.* 20 the Apostle returns to the strict line of his chain of proof: Christ has in fact risen, and that as the first-born of those who have fallen asleep. Paul deduces theologically the resurrection of believers from the Adam-Christ parallels: Christ is the Head of a new humanity that belongs to Him, the Founder of a new race, and what happened to Him will happen to all. Paul develops this view of the salvation-history consistently: the resurrection of all who are united with Christ will take place when He restores everything in the divine order at the 'end' and delivers up Himself to the Father (*vv.* 21–28). After that Paul makes some short, separate statements, lightly sketched, that again are calculated to act as *argumenta ad hominem:*

(a) the baptism for the dead, *v.* 29.
(b) the sacrifice of his own life, which would be senseless without the resurrection faith, *vv.* 30–32a.
(c) the basic principle of men concerned only to enjoy life, with its evil consequences, *vv.* 32b–34.

There is thus a dominant structure, roughly according to the scheme A-B-A (J. Weiss), as the dogmatic and logical core (*vv.* 20–28) is set in the midst of more palpable arguments.

H. Preisker paid too little attention to this structure in his article, 'Die Vicariatstaufe 1 Kor. xv. 29 ein eschatologischer nicht sakramentaler Brauch'.[49] He wanted to attach the verse to the 'magnificent eschatological portrayal' of *vv.* 23–28 and so to bring the vicarious baptism into connection with the resurrection of the righteous. In order that the end of the age and the resurrection of the dead might come, a definite number of 'righteous' had to be reached. In the earliest days of the primitive Church baptism had

[49] In *ZNW* 23 (1924) 298–304.

not been administered to all converts, hence a number of them died unbaptized. Accordingly relatives, or persons otherwise standing near to them, had themselves baptized on their behalf, so as to complete the eschatological number of the righteous and bring in more quickly the delayed end.

This attempted solution is unacceptable. A determination of time in this way, according to the number of the righteous, cannot be proved in the New Testament. Neither in the 'synoptic apocalypse' nor in the last book of the New Testament can such a *numerus clausus* be adduced among the signs of the parousia. Similarly Preisker's thesis, that there was a period in the primitive Church when baptism was not generally administered, cannot be supported by solid reasons. We have no right to doubt the general application of Peter's demand on the day of Pentecost that men become baptized (Acts ii. 38).

2. *The Grammatical Aspect*

The basic understanding of 1 Cor. xv. 29 is determined by the way in which the preposition ὑπέρ with the genitive is translated. In this connection the following interpretations are to be considered: (a) 'in favour of, in the interests of'—the most general use, even if it is considerably limited in the New Testament by περί with the genitive; (b) 'instead of'. That the preposition can take this sense in the *Koine* and in the New Testament is satisfactorily attested;[50] (c) 'for someone or something, in order to attain a goal' (final sense). In recent works much attention has been accorded to this.[51] It arises from the general meaning of ὑπέρ with the genitive, which, according to context, can indicate rather the interest for someone (= *dat. commodi*) or a reason (causal) or a goal (final), and is also cited in the dictionaries.[52] The linguistic basis is therefore broad enough to allow of very different interpretations; the exegesis of the passage must settle the issue.

[50] For the N.T. passages see especially Robertson, Grm. 630–2; further Radermacher 139, Abel § 490 (p. 224) with good examples from the papyri (Abel cites 1 Cor. xv. 29 with this significance).

[51] Foschini, op. cit. 94 (following P. Dürselen, Die Taufe für die Toten, 1 Kor. xv. 29, in *ThStKr* 1903, 291–308): 'For in βαπτίζεσθαι (or βαπτίζειν) εἰς, the preposition εἰς indicates the object towards which or in whose behalf, honour etc., the baptism tends, and this same sense can be rendered by ὑπέρ'. Cf. pp. 95f. Further especially M. Raeder, Vikariatstaufe in 1 Cor. xv. 29?, in *ZNW* 46 (1955) 258–60.

[52] Bauer, *Wörterbuch* col. 1659 lb; Liddell-Scott, *Greek-English Lexicon* 1857 A II, 1. According to Bauer the following N.T. examples should be mentioned: Jn. vi. 51; xi. 4; Rom. i. 5; xv. 8; 1 Cor. xv. 3; 2 Cor. i. 6; xii. 19; Gal. i. 4; 1 Thess. iii. 2. M. Raeder quotes three interesting examples from the classical literature (op. cit. 259. n. 10) after the exegete J. Elsner (1728).

The expression τί ποιήσουσιν *v.* 29a is translated by Bachmann (and similarly Schlatter): 'What will they (who get themselves baptized) achieve for the dead by this?' A different tone may be discerned in the rendering of J. Weiss: 'What should they resort to ... what will they do in the future?' Passages like Mt. v. 47; xix. 16; Mk. x. 17; xi. 3–5; Acts xiv. 15; xxi. 13 offer themselves for comparison. The meaning of the term and the passages cited for comparison tell in favour of Weiss' interpretation.

3. *Some Attempts at Interpretation*

(*a*) *With the Translation 'in favour of'*

It is an old view that baptism takes place with faith in the resurrection of the dead, which the baptized confesses in the baptismal creed (Chrysostom, Theodoret, Theophylact, Oecumenius, Epiphanius).[53] But οἱ βαπτιζόμενοι, which refers to a particular circle of persons, would then be a remarkable mode of expression.

Bachmann thinks that baptism takes place in the interest of one's own resurrection; the dead are the people themselves who get baptized 'so as not to belong to the dead' (Gutjahr). An unprejudiced reader can scarcely gather this from the wording of the statement.

Again, others are of the opinion that the saying has to do with the baptism of catechumens. They receive a final impulse to baptism in consideration of their relatives and friends who have died in profession of the Christian faith (Robertson-Plummer). This interpretation, which in this form is too indefinite, will occupy us again in considering the understanding of ὑπέρ as final (under (*c*)).

Allo has in view catechumens who, in their own baptism, desire to enable the dead of their family to participate in its grace; it is presumed that such had died in faith (with the 'baptism of desire') but did not attain to the joy of being baptized in water. The catechumens would have interceded for these dead at their own baptism by means of special prayers and ceremonies.

Stauffer gives a suggestion related to that of Allo:[54] it is an intercessory baptism for the dead on the analogy of the Jewish *oratio pro defunctis* (cf. 2 Macc. xii). Its power reaches down into Sheol and there serves to benefit men, who in their time on earth did not receive the sealing with the name of Christ. The strength of this exposition is the terminological association with 2 Macc. xii. 44, 46 and the link with the thought of resurrection. Nevertheless prayer and sacrifice for the dead are far from being the same as baptism for the dead. Moreover we know nothing of

[53] Panar. XXVIII, 6, 5 (GCS I, 318, 22–28 Holl.). [54] *Theol.* 202, and n. 544.

special prayers and rites which might have been connected with baptism. The whole idea remains completely hypothetical.

Schlatter takes another direction.[55] He interprets οἱ βαπτιζόμενοι in a figurative sense as indicating 'dying', and he appeals to the metaphorical statement of Jesus in Mk. x. 39; Lk. xii. 50, and to the equation baptism = death, assumed in Rom. vi. 4; Col. ii. 11. Essentially he thinks of the outstanding members of the primitive Church who had already died, but whose death ministered to the salvation of the dead. What Jesus had wrought in his death is applied to the death of his messengers. The addition of *v.* 30 is then meaningful: Paul even now does the same as they who suffered a martyr's death for Jesus.

The chief difficulty of this hypothesis is the metaphorical interpretation of βαπτίζεσθαι, which the readers could not light upon without further explanation. By adding the accusative (τὸ) βάπτισμα in Mk. x. 39; Lk. xii. 50, Jesus leaves no doubt that He is speaking of a special baptism or of a kind of baptism. But the readers could not arrive at the idea of considering death as 'baptism' merely on the interpretation of Christian baptism as a 'baptism of death'.

(b) With the Translation 'instead of'

The majority of recent scholars decide in favour of this (Cornely, Sickenberger, Kuss, Bousset, J. Weiss, Lietzmann, H. D. Wendland, etc.), as did Ambrosiaster before them.[56] Nevertheless Bachmann (p. 450) and Schlatter (pp. 433f) have raised an objection from the linguistic side: a representative baptism never takes place for *the* dead, but always for a particular dead person. It could at once be replied that the repetition of the cases of baptism justifies the plural; but it must be admitted that one would then expect ὑπὲρ νεκρῶν. However in *v.* 29b νεκροί stands without the article, and ὑπὲρ αὐτῶν harks back to it. A hint, therefore, is in fact provided that individual cases are in mind, not the collective sense but signifies 'for *their* dead', for particular dead people about whom they are concerned.

On the view of a vicarious baptism the expression τί ποίησουσιν must presumably indicate: 'What will [with the nuance, "what *ought*", cf. Rom. vi. 2] such people do in the future?' when, namely, they arrive at the discovery that in this practice they are in opposition to the denial of the resurrection. J. Weiss rightly recognizes that the saying has its thrust only if the deniers of the resurrection themselves, or some of them at least, participate in this custom.

Exegetically the understanding of the passage in the sense of a vicarious

[55] *Paulus Bote Jesu*, 420–5. [56] PL 17, 266.

baptism can be justified. The chief objections to it come from the historical point of view. Bachmann reproduces them in all their sharpness: (1) A direct report as to a usage of this kind among the Marcionites is first found in Chrysostom. Earlier testimonies to such a view and custom are uncertain. (2) According to Paul's mode of expression there is not the slightest limitation as to locality assumed, say, to Corinth or to Achaia; yet neither is there the least trace of such a custom in the Christianity of the first and second centuries. (3) If there had been even a slight beginning of a custom like this in Corinth and it had enjoyed Paul's approbation in his argument, it is thoroughly incomprehensible for it not to have become naturalized in the great Church generally, in view of the inclination towards sacraments and rites that rapidly established itself in the ancient Church. (4) There is no presupposition on the basis of which this view can be explained. It is foreign to the original Christian meaning of baptism.

We may grant that it can be concluded from the reliable report of John Chrysostom[57] that this custom had existed for a long time. Epiphanius[58] knows of a tradition concerning the same usage among the adherents of Cerinthus in Asia and Galatia. On the other hand the two passages in Tertullian[59] do not belong here, since they are manifestly only an exegesis of 1 Cor. xv. 29; they do not betray any original knowledge on the part of the African. Whether the baptism *of* the dead, as the giving of the Lord's Supper to the dead in Montanist circles, had anything to do with the representative baptism *for* the dead must surely appear doubtful.[60]

Since the material for Christianized Gnosis is small, the question arises the more acutely whether such a custom is attested in circles outside Christianity. Reitzenstein,[61] Bousset, J. Weiss, Lietzmann (ad loc), Clemen,[62] among others, affirms that there is. The representative initiation for the dead in the Dionysiac Mysteries is quoted as sure proof of this, as also Plato, *Pol.* II, 364f.[63] These texts may well have in view a

[57] Ad loc (Montf. X, 378C). [58] Panar. XXVIII, 6, 4 (I, 318, 15–22 Holl.).

[59] *De carn. resurr.* 48 (III, 100, 5–11 Kroymann) and *Adv. Marc.* V. 10 (III, 605, 15–24 Kroymann).

[60] E. Stauffer in RGG V, 1239 thinks that baptism of the dead and baptism for the dead amount to the same thing. However other ideas, precisely on African ground, may have been at work, cf. Bonnet in Angelos I, 116f. Schweitzer, *Mystik* 277, refuses a similar Mandaean testimony from Reitzenstein.

[61] *Mysterienrel.* ³233; *Vorgeschichte der christlichen Taufe* 43f. Does the inscription here cited, which gives information of the representative initiation of a certain Dionysios for his brother, have anything to do with a baptism?

[62] Op. cit. 162.

[63] See Fragm. orph. 208, reproduced by E. Rohde, *Psyche, Seelencult und Unsterblichkeitsglaube der Griechen*, Tübingen ⁹⁻¹⁰1925, II, 128 n. 5; Plato, *Pol.* II, 364b-365a (ed. Burnet IV)—Rohde (see above) thinks it has to do with old Orphic views that Plato only reproduces.

religious care for the dead, but they do not offer a convincing parallel. Schweitzer has given some justifiable criticism as to this narrow basis.[64] He, therefore, with A. Marmorstein[65] and Stauffer (see under (*a*)), seeks a connection with Old Testament and Rabbinic ideas. The sacrifice for the Maccabaean heroes (2 Macc. xii. 39–45) was offered for the sins of sorcery and idolatry (the fallen wore heathen amulets). Marmorstein cites in this connection the Rabbinic teaching from the Tannaitic period: 'If a man prays for one who is in hell, he casts him out of hell.'[66] He also endeavours to make credible an old teaching, according to which a sin-offering can be sacrificed for the dead (contrary to the later opinion of the Mishna).[67] But precisely his basic presupposition, that 'baptism among the first Christians was equivalent to the sin-offering of the older religious belief'[68] is very doubtful.

In fact, historically little room can be found for this view. Traces of ideas of this kind give the right to postulate that the custom was not impossible for Corinth. But the weighty objection still remains that Paul could not approve of such a custom, nor tacitly suffer it, if the Corinthians already had an inclination to certain 'magical' ideas of the sacraments (cf. 1 Cor. x. 1–13). If in spite of this many scholars have held fast to the idea of a vicarious baptism, that is probably due to the fact that no other satisfactory explanation was at hand.

(*c*) *With the Translation 'for' in the final sense*

The proposal to interpret ὑπέρ as final is not new.[69] On this view ὑπέρ would give the purpose which someone might wish to reach through the action in question. This grammatical possibility (see above under 2) does not remove the obscurity of the passage; the exegesis must try to make comprehensible the intention of those who get themselves baptized 'for the dead'.

B. M. Foschini postulates a final meaning when, in his monograph, he holds ὑπέρ to be synonymous with εἰς τοὺς νεκρούς. This expression he would approximate to the phrase βαπτίζεσθαι εἰς τὸν Χριστόν; it affirms a relation of belonging (that is correct, cf. § 4). In order to gain an approximate meaning for the passage he interprets it, with the aid of numerous question marks, as follows: 'Otherwise what shall they do who are baptized? for the dead? (that is, are they baptized to belong to,

[64] *Mystik* 276–8; cf. also G. H. Marsh, op. cit. 146ff. [65] *ZNW* 30. (1931) 277–85.
[66] Pesikta rabbati (ed. Friedmann, c. 20, p. 95B) after Marmorstein, op. cit. 279 and n. 5; cf. Bonsirven, *Judaisme* II, 96–98.
[67] Op. cit. 284. [68] Op. cit. 279.
[69] M. Raeder (in *ZNW* (1955 p. 259, n. 10) cites for it Jac. Elsner, *Observationes Sacrae in Novi Foederis Libros*, tom. II (1728) 127–31.

to be numbered among the dead, who are never to rise again?) Indeed, if the dead do not rise again at all, why are people baptized? for them? (that is, are they baptized to be numbered among the dead who are never to rise again?)'.[70] By means of the question, therefore, a negative answer is insinuated: the baptized do not become baptized on this account—to belong to the dead! In my judgment, however, the attempt is artificial and unconvincing.

In contrast to this the exposition given by M. Raeder, a pupil of J. Jeremias,[71] is worthy of consideration: the baptized here mentioned had resolved on their baptism in order to be united with Christian relatives or friends at the resurrection.[72] Admittedly it can be objected that this is not a lofty motive (possibly not even a religious one) for joining the Christian Church; but on the assumption that they confessed faith in Jesus Christ as Lord, the argument does not step outside the frame of primitive Christian views, and above all it fits excellently into the resurrection chapter. J. Jeremias points out in this connection that a linguistic distinction between νεκροί = the dead generally and οἱ νεκροί = deceased Christians, is consistently maintained throughout chapter 15; it is fully consonant with this exposition and adds strength to it.[73] It would still be possible to object that the idea in the brief phrase ὑπὲρ τῶν νεκρῶν is not directly stated but has to be filled out by the exegesis. But that equally applies to other comparable passages that have a final ὑπέρ. If, for example, it is stated in 1 Cor. xv. 3; Gal. i. 4 that Christ 'died for our sins', we interpret it as implying, since the thought is well known to us, 'in order to redeem us from our sins'. The idea suggested by M. Raeder and J. Jeremias is close to the context and so cannot be charged with being an unjustifiable intrusion. The further argument mentioned by the Apostle, with regard to his own person, also links up with it well: 'For what purpose do we ourselves face dangers every hour? I die daily. ... ' (*vv.* 30f). The Apostle constantly exposes himself to the danger of death in order that at the last he may attain to the resurrection (cf. 2 Cor. iv. 10f; Phil. iii. 10f).

In this last suggestion it may well be that an exegetical solution has been found which, in a simple and yet convincing way, settles an old *crux interpretum*. It makes no new contribution to Paul's view of baptism; but the eschatological expectation is confirmed which already shines forth from the key passage Rom. vi. 1–11.

[70] Foschini op. cit. 93; cf. his whole exposition, pp. 92–98.
[71] J. Jeremias in *NTS* 2 (1955/56) 155f agrees with her exposition.
[72] M. Raeder, op. cit. 290.
[73] J. Jeremias in *NTS* 2 (1955/56) 155f.

PART TWO

Biblical-Theological Construction

THE SALVATION-EVENT AT BAPTISM IN THE CONTEXT OF THE PAULINE THEOLOGY

CHAPTER ONE

The Salvation-Event at Baptism *in general*

§16. BAPTISM AS MEANS OF SALVATION (SACRAMENT)

WHEN one contemplates the fulness of the Pauline baptismal conceptions the question arises whether they allow of being gathered together into a unity and of occupying a definite place in the Pauline theology. The concept of sacrament immediately suggests itself for this purpose. Yet one cannot help being conscious of the difficulties of applying this concept, so firmly established and clearly defined in modern theology, to Paul. The critical direction of studies in the comparative history of religions frequently ascribes to Paul a share of responsibility for the development of 'sacramental piety'.[1] By 'sacrament' in this sense is meant an external means and sign through which supernatural power is mechanically released and conveyed. This view is said to have emanated from the world of Hellenism, especially from the Mystery Religions, for Judaism did not know such sacraments. The question has extensive ramifications, for it postulates nothing less than an initial break between the piety of the primitive Jewish Christian Church and that of the Gentile Christian great Church, even in the time of Paul. Its implications go beyond baptism and include above all the central cultus of the Lord's Supper.

There is no doubt that a strong yearning for something higher than earthly, transitory goods lived in the men of Hellenistic and Oriental syncretism, and the Mystery Religions knew of many signs and customs that purported to convey hidden powers of salvation to believers through their application Into this world Paul took the Gospel of Jesus Christ, the Redeemer and Bringer of salvation. It would be understandable if the Apostle to the Gentiles, who desired to be 'all things to all men' (1 Cor. ix. 22), had made use of this 'Hellenistic' sacramental idea in order to open to the 'Greeks' a door for faith. Nevertheless, his uncompromising will to hold firmly to the religion of the Cross of Jesus Christ, though it seemed as folly to the pagans (1 Cor. i. 23),

[1] Cf. Heitmüller, *Taufe* I, 14ff, 21f; *Taufe* II, 18ff; H. J. Holtzmann, *Ntl. Theologie* I, 455; Leipoldt, *Urchristl. Taufe* 57ff. Later scholars consider that this development took place after Paul; according to Oepke, *ThWI*, 541, baptism first became a 'physical-hyperphysical means of grace', at least in so far as it reached the leading circles, in the early Catholic era; cf. further A. von Harnack, *Mission und Ausbreitung d. Christ.* 4I, 250.

and his consciousness of being bound to the tradition of the primitive Apostolic proclamation of salvation (1 Cor. xv. 3) militate against this view. He himself is of the conviction that the Gospel he received through the revelation of Jesus Christ (Gal. i. 12), and laid before the leading Apostles in Jerusalem (Gal. ii. 2), is none other than that of the first Christian community. Whatever one's judgment on the total work of the missionary Apostle, who emerged from Diaspora Judaism and burst into the centres of Hellenistic culture, we found in his teaching on baptism (if we may trust the testimony of Acts) expressions and views that were already dominant in the primitive community in Jerusalem; these included baptism as a bath of cleansing from sins, baptism to the name of Jesus, baptism in unity with the work of the Spirit of God. His own characteristic formulations, like baptism as 'the circumcision of Christ' (Col. ii. 11), 'putting on Christ' (Gal. iii. 27), 'being buried with Christ' (Rom. vi. 4; Col. ii. 12), cannot be proved to be imports from the world of Hellenistic thought. It is therefore more than bold to assert that he borrowed his idea of the sacraments from that source. It would be a perverse methodology to attempt to come at his basic principles with the aid of such a concept.

It ought not to be forgotten that Judaism also was acquainted with numerous religious washings and baptisms, even if it be a debatable point how far they bore a sacramental character.[2] It was precisely Judaism that was in the forefront of the great baptismal movement, the broad stream of which we have been the better able to survey in recent years.[3] How closely primitive Christianity was in contact with it—perchance through John the Baptist?—is not yet decided. Paul at any rate is no innovator here. He created neither the institution nor the basic interpretation of baptism, but found them already in existence; it is rather a cause for wonder how he was able to combine his deeper, Christ-related reflections on baptism with the views he adopted. Without doubt it remains wholly within the bounds of possibility that in formulating his baptismal teaching he constructed at the same time a bridge to Hellenism—as in the case of the *Kyrios* idea, there were religious conceptions and usages enough which Jews and Greeks alike were able to hear and understand, even if the timbre varied at times.

For our investigation it seems best to operate first with a quite general overall conception; for this we propose the concept 'means of salvation'.

[2] On the question of Judaism and sacraments cf. Bousset-Gressmann, op. cit. 199–201; F. Gavin, *The Jewish Antecedents of the Christian Sacraments*, 1928; on baptism especially J. Thomas, op. cit. 4–60; Marsh, op. cit. 4–7.

[3] See especially the work of J. Thomas, and for the comparative historical material also R. Reitzenstein, *Die Vorgeschichte der christlichen Taufe*, 18ff, 43ff.

The expression is broad enough to include the views of the Jerusalem primitive community, independently of the question of a 'Hellenistic' sacramental idea—unless it were believed that the oldest Christian 'baptism' was the charismatic outpouring of the Spirit alone (Acts i. 5) and all the passages that speak of water baptism were eliminated as the work of a later redactor.[4] The yearning desire of those circles that give ear to the earliest Apostolic preaching is directed to the (eschatological) redemption (σωτηρία), with all its blessings of salvation (Acts ii. 21, 40, 47; xi, 14; cf. xiii. 26, 46f; xv. 1, 11), and baptism, according to the words of Peter, serves as an indispensable prerequisite to it (Acts ii. 38; cf. 40f).

That for Paul himself 'means of salvation' in its broadest sense can serve as a provisional leading concept is evident from the fact that in some way or other all the relevant texts have to do with 'salvation', or the idea stands in the background. The 'washing' in baptism introduces the process of sanctification, and is the precondition and warrant for inheriting the Kingdom of God (1 Cor. vi. 11; cf. 10). Baptism to the name of Jesus binds us to the Lord, who was crucified for us—and for what other purpose than to deliver us from eternal destruction (1 Cor. i. 13; cf. 18)? The fact that in baptism we 'put on Christ' brings us into so close a unity with Him, we become through Him participators in the blessing promised to Abraham (Gal. iii. 27; cf. 29). In the bath of baptism we are 'buried with Christ', to rise with Him also to life (Rom. vi. 4, 8; Col. ii. 12f), a life whose full, divine glory will be manifested only at the end (Col. iii. 3f). The 'bath of regeneration' bestows justification in grace and a title to the heavenly inheritance, according to the hope of eternal life (Tit. iii. 5; cf. 7). These are Pauline ideas, and they coincide with the very different ideas, such as are found in 1 Pet. iii. 21, in the one point, that baptism is the fundamental means of deliverance in the New Testament time of salvation. It was through this inclusive concept that Paul was able to make use of the comparison with the Old Testament 'type' of baptism (see above § 14). From this point of view baptism is a completely unified entity. As there is but one Lord, so there is only one faith and one baptism (Eph. iv. 5).[5]

[4] Windisch, *Taufe und Sünde* 92; Behm, *Die Handauflegung im Urchristentum*, Leipzig 1911, 165–176; von Stromberg, op. cit. 50, 89, 117, 157f; J. Weiss, *Urchristentum* 488f; Jackson-Lake, *The Beginnings of Christianity* I: *The Acts of the Apostles*, London 1922, I, 337–44; Lake-Cadbury op. cit. IV, 93; for criticism of this view cf. Coppens, *L'imposition des mains* 212–6 and *Confirm.* 136ff; P. van Inschoot, 'Baptême d'eau et baptême d'Esprit Saint', EphThLov 13 (1936) 653–66; Gewiess op. cit. 130–2.

[5] It is not enough, therefore, to ascribe to baptism only a *significant* role, as is consistently done in the work by M. Barth (*Die Taufe—ein Sakrament?* Zollikon-Zürich 1951). Barth writes (p. 56): 'The baptism of the disciples is the prayer for the heavenly glory which the death of Christ as the source of life attests'; and on Acts ii. 38 (p. 136): 'Repentance should

If it be desired to define this means of salvation more exactly, it will be pertinent to affirm: all salvation that is mediated comes from God. All things come from Him, and for Him we are created (1 Cor. viii. 6). This foundation of theological thinking lies at the basis of the Pauline soteriology. Baptism is not a human manipulation, a secret procedure through which a man may appropriate something hard to obtain. The blessings of salvation mediated through it are bestowed by God. Although baptism presupposes human co-operation for salvation, the decisive action comes from God alone. That is shown linguistically in the passive expressions by which the salvation-event in baptism is described. Βαπτίζειν is never employed in any other way when denoting that which the Christian experiences in baptism (1 Cor. i. 13; xii. 13; Rom. vi. 3; Gal. iii. 27). Paul speaks in the active only of his baptizing activity (1 Cor. i. 16, 17), and he uses the middle only of the Israelites, who received in the Red Sea the 'baptism to Moses' (1 Cor. x. 2). The other expressions also, which relate to the salvation-event in baptism, give God the pre-eminence in the action. The term ἀπελούσασθε in 1 Cor. vi. 11 is but an apparent exception, since it possesses—alongside two passive forms—a causative meaning ('you caused yourselves to be washed'). God alone is the one who redeems and makes alive (Col. ii. 12f; Eph. ii. 5). Even the late Epistle to Titus pointedly expresses our gracious deliverance by God; He has saved us not on the basis of our own works, that we ourselves have done, but solely on the basis of his pity, through the bath of regeneration (Tit. iii. 5). This Christian means of salvation is exalted high over all means of sorcery and magical manipulations. It belongs to a religion which defends God's primacy in everything. It is never loosed from God's will to save, to be delivered up to the unholy will of man. It always remains in the light of the *logos* and *ethos* and in the service of the true worship of God.

If enquiry be made after the operations of salvation, the blessings of salvation mediated through baptism, the ideas that are characteristic of the primitive Church reappear also in Paul, namely the forgiveness of sins and possession of the Spirit (Acts ii. 38; xxii. 16). The 'washing' of 1 Cor. vi. 11, in its context, can mean nothing else than cleansing from

therein begin and be certified actively, genuinely, concretely, and in a documentary fashion, to the effect that the man who has been seized by the preaching and its content now gets himself baptized. Baptism ought to be the sign of repentance' (cf. also p. 140). See further p. 332; (on John) 418–53; (on Tit. iii. 5) 454–71. In summary it is stated: 'In the act of baptism the baptized and the baptizer—and with them and through them the Church—confess before God and the world their knowledge of the meaning and effect of the death of Christ and of the operation of the Spirit of God. They confess in the water of baptism their desire for the baptism of the Spirit, and their sure hope or their trust to receive the baptism of the Spirit.' 'Knowledge' and 'confession' scarcely do justice to the realistically described saving effects of baptism.

the defilement of sin (*vv.* 9–10; cf. also καθαρίσας Eph. v. 26). This basic conception of the 'bath of baptism' is never lost (cf. Heb. x. 22). The role of the Holy Spirit, however, has characteristically changed. If in the Acts of the Apostles it signifies the great divine gift of salvation (ii. 38; viii. 16f; xix. 2–6), for Paul the Spirit is rather, in closest connection with the exalted Lord, the *Mediator* or the means of justification and sanctification (1 Cor. vi. 11). In manifest contrast to John's water baptism (Acts i. 5; xix. 3f), the Church lays all emphasis on the fact that its baptism brings with it the (charismatic) outpouring of the Spirit. This consciousness is still present at a later time (cf. Tit. iii. 6); Paul regards the Spirit as the gift of God (Rom. v. 5; viii. 15; Gal. iv. 6). But for his baptismal theology the *Pneuma*-concept renders him yet another service: the divine Spirit is the effective organ of the heavenly Christ (because of this, the process of sanctification takes place ἐν τῷ πνεύματι κτλ. 1 Cor. vi. 11), or, in impersonal categories, He is the divine power that goes forth from the Christ, filling those who believe in Him and uniting them in the 'Body of Christ' (1 Cor. xii. 13). By this means Paul has made the more external connection between baptism and Spirit in Acts (cf. viii. 16f; x. 47f; xix. 5) to become more inward, and at the same time he has tied more tightly the cords that united the believers to Christ.

In Paul, however, the greatest weight falls on those passages which describe the saving event in baptism as a dying and being raised with Christ. They must be dealt with later (see below §§ 21–23) in their context.

For the comparison with the views of the Church, the 'social' effect of baptism is still of significance. In Acts it is not a matter of secondary import that baptism makes one a member of the community of salvation (ii. 41 προσετέθησαν, cf. 47; x. 47f; xv. 8–11). It has even been thought that this is the oldest meaning of baptism, and that only later did the reception of the Spirit become bound up with baptism.[6] This interpretation, which depreciates baptism to become an almost juristic act of reception, and denies the religious, soteriological and eschatological character which it possessed from the beginning (cf. Acts ii. 38 with 33 and 21), is to be refused. It is certain that for the primitive Church, baptism is not only the indispensable condition for the individual's attainment of salvation (cf. viii. 36–38), it is also the religious act of reception into the community of salvation led by the Holy Spirit (cf. ii. 41f, 47; iv. 31; v. 9–11; ix. 31; xx. 28).

Paul took up this understanding of baptism in his own way and deepened it. For the Apostle, who formerly breathed in the particularistic

[6] G. Kittel, Die Wirkungen d. christl. Wassertaufe nach dem NT, *ThStKr* 87 (1914) 33–42.

atmosphere of Judaism, the step into Christian faith signifies the transition from the national and religious narrowness of Judaism into the broad spaces of a religion for humanity. This experience powerfully bursts into view in the Letter to the Galatians. If the Mosaic Law was to him as a burdensome guardian, that held him and his religious compatriots (cf. the 'we' of iii. 23–25) imprisoned in strict custody (*v.* 23), the coming of the religion of grace by Jesus Christ signified the falling from his shoulders of the sense of restraint and opened up the prospect to a new community of faith, no longer hindered by religious-national, social and sexual limitations (cf. the 'you' of *vv.* 26–29). That is the joyful message of the missionary to the heathen that he delivers to his readers: 'You *all* are sons of God through faith in the fellowship of Christ Jesus' (*v.* 26). The fellowship of Christ becomes a complete reality in baptism, wherein all have 'put on Christ'. Through his *Pneuma* the risen Lord enters into an intimate union with the baptized personally, and through that selfsame *Pneuma*, whom He imparts to all the baptized (cf. 1 Cor. xii. 13), He includes him in the community of the members of Christ, in the new 'Israel of God' (Gal. vi. 16). With steady gaze Paul the theologian seizes on this significance of baptism and coins the formula 'all one in Christ Jesus' (*v.* 28).

The Apostle develops the same idea yet more powerfully under the concept of the 'Body of Christ'. Through baptism believers are taken up 'in a single Spirit into a single Body', namely into the Body of Christ (1 Cor. xii. 13, 27). Baptism has the important function of integrating new members into this Body of Christ, and thereby to build it up. That happens through the one Spirit, the Spirit of Christ and of God, who fills and pervades all the baptized. If in Ephesians and Colossians the symbol of the Body is differently outlined—Christ the Head, the believers his Body (Eph. i. 22f; iv. 15f; Col. i. 18; ii. 19; iii. 15), this σῶμα with its members (cf. Eph. v. 30) is nevertheless conceived of in principle in the same way: it is the Body of Christ in which the baptized are united, Christ's growing community of salvation. This is illustrated by another symbol in Ephesians, that of the building of which the 'Apostles and Prophets' form the foundation and the headstone is Christ, which also grows continually through those who 'are built together to become a dwelling for God in the Spirit' (ii. 20–22).[7]

If Paul's extensive theological work has become apparent, in this

[7] The 'Apostles and Prophets' themselves should be considered as the foundation (gen. of apposition), since the teaching as such does not suit a picture where all the stones are persons (Dibelius ad loc). Christ is the stone that completes the building (cf. Jeremias in *Angelos* 1 (1925) 65–70 and 2 (1926) 119). The symbol is not consistently developed, because the idea of growth is in view. Cf. further Schlier, *Epheserbrief* ad loc (142ff).

consideration of the effects of baptism with respect to salvation, it becomes yet more luminous when we contemplate the significance of Christ for the New Testament means of salvation. It should immediately be said that for Paul, as for the Church, it is beyond question that the redemption of all mankind has happened through Jesus Christ alone, and the way of salvation is possible through Him alone (cf. Acts iv. 12 and Rom. iii. 23–25). Next to the prime assertion of the Pauline teaching of God, that there is one God, the Father, from whom everything derives and for whom we have been created, there is a second lapidary statement, that there is one *Kyrios*, Jesus Christ, *through* whom everything is and through whom we also exist (1 Cor. viii. 6). But alongside this basic conviction, which the entire primitive Church shared, one can perceive in Paul the effort to demonstrate an inner relation of baptism to Christ. For his baptismal theology he has fastened on the Church's proclamation that its baptism takes place 'to the name of Jesus' (Acts viii. 16; xix. 5; cf. ἐπὶ τῷ ὀνόματι Ἰησοῦ Χριστοῦ ii. 38; ἐν τῷ ὀνόματι Ἰησοῦ Χριστοῦ x. 48). This formula, which he takes over (cf. 1 Cor. vi. 11; i. 13), has pointed him the direction in which to work out the essence of Christian baptism: it is a means of salvation that can only be understood by reference to Christ. Paul prefers to use the shorter formula βαπτίζειν εἰς Χριστόν (Gal. iii. 27) εἰς Χριστὸν Ἰησοῦν (Rom. vi. 3a), εἰς τὸν θάνατον αὐτοῦ (Rom. vi. 3b), which allows him to express the close relation of the baptized to Christ. It is true that it does not appear originally to possess the 'mystical' colouring, which many scholars want to bestow on it ('to immerse in the mystic Christ'); but it forms a good bridge, all the same, to the Pauline ideas of 'putting on Christ' (Gal. iii. 27) and of 'being buried with Christ' (= Rom. vi. 4). The same tendency to exhibit the Christ-relatedness of baptism is illustrated in its characterization as 'Christ-circumcision' (Col. ii. 11); the 'Christ-genitive' hints that it may have been coined by the Apostle himself. He makes his most profound and characteristic utterance in Rom. vi. 3ff, where he describes the entry into the fellowship of Christ as a participation in the event that once happened to Christ Himself. Here the Christ-event of history gains an immediate significance for the present attainment of salvation by the Christian. The baptized man is drawn into the once-for-all event of salvation accomplished in the cross and resurrection of Christ, and with Christ he goes through death and the grave to the resurrection. He dies with Christ to the power of sin and is given over to a life for God. The risen Lord, to whom he is thereby united, bestows on him through his Spirit the powers of the divine life, the final goal of which is the bodily resurrection and the utter conquest of the power of death (cf. Rom. viii. 11). Without pursuing this thought further at present, it should now be plain that Paul's creative theological activity becomes the greater, the more closely he associates baptism with Christ and blends it with his 'Christ-mysticism'.

For the more precise definition of the Pauline theology of baptism, therefore, the question we shall immediately go on to consider is of decisive importance, namely in what relation the salvation-event in baptism stands to the great saving act of Christ. In this connection we must look out for the constructive line of his soteriology, to which the 'means of salvation' in baptism belongs.

§17. CHRIST'S ACT OF SALVATION AS THE FOUNDATION OF THE SALVATION-EVENT AT BAPTISM

It can be no accident that the most instructive chapter of Paul's baptismal theology (Rom. vi), containing his most characteristic and deepest thought on the subject, follows immediately on the profound conception of the Adam-Christ parallels (Rom. v. 12–21).[8] Certainly it meets *vi verborum* an objection arising out of the bold principles of the Pauline soteriology (Rom. vi. 1); but at the same time it signifies a deliberate setting of the baptismal event within the frame of the divine economy of salvation. The expression συνεσταυρώθη (*v.* 6) shows that Paul bases the salvation-event in baptism on the historical act of salvation wrought by Jesus and he never looses it from the act; i.e. he founds it on that saving act, the universal significance of which he has made clear in the contrast with Adam's far-reaching act of ruin.

By this means a fundamental insight has been gained. Paul knows and recognizes only one source of salvation: the cross of Jesus Christ. He does not teach a miraculous effectiveness of holy signs and rites, isolated from the one great saving event on Golgotha.

Paul thinks, in accordance with his Jewish-Semitic inheritance, in terms of the salvation history. God sent His Son in the 'fulness of time' (Gal. iv. 4), and this event is the most incisive intervention in the history of mankind, for it is the turning point from ruin to redemption. From this point of view there are to him only a few figures of significance: Moses, the mediator of the Law (Gal. iii. 19), and Abraham, the recipient of the (Messianic) promises of blessing (Rom. iv. 13–25; Gal. iii. 8–18). In comparison with them Christ stands as the end of the Law (Rom. x. 4; Gal. iii. 24f) and the heir of the promise (Gal. iii. 16). But

[8] This is emphasized also by C. H. Dodd, *Romans* p. 86; L. S. Thornton, *The Common Life in the Body of Christ*, 56ff; A. Nygren, *Römerbrief*, 171f; E. Best, *One Body in Christ*, 56ff.

the light afforded by the salvation history sheds its full brilliance on Christ only when He is apprehended as the corresponding type to Adam, the first man. As Adam was the head of earthly humanity, so Christ is the head of the new humanity, which is restored in the image of God and will bring to view the divine likeness in body and soul (1 Cor. xv. 21f, 45–49). As sin and death came into the world through the first Adam, the second Adam is the bringer of grace and life, but in incomparably higher measure than the first founder of the race lost it for all (Rom. v. 12–21).[9]

As a basis for the theology of baptism the *Adam-Christ parallel* is of supreme importance because it explains how the salvation gained by the one man, Jesus Christ, can in principle benefit 'the many'. His act remains the act of an individual: his personal obedience stands over against the disobedience of Adam (Rom. v. 19); but at the same time the 'many' will be made righteous[10] (κατασταθήσονται) through his act of obedience. His act has a like significance for mankind as Adam's act, only with positive instead of negative auspices; but this is not a simple settlement of accounts, a restoration, rather it signifies a tremendous surplus, as it were (ὑπερεπερίσσευσεν *v.* 20), which Christ has achieved for the salvation side of the balance.

That Adam's sin could have such calamitous effects and that all died 'in him' (1 Cor. xv. 22)[11] reflects a mode of thought for which ancient views of the solidarity of natural human social groups like family, tribe, nation have been decisive.[12] The fate in which the

[9] On this see Prat II 209–11; Weinel, *Theol.* 315–17.

[10] By the translation 'be represented' (e.g. Weinel, *Theol.* 224) the act appears only as a juridical declaration (cf. Protestant writers, especially Schlatter, ad loc). This is not true of this concept, however, cf. Bauer, *Wörterb*, col. 771, 3; Lietzmann ad loc. Moreover it is actually excluded by reason of κατεστάθησαν in the previous sentence, for men have *in fact* become sinners (cf. *v.* 12), cf. Sickenberger ad loc.

[11] Kuss, op. cit. 43, holds that a local meaning is possible in 1 Cor. xv. 22 (with appeal to Heb. vii. 9f). To infer from the following ἐν τῷ Χριστῷ (22b) a mystical-realistic fellowship of fallen and doomed man with the founder of the race, Adam, is impossible, as Deissmann recognized, *Die ntl. Formel* ... 124f (referring to 1 Cor. vii. 14). The future ζωοποιηθήσονται with ἐν τῷ Χριστῷ demands that we think of the *Pneuma*-fellowship of those who are to be raised with the (similarly) *Pneuma*-Christ; cf. on this K. Deissner, *Auferstehungshoffnung* p. 20; H. Moliter, *Die Auferstehung der Christen und Nichtchristen nach dem Apostel Paulus* (NtlAbh. XVI, 1), Münster 1933, 37f. Ἐν τῷ Ἀδάμ, can also be understood in an instrumental sense; the change in the content from the ἐν of 1 Cor. xv. 22a to the ἐν of 22b need not disturb any, for the linguistic formulation is influenced by the parallelism; the *tertium comparationis* lies in the *fact* of the union with Adam or Christ, not in the *mode* and *manner* of this connection of the members with the differing heads of humanity. Cf. J. Freundorfer, *Erbsünde und Erbtod beim Apostel Paulus* (NtlAbh. XIII, 1–2), Münster 1927, 256f. J. Jeremias in *ThW* I, 141, A7: 'ἐν τῷ Ἀδάμ is probably an analogical formation to ἐν τῷ Χριστῷ'.

[12] Moore, *Judaism* I, 475f; cf. Wrede, *Paulus* 50f; Tr. Schmidt, op. cit. 223f; Molitor, op. cit. 36ff. More recent authors assume a connection between the Pauline view and the widespread myth of the primal man, so J. Jeremias in *ThW* I, 142f; Wiencke, op. cit. 17–20; Bultmann, *Theol.* 177. 294.

human race finds itself is frequently attributed to Adam in Jewish-apocryphal[13] and Rabbinic[14] literature, although men are not thereby relieved of the burden of their own sins. How this subsuming of the entire race under its head, this representation by the first of the race for his entire succession was originally explained, it is difficult to say. The naive-realistic idea of Ex. rabba xxxi 1f, according to which all the future righteous were contained in Adam, finds a parallel in Heb. vii. 10, according to which Levi was 'in the loins of his father' (his ancestor) Abraham, when the latter met Melchisedek, and the son was tithed by his father (*v*. 9).

Here we come upon a principal category of Pauline thought, which the Apostle has taken over from his Jewish spiritual inheritance: the idea of 'corporate personality'. The Semite thinks largely in terms of the corporate body and of solidarity, so that a member of the family or tribe stands and acts for the entire family, and the community is immediately affected by the destiny of one of its members.[15] That applies in especial measure to the founder of a group; he is not only an individual person, but comprehends in himself the whole community that is associated with him and derives from him. The people of Israel calls itself after its ancestor Jacob-Israel and feels itself united together in him in its twelve-tribe-union. Adam, as the founder of the entire human race, is representative of mankind; those who derive from him and are united with him participate in him and his destiny. The significance of this conception of racial solidarity for Pauline theology has been recognized in recent research, especially in England; its effects are particularly manifest in the Adam-Christ parallel, but to a certain extent it also explains the conceptions of 'life in Christ' and the 'Body of Christ'.[16] The difficulty that arises for our thinking through the distance between the once-for-all event of the cross and resurrection of Christ and our attainment of salvation ensuing here and now at any given time, is dissolved in that mode of thought. Because Christ 'was delivered for our sins and raised for our justification' (Rom. iv. 25), his death and resurrection benefit us when we appropriate Him to ourselves (in faith and in

[13] 4 Esd. iii. 7; vii. 11, 118; syr Bar. Apk. xvii, 3, xlviii. 42f. Cf. Volz. *Eschat.* 300.

[14] Billerbeck III, 227f. Moore I. 476 reproduces an impressive passage from the Tanchuma, according to which God causes all the generations to pass by Adam and to accuse him of his calamitous act.

[15] Cf. J. Pedersen, *Israel, its Life and Culture*, I–II, London 1926, 263–79; H. W. Robinson, The Hebrew Conception of Corporate Personality, *Werden und Wachsen des Alten Testaments* (Beiheft 66 *ZAW*), Berlin 1936, 49–66.

[16] Cf. Dodd, *Romans*, 86–88; Thornton, *The Common Life in the Body of Christ*, 34–65; Best, *One Body in Christ*, passim, especially 34–43 (and the authorities mentioned by him); W. D. Davies, *Paul and Rabbinic Judaism* 36–57; Nygren, *Römerbrief* 174–6.

baptism). Because Christ died and rose as Representative and Substitute of redeemed mankind, we also are 'buried with Him and raised with Him' in baptism (Col. ii. 12). So soon as we establish through faith and baptism the union with Him as our spiritual founder of the (new) race, we participate in that which happened to Him: his death becomes our death, his resurrection becomes our resurrection.

This relation is not reversible. Christ always remains the First, the 'Beginning' (ἀπαρχή 1 Cor. xv. 20, 23), the Leader of salvation, who joins to Himself those who follow Him, includes them in his redeeming event and finally brings them to the bodily resurrection, to conform them to the complete likeness of his glory (Rom. viii. 29; 1 Cor. xv. 49). The historical once-for-all event that transpired on the cross stands immovable in its place and remains prior to that which we experience in baptism. Therefore we die 'with Christ', it can never be the reverse, and on the basis of his resurrection we shall rise through Him and in Him and with Him. The distance of time and the repetition of baptism for those who subsequently believe and come to baptism play no role in this view. All who attach themselves to Christ, irrespective of the time of their doing so, are taken up into the once-for-all event and in Him Himself.

In this connection the *manhood* of Christ is especially emphasized (ἀνθρώπου Rom. v. 15; δι' ἀνθρώπου 1 Cor. xv. 21; ὁ δεύτερος ἄνθρωπος 1 Cor. xv. 47). Our union with the first Adam is that of a community of race into which we enter through birth. Christ similarly becomes representative of the race of man through the incarnation (Gal. iv. 4) and as such the first born and founder of a new humanity, which is again created after the image of God (cf. Col. iii. 10). In 1 Cor. xv Paul exhibits the difference between the old, terrestrial and corruptible humanity and the new humanity, glorified in the Spirit through the resurrection. The first Adam becomes only a living ψυχή, the last a life-creating πνεῦμα (so Paul deduces from Gen. ii. 7 by his own peculiar exegesis, *vv.* 45f). The first man is taken out of the earth, the second comes from heaven (*v.* 47). One may perceive precisely in his bold exegesis, which is not demonstrable in Jewish literature in this form,[17] how Paul has struggled over this important substructure of his theology. If in 1 Cor. xv the consequences of the Adam-Christ parallel were important for the bodily resurrection, and therefore for the consummation

[17] Cf. Billerbeck III, 477f; J. Jeremias in *ThW* I, 142, 5ff. Lietzmann, 1 *Cor.* pp. 85f, would recognize in Paul's exegesis, that infers from the psychic nature of the 'first Adam' the *pneuma*-nature of the 'second Adam', an opposition to the Rabbinic tradition, in so far as it lay before Philo. Contra Deissner, *Auferstehungshoffnung* 37 and nn. 3 and 4; J. Jeremias in *ThW* I, 143, 6ff.

of salvation, equally plainly were they so in Rom. v. 12–21 for his teaching on redemption. That which is presupposed in 1 Cor. xv is developed in detail in Rom. v: in virtue of his humanity Christ is able to convey the surpassing wealth of his grace on others since He is in the strict and truest sense, the Mediator.

This mediatorial activity of the new Head of mankind, who is bound up with us and yet brings to us the saving powers of God, comes to expression in Rom. v in the rich use of the preposition διά. The Apostle can say of Adam that the verdict of condemnation and judgment took its rise from Him (ἐξ ἑνός, *v.* 16), and that death exercised its ruinous sovereignty through him (διὰ τοῦ ἑνός, *v.* 17). In exactly the same manner the righteous act (δικαίωμα *v.* 18) and the obedience (*v.* 19) of the 'one man', Christ, becomes for the many the mediating cause of their blessing and deliverance unto eternal life. Christ has become the Mediator of the reign of grace that promises life, as the resounding διὰ Ἰησοῦ Χριστοῦ κτλ at the conclusion of *v.* 21 declares.

Whether, and to what extent, all numerically gain the life of the glory of Christ is not stated by Paul in this context, the subject of which is the saving significance of Christ, that in principle is universal in its scope. The sayings that limit the personal circle of those who are actually saved[18] are associated with the *reception* of salvation by individuals, and they are anchored in the eternal decree of God (Rom. viii. 29f). As the baptismal theology of Paul is unthinkable without the view of Christ as the Head of humanity, this universal aspect has its complement in the soteriology that is related to the individuals, and it finds its clear expression in the demand for saving faith and baptism.

At this point an important difference reveals itself between Adamitic and redeemed mankind: if we are born into the Adamitic race of man without any action on our part, we are baptized into the 'race of Christ' only with our own decision; that is, we first become members of the new, redeemed humanity when we ourselves decide on it in faith and let ourselves actually be incorporated through baptism. God, who created us without our aid did not wish to redeem us without our will.[19] The foundation of the new humanity is different from that of the old: it is no longer a matter of physical descent, the 'flesh', but of faith in Christ and the 'Spirit'.

With this interpretation of Christ as the Head of the new humanity Paul unites the further concept of the representation of the one for all in

[18] Cf. the antitheses τοῖς μὲν ἀπολλυμένοις—τοῖς δὲ σωζομένοις ἡμῖν 1 Cor. i. 18; further 2 Cor. ii. 15f.

[19] Augustine, Sermo 169, 13 (PL 38, 923): '*Sine voluntate tua non erit in te justitia Dei ... Qui ergo fecit te sine te, non te justificat sine te. Ergo fecit nescientem, justificat volentem.*'

the foundation principles of his soteriology. There are several texts that unmistakably express it (especially 2 Cor. v. 14f, 21; Gal. iii. 13; 1 Tim. ii. 6). In the light of these statements it is less significant that a disagreement in measure prevails on the issue as to how far the preposition ὑπέρ exactly represents ἀντί.[20]

> That ὑπέρ can really have the meaning of substitution is rendered certain by the rich material of the papyri; e.g. a writer representing the illiterate refers to his function as ὑπὲρ αὐτοῦ.[21] P. Feine is of the opinion that in all the N.T. passages (he quotes 17) it is sufficient to accord it a literal rendering 'for the benefit of'.[22] But if the idea of substitution plainly springs out of the context, as in the above mentioned passages, one should have no hesitation in translating the preposition itself 'in place of'. Perhaps a conscious ambiguity is also permitted.[23]

From the viewpoint of method it is of no account that a number of passages can be quoted in which this conception is doubtful, including perhaps those with παραδιδόναι ὑπὲρ ἡμῶν.[24]

In 2 Cor. v. 14f 'the essential soteriology of Paul appears in its whole power and fulness' (Allo). The idea of substitution is moulded in the pregnant form:

One died for (instead of) all.
Consequently *all* died.

A 'principle of solidarity' is stated there, 'that makes of the death of Christ our death, or the life of Christ our life'.[25] Only it must never be left out of account that this relation is never reversible or applicable to others: Christ alone could take the place of all; others in the generality of mankind could not assume this function, as it presupposes a continuance *in solidum*. Here we see that the concept of representation is bound to the Adam-Christ parallel: Christ is the Head within the new humanity, and

[20] Cf. Radermacher 116; Moulton-Thumb 171; Robertson-Stocks 174f; Abel § 490; Bultmann, *Theol.* 291; K. H. Schelkle, *Die Passion Jesu in der Verkündigung des NT*, Heidelberg 1949, p. 134.

[21] Deissmann, *Licht vom Osten* 285 and n. 2; Bauer, *Wörterb.* col. 1659, see under ὑπέρ 1c.

[22] *Theol.* 182 centre page. His list p. 193, n. 2 is incorrect; Eph. v. 2 is lacking and 1 Cor. v. 7 should be in parentheses, since the variant reading ὑπὲρ ἡμῶν is not satisfactorily attested.

[23] Cf. Tobac, op. cit. 142; Schelkle, op. cit. 133f.

[24] Rom. viii. 32; Gal. ii. 20; Eph. v. 2, 25; cr. 1 Cor. xi. 24. Yet the expression ὑπὲρ τῶν ἁμαρτιῶν ἡμῶν (Gal. i. 4; cf. 1 Cor. xv. 3 etc.) above all is close to the idea of sacrifice, which does not necessarily have to include the idea of the *satisfactio vicaria*, see further in the text. K. F. Euler, *Die Verkündigung vom leidenden Gottesknecht aus Jes. 53 in der griechischen Bibel* (BWAT IV, 14), Stuttgart-Berlin 1934, 139–43, distinguishes two series of ideas, one of the suffering Christ, which is connected with παραδοθῆναι (139), and the other of the redeeming Christ, which is associated with the watchword περὶ (ὑπὲρ) ἡμῶν (141).

[25] F. Prat, *Theol.* II, 243; cf. Amiot I, 191.

no other member can take over this leading and comprehensive position.[26] This peculiarity of the concept of representation in the Pauline soteriology will become plainer when we examine other occurrences of the idea.

The concept of representation can be demonstrated both on Jewish and on Roman-Hellenistic ground. In the Old Testament it is needful to be cautious in applying the idea of the *satisfactio vicaria*. In interpreting the difficult views of sacrifice it is true that P. Heinisch, with other scholars, still considers that in the making of a sin-offering sin is symbolically transferred to the beast, and God in His mercy is satisfied with the life and blood of an animal instead of that of the man who has merited death through his sin;[27] but the doubts that can be advanced against such an interpretation of the sin-offering are considerable.[28] Above all the sacrificial animal, laden with sins, would have to be counted as unclean, but it is regarded as very holy (Lev. vi. 19); and to substitute for it a meal offering is not allowed (Lev. v. 11). The offering of the ram that Abraham brought in place of his son (Gen. xxii. 13) is to be understood from the situation; it does not necessarily provide clear evidence for the sacrificial idea; at most there are signs present of a view that only later became more deeply developed. The wish of Moses, that God would strike him out of His book (the book of life) rather than that He should not forgive the people (i.e. punish them with death Ex. xxxii. 32f), does not certainly imply the idea of representation.[29] The concept of representative atonement first becomes plainly revealed in the figure of the suffering Servant of God, Is. liii,[30] at a time when a martyr theology is beginning to develop.[31] The idea becomes dominant

[26] Cf. Tobac 143; R. G. Bandas, *The Master-Idea*, 213–24.

[27] P. Heinisch, *Theologie des AT* 191; Wiencke, op. cit. 67; A. Médebielle in his detailed article 'Expiation' in DB Suppl. III, 1–262 finds strong support for his view in the translation of Lev. xvii. 11 in the LXX (cols 70f). P. Volz also thinks in terms of a substitutionary offering, Jes. II (*Kommentar z.AT*, ed. by Sellin IX, Leipzig 1932) p. 193, appealing to Gen. xxii. 13 and Lev. v. 14ff. The concern here is for the original O.T. view of the sin-offering; that this has undergone a development towards the idea of representation is undeniable. Cf. G. Dalman, Jes. 53, *Das Prophetenwort vom Sühneleiden des Gottesknechtes*, Leipzig [2]1914, 27–29; D. Schötz, *Schuld- und Sündopfer im AT* (Bresl. Stud. z. hist. Theol. 18), Breslau 1930, 106–14.

[28] Cf. B. Stade, *Bibl. Theol. d. AT* I, Tübingen 1905, 160; W. Eichrodt, *Theologie des AT*, [5]I, 101, n. 341; F. Nötscher, *Bibl. Altertumsk.* 327 and n. 2.

[29] D. Schötz, op. cit. 108, R. Simali (c250) interpreted Is. liii. 12 in the light of Ex. xxxii. 32, and so wanted to understand Moses as the atoning Servant of God who offers his life for the people (cf. Billerbeck I, 483); but this interpretation is isolated and perhaps even anti-Christian, cf. J. Jeremias in *ThW* V, 684, 27ff.

[30] Cf. the commentaries, further Dalman, *Jes.* 53; Lagrange, *Judaisme* 368–381; Médebielle, op. cit. 90–100; C. R. North, *The Suffering Servant in Deutero-Isaiah*, London [2]1956; W. Zimmerli J. Jeremias in *ThW* V, 664–72; 680–98; H. Haag, 'Ebed-Jahwe-Forschung 1948–58', in *BZ* (NF) 3 (1959) 174–204 (with literature).

[31] On this cf. W. Wichmann, *Leidenstheologie*; K. F. Euler, op. cit. 139–41; E. Stauffer, *Theol.* 79–81; 314–7; H. W. Surkau, *Martyrien in jüdischer und frühchristlicher Zeit* (FRLANT NF. 36), Göttingen 1938, 57–82; J. J. Stamm, *Die Leiden des Unschuldigen in Babylon und Israel*, Zürich 1946; E. Lohse, *Märtyrer und Gottesknecht*, Göttingen 1955(with literature).

in late Jewish literature (perhaps it is already in Dan. xii. 3),[32] especially in connection with the Maccabaean Martyrs (2 Macc. vii. 38; 4 Macc. i. 11; vi. 28f; xviii. 4), and then in Rabbinic literature.[33]

In the Roman-Hellenistic sphere the idea of representation is especially rooted in the law.[34] The New Testament itself testifies that a slave can represent his master (Philem. 13). If it be asked from what source the conception in 2 Cor. v. 14f has come, recourse should not immediately be made to such Hellenistic views, since the idea of a representative atoning death is deeply rooted in Judaism and would be familiar to Paul from there. A. Deissman, it is true, considers that we here have one of those cases where the Semitic and Hellenistic worlds come into contact, so that Paul united well known ideas of his Jewish upbringing with current Hellenistic legal conceptions.[35]

Further light on the idea of representation[36] may be gained especially from the passages that treat of the Maccabaean martyrs.[37] The venerable Eleazar prays in 4 Macc. vi. 29: 'Take my life as a "substitute life" (ἀντίψυχον) for them (the members of his people).' The same expression occurs in xvii. 21 in a pregnant setting, the martyrs of the Maccabaean age have become, as it were, an ἀντίψυχον[38] for the sin of the people, i.e. for the life of the people forfeited through sin. In 4 Macc. vi. 28 ὑπέρ occurs with the same application as in 2 Cor. v. 14f. God will accept as a satisfaction the punishment of the individual in the stead of his compatriots (τῇ ἡμετέρᾳ ὑπὲρ αὐτῶν δίκῃ). In 4 Macc. xvii. 20; xviii. 4 it is declared to be δι' αὐτούς.

The Jewish conception of vicarious atonement is particularly rooted in their high esteem for merit.[39] 'The innocent death of a righteous man represents in Jewish eyes a merit that God reckons to those who stand with this righteous man in a great community, in the unity of Israel.'[40] Vicarious atonement, however, is made possible through the solidarity

[32] Volz, *Eschatologie*, asks whether the passage has in view a representative suffering or a *thesaurus meritorum*. Goettsberger, *Das Buch Daniel*, Bonn 1928 ad loc, thinks only of instruction of fellow-countrymen, according to xi. 33.

[33] Cf. Weber, *Jüdische Theol.* 326–30; Dalman, *Jes.* 53. 23ff; Billerbeck II, 275f, 279–82; Moore I, 546–52; Wichmann, op. cit. 51–80; Surkau, op. cit. 34–57; 65–74; E. Lohse, op. cit. 31–37; 64–110.

[34] Cf. L. Wenger, *Die Stellvertretung im Recht der Papyri*, Leipzig 1906; the linguistic investigation (7–12) shows that the preposition gives no certain criterion. The idea of representation itself has a broad application, alike in constitutional and civil law (18–109, 157–269).

[35] *Licht vom Osten* 285, n. 1.

[36] For older views see Prat II, 242ff in the footnotes; cf. Volz. *Jes.* II, 193: 'The forensic probably has a stronger effect here than the cult'; Bultmann, *Theol.* 291.

[37] Cf. E. Lohse, op. cit. 66–72.

[38] Cf. Médebielle, op. cit. 108 (middle); in Ignatius the term has already become worn and signifies 'substitute', 'ransom money', Eph. xxi. 1; Smyrn. x. 2; *Pol.* ii. 3; vi. 1

[39] Cf. Dalman, *Jes.* 53, 19ff; 36ff; E. Lohse, op. cit. 102ff.

[40] E. Lohse, op. cit. 104.

of the members of a community; once more, accordingly, we are led to the idea of 'corporate personality'.

Paul does not refer to the 'merit' of the fathers or the righteous and martyrs in his teaching on salvation by grace, but he applies the idea of 'reckoning' by God to Christ and to those represented by Him (cf. 2 Cor. v. 19, μὴ λογιζόμενος). The Jewish roots are undeniable, but the fact that it is Christ, the new Adam, who is in mind creates a peculiar Christian view. Christ is the one great Representative of mankind; God reckons his death as an atonement for the sins of all and so effects the 'reconciliation' of all with Himself. 2 Cor. v. 18–21 makes it plain that we are here dealing with an act of the grace of God that proceeds from his will to save men. The entire plan of salvation, that culminates in our becoming a 'new creation in Christ' (*v.* 17), is a work of God, as *v.* 18 clearly states: 'It all comes from God. ...' But God's action, directed to our being 'made righteous' (*v.* 21), is made possible through the fact that Christ (as corporate personality) includes, represents and takes the place of us all.

In this idea of representation on the basis of the solidary unity of Christ with mankind, neither juristic nor 'mystical' views can be viewed as exclusively normative. The statement, 'If one died for all, then all in consequence died', receives from Prat the brief comment, 'ideally and mystically in Him and with Him'.[41] But 'ideally and mystically' are unsuitable expressions for this conception of corporateness and solidarity. The former *really* represents and takes the place of the race united to him. We do not die 'mystically' on the cross of Christ on Golgotha; rather the death of the one in God's eyes passes for the death of all. Again, this is not simply a juristic fiction or arrangement, as if God simply reckoned the death of Christ to our account; rather Christ's death really becomes our death, so soon as we die 'with Him' in baptism. Even if the mode of expression in *vv.* 14 and 19 has a juristic sound, the salvation-event for Paul nevertheless amounts to a new creation (*v.* 17). Thus the idea of representation, when linked with the conception of Christ, the Founder and Representative of a new humanity, gains a stamp all its own.

By this means the difficulty as to how one should conceive of people 'dying' who had not yet existed is resolved. Christ alone dies on the cross of Golgotha as our Representative. Our personal appropriation of

[41] *Theol.* II, 243; Bandas, op. cit. 251f, speaks of the mystical participation of the members in the action of the Head, but then says: 'These events took place juridically on Calvary and in the grave, but effectively through participation in the Spirit of Christ through baptism.' Similarly Amiot I, 191. The idea is interpreted mystically also by Weinel, *Theol.* 245, and by means of the Gnostic myth by Bultmann, *Theol.* 294.

salvation in baptism is different: there Christ's cross and resurrection are already existing factors of salvation; we die ('sacramentally') with Christ, we are crucified with Him (Rom. vi. 6) and rise with Him.

The ἵνα-sentences of 2 Cor. v. 15 and 21 show that Paul uses the idea of representation simply as a basis to make comprehensible how God can extend to all men the salvation won by Christ as an individual personality. The purpose of representation is that 'all' should attain salvation, that we should become 'the righteousness of God' in Christ. How it happens is not said here; to understand that, the baptismal statements must be called in. Paul has not at all excluded them here; only he overleaps the stage of the (sacramental) appropriation of salvation because his tendency, as so often, is an *ethical* one. In *v.* 15 he skilfully and impressively joins to the contrast of death and life: Christ died for all, in order that the living should no longer live for themselves, but for Him who died and rose for them. The *fact* declared by the Apostle can be briefly stated: Christ *died* for all to save their *life*. But this fact lays on us the obligation to return that love (cf. *v.* 14a): hence the *deduction* and *exhortation*: our life should belong to Him who died and was raised for us. It is a mutual arrangement: Christ did that *for us*, and so we should live *for Him*.

The concept of representation thus supports the Adam-Christ parallel and creates the possibility for the redeeming act of the one to pass over to the redemption of the many. The salvation won by Christ in principle is accessible to all men; factually it is for those only who take the subjective way of redemption. God of his own initiative does everything needful to open to men entrance into the sphere of salvation; but He also leaves a definite place for the co-operation of men. Here lies the significance of a means of salvation that emphasizes the truth, 'All salvation comes from God', yet at the same time explains why not all men attain that salvation.[42]

§18. BAPTISM AS A MEANS ALONG WITH FAITH OF APPROPRIATING SALVATION

As an interpreter of the Gospel Paul has an urgent desire to make his voice heard on the 'subjective' element in salvation. In Judaism the way of salvation leads through the Law, and that in its concrete form developed in Mosaism and Rabbinism; in sharp antithesis to this, Paul sets forth his teaching on justification in the great dogmatic chapters of the Letters to the Galatians and Romans: man is justified not by

[42] The book that more than all others gave the impulse to this was A. Deissmann's *Die ntl. Formel 'In Christo Jesu'* (1892). Works on Pauline mysticism follow his lead.

works of the Law but solely through faith in Christ Jesus (Gal. ii. 16; Rom. iii. 20–22).

> This 'subjective' way of salvation is also 'objective', in so far as by that is meant the establishing of definite, generally obligatory acts, in opposition to purely inward or wholly individual modes of behaviour; and it is 'universal', in so far as it is open to all men, Jews and pagans alike, without exception (cf. Rom. iii. 22; Gal. iii. 8). In this context 'subjective' means simply the personal appropriation of salvation by the individual.

This contrast with the Jewish *nomos,* which was considerably strengthened by the Apostle's personal experience under the taskmaster, and by his bitter struggle with Judaism, unquestionably led him to focus the subjective way of salvation primarily on the formula, 'faith in Christ Jesus'. But the formula tends to be abused; it should not be permitted to becloud the other demands for the attainment of salvation —demands that, in truth, are contained within it and to which baptism especially belongs.

In historical critical analysis there have not been wanting those who have urged the recognition in Paul not of a single, unified (subjective) way of salvation, but of several tracks running parallel to each other. For an unconscionable time a struggle took place, fated by the Reformers' way of stating the issue, on the Lutheran doctrine of imputation, with a juridical kernel that cannot be denied; since the latter part of the nineteenth century, however, attention has been increasingly directed to the Pauline statements about 'life in Christ'; there has been a desire to understand them no longer in a moralistic sense but rather to bring them into connection with mysticism. A change has gradually taken place in the interpretation of the New Testament texts, especially under the influence of the religious-historical method, that breathed as it were, in the air of the Hellenistic world. With the recognition of the ontological-realistic element[43] it has become necessary also to pay closer attention to the sacraments. A. Schweitzer gives it as his judgment, 'The recognition of the sacraments in Paul has become, if possible, an even more difficult matter to theological science than that of the

[43] Thanks to its teaching on grace and the sacraments, Catholic exegesis has never lost the sense of the real character of the new life after baptism (cf. e.g. Ad. Maier, Bisping, von Henle). Among others who have recovered its importance in the Protestant camp may be named H. Lüdemann, *Die Anthropologie des Apostels Paulus* 1872; O. Pfleiderer, *Der Paulinismus* 1873; W. Wrede, *Paulus* 1905; also—admittedly falling into the other extreme—the religious-historical school (Heitmüller, Bousset etc.). Cf. A. Schweitzer, *Geschichte der paulinischen Forschung* 128–31, 152–70.

quasi-physical, realistic character of being dead with Christ.'[44] Hence three different ways of looking at the problem have come to pass: one starting out from faith, a second that is 'mystical', and a third 'sacramental'. From this H. Weinel, in his *Biblische Theologie*, has drawn the deduction that for Paul there was a threefold 'way of salvation'.[45] A. Deissmann also endeavoured to establish a distinction between mysticism and the sacrament.[46] The majority of critics hold these two phenomena of religious reality together, yet many still feel acutely the tension between 'juridical' and 'mystical' teaching on justification, which apparently follow hard on each other in the Letter to the Romans (chs. 1–5 and 6–8). This assertion of a double carriageway in the Pauline teaching on justification has a considerable history.[47]

> It has recently been espoused by A. Schweitzer. He poses the question with sharpness: 'Did Paul, in the Epistle to the Romans, really succeed in providing the doctrine of righteousness by faith with proof drawn from its own presuppositions, and thus in setting it on an independent basis?'[48] He gives the answer that in any case it is impossible to derive the quasi-physical redemption doctrine of the mysticism of life in Christ from the doctrine of righteousness by faith.[49] He ascribes the priority to the mysticism, from which alone the doctrine of redemption has been developed.[50]
>
> Oepke opposes this strong confrontation: 'Paul is far removed from an abstract distinction between the juridical and mystical series of concepts. His forensic justification flows in full stream into the fellowship of Christ in the Spirit.'[51]

Protestant theologians are constantly contrasting the value of baptism and *faith*. The way of justification through faith is frequently described without mentioning baptism,[52] and the fulness of the Pauline fellowship with Christ is transferred to faith.[53] Certainly, another tendency does exist which sets the eminent significance of baptism in full light. The

[44] *Mystik* 18; he cites (18f) as particularly significant Deissmann, who even disputes that for Paul baptism mediates access to Christ; baptism is not the origin but the seal of fellowship with Christ (*Paulus* 115).

[45] Pp. 236–51.

[46] *Paulus* 115f. We return to this theme below in § 24.

[47] On this cf. the comprehensive review in Wissmann op. cit. 4–27; further W. Mundle, *Glaubensbegriff* 132ff.

[48] *Mystik* 214.

[49] Op. cit. 215.

[50] Op. cit. 216.

[51] *ThW* I, 539, 4–6.

[52] Schlatter, *Theologie d. NT* II 265–9 (he first treats of the sacraments under the doctrine of the Church 490–506); also Feine, *Ntl. Theol.* 229ff (he discusses the sacraments in connection with the tradition of the Church, 321ff).

[53] W. Beyschlag, *Ntl. Theologie* ^{2}1896 II, 185ff; Wrede, *Paulus* 67ff; Deissmann, *Paulus* 125ff.

elder Paul Althaus expounded the sacraments as means of really bestowing grace;[54] in this he was followed by F. M. Rendtorff[55] and others. E. Sommerlath even devotes his attention to baptism *before* faith, and sees it as the means of subjectively appropriating the new life.[56] W. Mundle decisively contends for the fundamental importance of baptism: 'Baptism moves into the centre of the Pauline teaching on justification, and indeed of the Pauline religious outlook generally.'[57]

On the Catholic side the 'sacraments' always have found a greater consideration in connection with the personal appropriation of salvation. Whereas Prat links the teaching on sacraments to that on justification without providing adequate reasons,[58] Tobac[59] and Bandas[60] both expound their inner connection: baptism and faith are the means of appropriating to oneself the effects of redemption. Here, rather, the danger is of assigning to the sacraments their place in too schematic a fashion, and of leaving out of account their organic connection with the Christ event. Paul is not concerned for an isolated application of the blessings of salvation but rather with the living fellowship of Christ.

First we must ask: Is baptism demanded for justification with the same general necessity as faith? In this connection it should be borne in mind that there was not the same reason for polemic against the Jewish doctrine of justification by fulfilling the works of the Law as there was in the matter of faith. Baptism was practised in early Christianity without any opposition and it was applied alike to Jews (Acts ii. 37, 41; viii. 36–38), and to pagans (Acts x. 47f).

From the manner in which Paul speaks of baptism, it is clear that for him it possesses the same importance as faith. In Gal. iii. 26f he ascribes personal fellowship with Christ first to faith and then similarly to baptism. There is no compelling reason to account for the change. Earlier he described the *nomos* in his destructive role as the increaser of sin (*v.* 19), as a prison warder (*v.* 23) and a strict pedagogue (*v.* 24). In contrast to that he now shows the power of faith to liberate and to bless. Faith is therefore the dominant point of view in his antithesis to the Law. Nevertheless Paul guides the thought over to baptism, obviously because it enables him to speak yet more clearly of our fellowship with Christ and with one another, in which fellowship we become free sons of God and heirs of the promised blessing.

[54] *Die Heilsbedeutung der Taufe im NT*, Gütersloh 1897, 156–60 and 300f.
[55] *Die Taufe im Urchristentum im Lichte der neueren Forschungen*, Leipzig 1905, 13ff.
[56] Op. cit. 72–84.
[57] *Glaubensbegriff* 137; cf. (as also for the following) the entire section 114–40.
[58] *Theol.* II. 305ff; cf. Amiot I. 217ff.
[59] Op. cit. 225–243.
[60] Op. cit. 321ff.

The easy transition from faith to baptism takes place through the ἐν Χριστῷ Ἰησοῦ, which occupies the key position at the end of *v.* 26. Since this expression possesses a certain emphasis, and the explanatory sentence of *v.* 27 attaches to it, it is best to make it dependent on υἱοὶ θεοῦ ἐστε and not on πίστεως, especially as πίστις ἐν in the sense of 'believe in' has a clear parallel only in Mk. i. 15.[61] This fellowship of Christ through baptism becomes a fellowship established and recognizable (cf. iv. 6) through the πνεῦμα and brings us into the sonship of God.

The connection between faith and baptism is similarly close in Col. ii. 12. Here baptism stands in the forefront and appears first in the field of view as 'Christ-circumcision'. But as soon as Paul describes resurrection with Christ he speaks of faith, manifestly because the power of God to raise the dead presupposes faith. Hence he can talk about faith or baptism according to the prevailing viewpoint. Some have manifested an anxiety to point out that in the Letter to the Galatians the concepts of juridical and mystical justification, of πίστις and πνεῦμα, are still united and inwardly connected, whereas in the Letter to the Romans they appear in separation (Rom. iii–vi); nevertheless the succession does not imply an opposition. Rom. v. 1 may be viewed as providing a bracket to clasp them together, for it looks both backwards and forwards. It is consonant with the practical tendency of vi. 1–14, that baptism first emerges in the description of the outworking and obligations of justification by faith. The thesis of dying to the power of sin occasions a backward glance to the figure of baptism by immersion. To attribute a development such as has been suggested between Galatians and Romans is to do an injustice to Paul, as is evident from the later passage, Col. ii. 12, which does not permit a separation between the two points of view.

Any limitation in the application of baptism, e.g. by postulating that it is not required at all times or for all people, is unknown to Paul. To him it is for every man the regular means of becoming a Christian. If, therefore, he knows only faith in Jesus Christ as the way of justification, to him baptism as the means of salvation is equally universal. But in what relation do they stand to each other? Does baptism only have the function of serving as an external and legal reception into the Church? This interpretation, which appeals for support to Acts ii. 41 (προσετέθησαν), is even less possible for Paul than it is for Acts, by reason of

[61] With Zahn, Burton, Oepke, Schlier, against Sieffert, Lietzmann, Lagrange.

the Apostle's more profound understanding of baptism. Baptism mediates the Spirit (1 Cor. vi. 11; xii. 13), sanctifies and justifies (1 Cor. vi. 11), and causes the baptized to go through a process of being buried and raised with Christ (Rom. vi; Col. ii. 12); more profound and more inward declarations cannot be made even for faith. Or should we think of baptism as an outward act of confession of inward faith (cf. Rom. x. 9; 1 Cor. i. 13)? But this would not do justice to the Pauline statements that stress the effects for salvation of the Christian 'bath' of water. Baptism includes an inner salvation-event to which the outward confession is only a precondition.

Faith and baptism belong together, but they are at all times significant in themselves. In one relationship faith is the presupposition of baptism, in another it has a fundamental and independent position. Baptism without faith in Christ is unimaginable for the thought of the primitive Church (Mk. xvi. 16; Acts xvi. 31; Jn. i. 13). Baptism is the act in which a man makes confession to Christ the Lord (Rom. x. 9f) and in which, conversely, the name of Jesus was probably called over the baptized (Jas. ii. 7; 1 Cor. vi. 11). But faith is not on that account simply a preliminary step. By it a man is justified, and it retains its significance beyond the once-for-all act of baptism. The mutual relation could be described as *complementary*. Genuine faith, which is obedience towards the Word of God (Rom. x. 16; 2 Thess. i. 8), leads to baptism, as Paul himself also submitted to this act (Acts ix. 18: xxii. 16). We find no mention of baptism in Paul's compendium of the doctrine of justification, Rom. iii. 21–26, because for him baptism is included in the διὰ πίστεως Ἰησοῦ Χριστοῦ of *v.* 22.

Baptism, however, over against faith, also signifies a new step, namely the outward manifestation of faith and the incorporation into the *Church*. The indissoluble relation of inward faith to the outward confession finds clear expression in Rom. x. 9f: 'If you confess with your mouth Jesus as the Lord and believe in your heart that God raised Him from the dead, you will be saved.' Paul adds to this by way of explanation (though in reverse order): 'For with the heart a man believes in order to become righteous, and with the mouth he confesses in order to be saved.' The two synonymous expressions, 'become righteous' and 'be saved', show that inward faith and outward confession are alike indispensable. The whole passage probably has baptism in view (cf. § 12). Moreover for Paul there is no personal fellowship with Christ without belonging to the Church (cf. Gal. iii. 28; 1 Cor. xii. 13, 27). The connection between belonging to Christ and belonging to the Church is, as Gal. iii. 27f shows, both inward and not to be abrogated.

The one Spirit, who unites the believer with Christ in baptism, incorporates him also in the 'Body of Christ' and therein joins all the members of Christ together. Therefore the laconic statement can be made (in Eph. iv. 4), '*one* Body and *one* Spirit'. We cannot belong to the Lord without faith and baptism, but by this means we also belong to the unity in Christ of all who believe and are baptized (cf. Eph. iv. 5). Thus faith is completed in baptism. 'Through baptism a man participates fully in the baptism of the Church and of Christ. His personal faith then becomes the faith of Christ and of the Church; its structure does not change, but its deeper nature is transformed; it is this faith in full strength that saves.'[62]

A man receives no other salvation through baptism than through justifying faith. But Paul would not understand it if anyone refused to be baptized; to him such an attitude would no longer be genuine faith. 'It is only because faith has an inner relation to baptism that it becomes effective.'[63]

Just as faith is already present before baptism, it also extends beyond baptism and remains the fundamental power of the Christian position. The life of Paul is a 'life of faith that reposes on the Son of God, who loved me and gave himself up for me' (Gal. ii. 20). Through faith Christ dwells in the hearts of Christians (Eph. iii. 17).

Accordingly, from this aspect, too, the position of baptism as the foundational means of salvation is not to be shaken. On the contrary, if Paul, with his concern to emphasize faith over against the works of the Law, recognizes its absolute value and aspires to give its meaning a theologically deeper basis, that is proof that this means of salvation signifies to him an indispensable stone in the structure of his theology.

§19. THE 'SACRAMENTAL' CHARACTER OF BAPTISM

For the question as to how far Paul ascribes a 'sacramental' character to baptism as a means of salvation, it is important to determine what significance he attaches to the external and visible element, the sign, the 'symbol'. Many find in him a depreciation of the outward sign in favour of an ethical or mystical-personal piety; others stress the 'symbol', in order to construe the salvation-event that takes place in baptism as a 'mystery', for which the outward and visible process of the sacred action is essential. The interpretation that prevailed in Protestant theology in the last century, according to which the sacraments in Paul's view

[62] J. Duplacy, 'Le salut par la foi et le baptême d'après le Nouveau Testament', *Lumière et Vie* 27 (1956) 3–52; the citation pp. 42f.

[63] Bandas, op. cit. 356; cf. also Tobac, op. cit. 257.

operated only on the ethical plane,[64] has been overthrown, especially through the labours of Heitmüller and the religious-historical school; today it can be regarded as abandoned.[65] A. Schweitzer is chief representative of a view which sets in relief Paul's 'mysticism of being-in-Christ' and so denies any importance to the external event in baptism. Whereas he considers the effects of baptism to be mystical and real, he holds that the external and visible aspect of baptism is wholly unimportant.[66] M. Barth goes so far as to repudiate all sacramental effects. Water baptism mediates neither the forgiveness of sins nor the Holy Spirit, but only a human work of faith and obedience, a preparation for the reception of salvation, the 'baptism of the Spirit'.[67] On the Catholic side a lively discussion has developed in recent times over the 'Mystery-religion theory' of O. Casel;[68] he focusses his whole attention on the 'symbol', and would interpret it as an event akin to the cultic acts of a mystery religion. On this estimate of the 'symbol' he builds his special theory of the 'Christian cult-mystery'. Accordingly it is necessary to investigate whether his concept of 'symbol' holds good for Paul.

First, a number of conceptions that are frequently encountered must be briefly explained.

1 The metaphor: a non-literal, purely figurative mode of expression; e.g. 'He was built up in his faith.'

2 The simile: a figurative mode of expression which illustrates an actual fact; e.g. 'you are built on the foundation of the Apostles and Prophets'; often with a greater pictorial reality, as 'temple of the Holy Spirit'.[69]

[64] Cf. von Dobschütz, *Sakrament und Symbol* 30: 'The figurative language of primitive Christianity is to be understood as ideal, not realistic; it does not at all correspond to cult symbolism; it derives from an outlook that is through and through spiritualized.' Further 38f: 'The effect is always thought of as ethically mediated; the writers are fully conscious of the figurative nature of the mode of expression.'

[65] Along with Heitmüller, cf. the works of Bousset, Clemen, Leipoldt, etc., and for a change in the Protestant interpretation, cf. O. Schmitz, Sommerlath, Wissmann, Schweitzer, Weinel, Stauffer, Cullmann, the commentaries of Oepke, Althaus, Schlier and the articles in *ThW*.

[66] On this see below under II, pp. 133ff.

[67] M. Barth, op. cit. (cf. above p. 107, n. p. 5). A discussion of this compendious work would take us too far from our purpose here. Cf. the reviews by W. Bieder in *ThZ* 9 (1953) 161–73; J. Héring in *RHThR* 33 (1953) 255–60; Ch. Masson in *Revue de Théologie et de Philosophie* 3 (1953) 21–30; (Catholic) P. Benoit in *RB* 60 (1953) 620–3.

[68] An account of it as far as 1947 is given by Th. Filthaut, op. cit. For the further course of the debate see B. Neunheuser, 'Mysteriengegenwart, Ein Theologumenon inmitten des Gesprächs', *ALW* 3 (1954) 104–22; the same in *ALW* 4 (1956) 316–24; the same in *Studia Patristica* (TU 64), Berlin 1957 54–63; J. Grotz in *Geist und Leben* 28 (1955) 381–6. Reflections from the Protestant side are given by G. Heintz, 'Die Gegenwart Christi im Gottesdienst', *Monatschrift für Pastoraltheologie* 43 (1954) 266–79.

[69] For further clarification of these concepts, which are less important to us, cf. the work of Straub.

3 The allegory: a figurative replacement of a person or thing by one of another kind; e.g. Jesus the good Shepherd.
4 The symbol: an object or event which represents and contains a deeper meaning; e.g. anointing as equipment with the Holy Spirit. (The special significance of 'symbol' in Casel's view is discussed below.)
5 The sacrament: an *effective* symbol. It brings about what it represents. Under the term 'sacrament' the effect is often included; i.e. more precisely, a sacramental sign.
6 The rite: the external forms and usages employed in the administration of a sacrament. The essential rite is identical with the sacramental sign.

I. *The View of O. Casel on the Rite of Baptism as a 'Cult-Symbol'*

For men of ancient times an image was not simply a sign to awaken remembrance, an intentional object. And a symbolic event did not merely awaken definite thoughts; it made one see something real, something that the beholder immediately received into himself and experienced. In the religious sphere the idea was extended to include powers which streamed over one, a real change that was accomplished in accordance with the external symbol. Perhaps Heitmüller was right in his view that our modern distinction between symbol and sacrament in relation to cult actions was foreign to ancient modes of thought.[70] It is an undeniable merit of O. Casel and his colleagues that they have vigorously emphasized this close, organic connection between external sign and inner event.[71] Anyone who grants that Paul understood baptism as a real and effective means of salvation will also admit an inner union of sign and salvation-event.[72]

With the cult images discussed by Casel, regarded as embodiments of divine powers, we would especially draw attention to the δεικνύμενα in the Mystery Religions, i.e. definite objects and representations that allude to a meaning connected with the Mysteries (especially their cult legends). For example, a golden serpent that

[70] *Im Namen Jesu* 324; cf. *Taufe* I, 15.

[71] *GGM* 82–95. Cf. the worship of the image of the Beast in Rev. xiii. 14f; xiv. 9, 11; xv. 2; xvi. 2; xix. 20; xx. 4. For the thought of the ancients cf. Kleinknecht in *ThW* II, 386, 29–35: 'image' is not to be understood as something that is present only in the consciousness, as foreign to reality; it participates in reality, indeed it is actually the reality itself.

[72] Cf. Sommerlath, op. cit. 75. Protestants now often admit this conception of the sacraments; they no longer regard it as Biblical, however, but as a product of development in the ancient Church, cf. Wiegand in RGG ²V, col. 73; further von Harnack, *Mission und Ausbreitung* I, 250: 'After him (Paul) the sluices are all open, and the Mysteries—and with them their Mysteriosophy—steamed in. In Ignatius, sixty years after Paul, the entire Hellenic theology has been given entrance and swallowed down.'

was drawn 'through the bosom' of the Sabazios initiate relates to the idea that the god united himself (sexually) with the initiate.[73] Little images, originally used in the temple (*telesterion*) were worn in daily life, closely kept in secret, but certainly venerated as magical objects.[74] Here we see the transition from symbolism to magic and discover the extreme limit to which the Christian faith can be drawn. Firmicus Maternus, who attests the custom of handing over (*tradere*) such signs and symbols (*signa et symbola*) to the initiates, considers these δεικνύμενα to be the invention of the devil.[75]

Catholic theology has always held firmly to the old sacramental axiom: *sacramenta efficiunt, quod figurant*; but later it was less taken up with the sign, the symbolic character, than with the operation that takes place. Söhngen characterizes this external-mechanistic way of looking at it as follows:

'The sign as such is reduced in value to the external significance of a suitable and attractive packing, in which the heavenly fuel is wrapped and which can therefore be regulated, divided and received. The spiritual bond between the bestowal of grace and the significance of the sign is cut asunder in that view; and grace itself is emptied of its spirituality, because the sign is shorn of its spiritual meaning.'[76]

Such tearing asunder of the figurative aspect of the sign and the dogmatic estimate of the operation (*effectus*) in isolation from it has the appearance of a magical interpretation (although actually this does not need to be the case). But Paul is not a witness for sacramental magic.

The endeavour, therefore, of more recent theologians again to draw more tightly the bond between 'symbol' and the reality of grace has much in its favour.[77] But Casel gives the 'symbol' a yet deeper meaning. The sacramental sign should be objective, immediate and visible in its accomplishment. The act of salvation wrought by Christ becomes objectively re-presented, i.e. it does not gain its presence simply in or with the recipient.[78] Through the rite a man, illumined in faith, sees the reality of the saving work of Christ in the recipient. The saving work must first be there (set in the present); not till then can the man be incorporated in it ('first' and 'then' are meant not in a temporal but in a logical sense).[79]

[73] Cf. Th. Hopfner in PRE XVI, 1324.
[74] Hopfner, op. cit. 1325.
[75] *De err. prof. rel.* 18 (Halm. 102, 13–16).
[76] *Symbol und Wirklichkeit* 58.
[77] Cf. again the positive view in Söhngen, op. cit. 76ff, 96ff.
[78] *GGM* 96–101; cf. Filthaut, op. cit. 43.
[79] Ibid, cf. Filthaut, op. cit. 44.

It will be perceived at once how this view of Casel's is orientated to that which takes place in the Mysteries (as he understands it). But Casel's estimate of the 'symbol' can be illuminated in yet another way. He brings the sacraments into close relation to the 'Christ-mystery' itself. In so doing he sets out from a theological interpretation of images that regards the theology of ikons and of their prototype as one. Through the ikon the *mysterium* of the Word made flesh becomes present with power to effect salvation.[80] Casel then states: 'That which is true of Christ as the image of the Father holds good analogously of his sacraments. Christ, in separating from the world and withdrawing his visible presence from his disciples, has bequeathed them to his own, that they may know and possess Him all the more surely in his divine presence; that they may not only spiritually discern in them the pledge of his existence and life, but actually handle, taste and experience them in a palpable manner.'[81] 'That which may be seen, heard and tasted in them is the transparent pledge of divine, invisible reality.'[82] 'As Jesus Christ is the visible image of the invisible God, so the sacraments of Christ are the visible symbols of the invisible act of salvation. As the believer sees the Father immediately in Christ, so he sees the redemptive act immediately in the sacrament of Christ.'[83]

V. Warnach, who has taken up the Mystery teaching of Casel and developed it, gives his judgment as follows: 'The ὁμοίωμα in baptism is the appearance and presence in a cultic symbol of the divine or saving-history reality, more exactly of the Christ-event itself. Therefore baptism is characterized as ὁμοίωμα τοῦ θανάτου αὐτοῦ, not because we experience in it a "mystical" death, similar to or the equivalent of the death of Christ on the cross, but because in it the death of *Christ* himself appears in a cultic form (a rite) and becomes effectively present.'[84]

What are we to say about this?

1. According to Casel-Warnach an essential significance is ascribed to the rite, in that the death of Christ appears in this cultic form. The external rite is understood as a *symbol*, through which the baptized is transplanted into the event of Christ's death. But it is questionable whether Paul ascribed to the rite such a far-reaching influence that it makes Christ's act of salvation objectively present. This only can be said with definiteness, that he did not grant any decisive influence to the experienceable and psychological element in baptism. It is, indeed, a feature that divides his teaching from the Mystery religions, that he has

[80] *GGM* 95; that this theology later becomes influential cannot be denied. Cf. Cyril of Jerusalem, *Myst. cat.* 3. 1 (Quasten 87, 30–34).

[81] *GGM* 95. [82] *GGM* 96. [83] *GGM* 105.

[84] *ALW* 3 (1954) 310f.

excluded from the Christian cultus everything that is theatrical and pompous and every suggestive-hypnotic element.

> In this respect Casel excellently brings out the unique element in the Christian sacraments over against the heretical Gnosticism: 'Where (in Gnosticism) cultic ceremonies are to be found, they are mere symbols, sensible representations, psychical helps, as it were, to induce purely inward experiences that urge on ecstasy; thus they are essentially different from the Mysteries of the Church, that operate objectively and contain the salvation-event. Despite all their apparent spirituality and elevation, the former are anthropocentric and anthroposophical, while the sacraments of the Church are theocentric and christocentric.'[85] Casel rightly emphasizes the plainness, simplicity and naturalness of the Christian symbols and their verbal succinctness.[86]

Paul did not ascribe a greater objectivity to the sacramental signs. In the texts the figure or image attaches mostly to the persons: '*We* have been buried with Him' (Rom. vi. 4), '*you*, who have been buried with Him' (Col. ii. 12). He never calls baptism a 'grave', as does Cyril of Jerusalem.[87] Of more objective expressions or designations we find in his writings only 'bath of water' (Eph. v. 26—whereas 1 Cor. vi. 11 offers the more personal style); 'bath of regeneration' (Tit. iii. 5), unconnected with the conception of dying and rising with Christ, which is the prototype of the Christian baptismal mystery in the meaning of Casel; and finally 'Christ-circumcision' (Col. ii. 11), again, remarkably enough, a figure that rests on the Jewish rite, not on one after the order of the Mysteries. It cannot be demonstrated that Paul anywhere 'represents' a quasi-Mystery Religion occurrence and interprets Christian baptism as a '*mysterium*'.

2. It is equally questionable whether ὁμοίωμα in Rom. vi. 5 can be understood as 'image' (cf. § 7). The expression could call to mind the Platonic archetype-image-scheme, but it certainly does not fit into the Pauline thought.[88] Warnach himself objects to such a Platonic interpretation, for it has to do with a making manifest of the reality of Christ on the plane of the concrete salvation-history.[89] But the concept ὁμοίωμα in Rom. vi. 5 is not directly identified with baptism; various possibilities of interpretation remain open, yet the term appears to be overburdened when it is made to denote a 'cult-symbol' in this special sense, particularly as it is not employed by Paul anywhere else with such a meaning.

[85] *GGM* 93. [86] *GGM* 97. [87] *Myst. cat.* 2. 4. (Quasten 84).
[88] Cf. Kleinknecht in *ThW* II, 385, 37–387, 7. [89] *ALW* 3 (1954) 355 n. 216.

3. The parallel drawn by Casel between Christ and the sacraments through the concept of images would seem to be too early for Paul. If Christ is called the 'image of God' (2 Cor. iv. 4; Col. i. 15), the Apostle nowhere draws a line from this declaration to the sacramental texts. God has indeed determined that we should become conformed to the 'image of his son' (Rom. viii. 29). But for Paul that is a personal series:

God,
|
Christ, the 'image of God' absolutely,
|
The Christian after the 'image of Christ' (Rom. viii. 29)
or after the image of God Himself (Col. ii. 10).

Behind this stands the Adam-Christ parallel: the 'second Adam' restores the original image of the glory of man. For us it holds good: as we have borne the image of the earthly man, so we (after the resurrection of the body) shall bear the image of the heavenly. But the sacraments are not in view in this connection.

Casel's interpretation of 'symbol', therefore, represents an exaggeration of Paul's teaching. The Apostle establishes an inner connection between Christ's act of salvation and the salvation-event in baptism, but he does not regard it as apportioned in individual phases present in the 'symbol'. However noteworthy Casel's 'symbol' theory may be for later times, it is hardly authenticated for Paul. It can only stimulate a more careful investigation into the significance of the sacramental sign and rites.

II. *The Positive Significance of the Outward Sign*

Paul's thinking is highly figurative and plastic. If, when urged on by the fulness and impulse of his theological thoughts, he does not always hit on a fortunate choice of images, and at times proceeds quite violently in working them out,[90] his preference for the plastic expression nevertheless bestows on his presentation a great perspicacity and freshness. This peculiarity of his language must be taken into account in his theology of baptism and the distinction observed between the real event and certain plastic modes of speech which he employs. In the strict sense the sacramental sign is more than a means of illustration, more also than a mere symbol; it is an operative sign that actually sets in being those effects to which it points. The fundamental question is whether, in

[90] Cf. the changing and sometimes inconsistently applied figures in 1 Cor. iii. 6–17; vi. 12–20; ix. 7–11, 24–27; 2 Cor. v. 1–8; Eph. ii. 19–22; v. 26–27 etc. Cf. Straub, op. cit. 13: 'Generally speaking figurative language is the weak point in the rhetoric of Paul'; on the heaping up and changing of figures see 121ff.

Paul's thought, we can really describe the saving means of baptism as a 'sacrament' in this sense. If Casel's interpretation along the lines of the Mysteries be refused, and with it an immediate influence of the 'Hellenistic' sacramental conception, it is not therefore necessary to exclude a realistic 'sacramental' interpretation, in favour, say, of a purely symbolic and transferred estimate of his utterances. In fact, the Pauline baptismal texts only allow of being interpreted in a realistic sense. Since scholarship, including the Protestant camp, widely admits this fact,[91] we may spare ourselves a detailed proof of it. On this basis, however, we might yet establish to what extent Paul gave consideration to the rite.

As an example of a strong depreciation of the external and figurative element, A. Schweitzer may be cited: 'In the Hellenistic Mystery religions the symbol is enhanced and solidified into reality. Through the believer's intensively imagining the symbolized experience and undergoing it in an imitative act, it becomes for him reality. In Paul, however, there is no staging of symbolism. He is content simply to assert the incomprehensible view, that the historic fact of the dying and rising again of Christ realizes itself in the believer.'[92] On Rom. vi. 3–6 he writes: 'He makes no use of the symbolism of the ceremony to explain what happens. He does not make it an object of reflection. In Rom. vi. 3–6 he nowhere suggests that he thinks of baptism as a being buried and rising again with Christ because the baptized plunges beneath the water and rises out of it again. These ingenious explanations have been read into his words by interpreters.'[93] And a general statement, 'For Paul the symbolism of the ceremony plays no particular part'.[94]

With regard to its figurative significance, Paul represents baptism as a particular occasion in accordance with the manner of its administration and the characteristic stamp it already possessed. So far as may be ascertained, he never altered anything in the rite. What attitude, then, did he take to the symbols and the symbolic proceedings?

1. Paul valued the external sign element in baptism as it had been handed down.

In accordance with its element (water) and its practice from earliest times (cf. the Jewish baptisms, the baptism of John) he understood it as a cleansing, a washing away of sins (1 Cor. vi. 11; cf. Eph. v. 26). He also received with respect other customs and signs such as the Lord's Supper (1 Cor. xi. 23ff) and the laying on of hands (1 Tim. iv. 14;

[91] On this see p. 128, n. 65.
[92] *Mystik* 16.
[93] Op. cit. 19f.
[94] Op. cit. 20.

v. 22; 2 Tim. i. 6; cf. Acts vi. 6; xiii. 3), and he accords to them the significance which Jesus and the primitive Church gave them.

2. In a certain measure Paul sought to extend the traditional symbolic meaning of baptism and to deepen it.

In Eph. v. 26 there is a development of the original figure of the cleansing bath: through the bath of water Christ has washed the Church from all defilement and made it glorious. We might compare the baptism of John, through which as many of the people of God as possible should be prepared for the Messiah; the image of the Church as a bride also appears in Jn. iii. 29. But the figure is differently presented: with John we have a baptism in preparation for the Messiah, with Paul a bath of cleansing through the blood of the Messiah; with the former we have a bride and a wedding, with the latter a wife and the married state; with the former an essential connection with repentance, with the latter a purely sacramental application of salvation. That Paul also linked this with the pagan custom of a bridal bath is hardly likely. In any case, the execution of the picture in Eph. v. 26f betrays his own handiwork. In this passage baptism for him is no longer a mere anchor to save an individual but the constituting of the community of salvation; and the drawing is an original sketch!

How far the Apostle in the late Letter to Titus (iii. 5) catches at a figurative motif in the expression 'regeneration', a motif that can be demonstrated elsewhere in early Christian testimonies (1 Pt. iii. 3, 23; Jn. iii. 5; Justin I *Apol.* 61, 3, 4, 10; 66. 1; Dial. 138. 2), or whether he is taking out a terminological loan from Hellenism, it is hard to say, for he does not give any further exposition of this figure (purposely?), but he does engage in further explanation of the *fact*, the salvation-event. This is rather a witness to his reserve (contrast Justin I. *Apol.* 61. 10).

Moreover, to make a typological use of the events in the wilderness wanderings in the interests of baptism and the eucharist (1 Cor. x. 1–5) is only possible when the figurative and pictorial elements are made a point of departure. The point of comparison does not lie in the sacramental effect but in the external procedure: Israel's envelopment in the cloud and in the sea is interpreted by Paul as a 'baptism', the eating of the manna and drinking from the rock as a prefiguration of the eucharistic meal. The comparison was by no means strange (cf. Jn. vi. 31ff). But Paul employs it with an ethical goal in view, not from the aspect of liturgy and ritual.

3. Paul also threw into relief new figurative interpretations of the rite of baptism.

Above all the interpretation of baptism by immersion as a being buried with Christ (in order to rise with Him) must here be taken into account (Rom. vi. 4; Col. ii. 12). Today we can no longer establish with certainty whether Paul came to this interpretation entirely of his own accord, or whether he was able to appeal even at this date to the primitive Christian outlook. We know too little of the liturgical life, and especially of the liturgical views, of the early Church. Nevertheless, it is most probable that Paul himself was responsible for coining this idea in connection with the rite. This favourite conception of the great theologian is not demonstrable in the early period of Christianity outside his Letters, and the later testimonies could well go back directly to the Pauline texts. Rom. vi. 3 (ἢ ἀγνοεῖτε) presupposes only the knowledge of the relation of baptism to the death of Jesus.

That he, however (contrary to the opinion of Schweitzer), holds to the rite of immersion is scarcely to be doubted, in view of Rom. vi. 4 and Col. ii. 12. Both times he uses the expression 'to be buried with', although, in Rom. vi. 4 especially, 'to die with' would actually have suited his purpose better. Admittedly, it is only a fleeting allusion to the rite; but that the latter provided him with the impetus is not to be contested.

According to Gal. iii. 27 the baptized has been (through plunging in the baptismal water?) 'clothed with Christ'—a peculiar image that testifies to the real ability of the Apostle for picture thinking. The expression 'Christ-circumcision' (Col. ii. 11) can certainly be intended more metaphorically. It is prompted by the 'putting off' a little part of the flesh, with which Paul compares the 'putting off the body of flesh' in baptism. Borderline questions raise themselves here, how far the thought of Paul is determined by the rite and how far it is determined by theological reflections (cf. below 5).

> The influence of 'metaphors and metonomies' on Paul's thought has been investigated by V. Heylen.[95] He thinks that they should first of all make acceptable a fact or rule. 'Metaphorical expressions by themselves do not permit us to determine the exact nature of elements of which the fact and the rule are a consequence' (288). He maintains that in his use of pictures Paul is not interested in the picturesque; he desires above all to put to use the power of conviction that is contained in this literary usage (289f). Straub comes to similar results.[96]

[95] 'Les metaphores et les metonymies dans les épîtres Pauliniennes', in *EphThLov* 12 (1935), 253–90.

[96] Straub speaks (op. cit. 154f) of the 'concentration of interest on the message entrusted to him (Paul)', of his being dominated by the 'didactic intention'.

4. Paul exercises reserve with regard to the liturgical language of symbols and limits himself to the essential rite.

In comparison with later liturgiologists and mystagogues, like Cyril of Jerusalem and Ambrose of Milan, the marked reserve of Paul towards liturgical forms of expression is striking. His language is rich in imagery for the illustrating of his theological thought, but not from the viewpoint of liturgical symbols. It may be granted that the rite of the administration of baptism had not yet developed so richly; many of the new forms came only later (e.g. exorcism and anointing with oil). But it is not this alone that makes the difference between Paul and the 'liturgiologists'. They extend the exposition of the rites in every conceivable respect. Paul e.g. employs the imagery of clothes without reference to the liturgy, purely in the ethical sense of stripping off evil works or the 'old man' (Rom. xiii. 12; Eph. iv. 22; Col. iii. 8). Cyril contemplates the liturgical procedure in baptism and reads out of it a threefold instruction: the 'taking off' the old man with his actions; the imitation of Christ, who was made naked on the cross; and the likeness with the first man in Paradise.[97] The manner in which Cyril gives separate interpretations to the anointing of the forehead, ears, nose and breast[98] is completely foreign to Paul. Paul fixes his eye only on the essential rite, the real sacramental sign, and plumbs the depths of its meaning; i.e. he brings to light that which it intimates for the inner salvation-event and that which it effects in its intimation. He is satisfied at any given time with *one* meaning and concentrates all attention on this uniformly described salvation-event.

5. Paul is more strongly motivated by his central theological conceptions than by the liturgical rite.

If Paul permits himself to be stimulated by the external sacramental sign to an interpretation of the sacramental salvation-event, he does so not in order to keep on drawing new thought from the rite, but only to reproduce in a fresh and impressive manner, through the figurative character, the principles of salvation that are already established for him. He therefore avoids disparate trains of thought that lead away from what is essential. For example, he does not concern himself at all with adducing considerations about the water, its manifold powers to bless in the realm of nature, its significance in the religious customs of the nations etc., as Tertullian essays to do.[99] That would divert him from his central idea—being washed clean and consecrated through Christ, or dying and rising with Christ. Paul's mode of thought is concentrated

[97] *Myst. cat.* 2. 2 (Quasten 81f).
[98] *Myst. cat.* 3. 4 (Quasten 89f).
[99] *De bapt.* 3–5 (I. 202–6 Reiff.-Wiss.).

christologically, and his major concern in baptism is ever the soteriological. Accordingly, the stream of his thought is especially channelled in the idea of dying and rising with Christ. The bestowal of the Spirit that ensues in baptism (Gal. iv. 6; Rom. v. 5) is also bound by the Apostle with the christocentric view. Strictly speaking *Pneuma*-existence belongs to the Risen Lord (Rom. i. 4; 1 Tim. iii. 16), and He draws us through his Spirit into this mode of being (cf. 1 Cor. xv. 45; Rom. viii. 9ff). The πνεῦμα who dwells in us is the πνεῦμα Χριστοῦ (Rom. viii. 9), hence the fellowship of Christ and the possession of the Spirit are essentially identical (1 Cor. vi. 17).

That Paul is no pronounced liturgiologist is finally confirmed through his admission that he himself baptized only a few people and that he feels himself called to the proclamation of the Word (1 Cor. i. 14, 17). This attitude of the missionary and preacher is the dominating impression conveyed in all his utterances, even when he describes the sacramental saving event;[100] to him the most important thing was the central content of the message of Christ, the purity and genuineness of the teaching, the rending power of the moral imperative, deeply rooted withal in faith, and the prophetic and inspiring outlook on the consummation of salvation.

Looking back we may affirm that Paul considered the salvation event in baptism as 'sacramental', but that his thought is not determined by a strongly marked 'sacramental-ritual' or 'liturgical' interest, i.e. by the external sign. To him the decisive thing is not rite and liturgy, not symbolic character and Mystery event, but the profound conceptions of his Christ-related doctrine of salvation. In this he stands much more firmly in the tradition of primitive Christianity than the religious-historical school will admit. An opposition between him and the primitive community, or between him and Jesus Himself, is the less plausible as one is compelled to admit that such a 'sacramental' view has already sprung into being on the Palestinian native soil of the Gospel, namely the mediation of salvation through outward signs and usages, or the bestowal of the blessings of salvation with the aid of holy actions that are bound to the one Mediator of salvation, Jesus Christ.

[100] Cf. K. Pieper, *Paulus* 59ff; F. W. Maier, Art. Paulus in *LThK* VIII, 38f.

CHAPTER TWO

The Sacramental Dying and Rising with Christ at Baptism considered in Detail

§20. CRITICISM OF RECENT EXPOSITIONS

THE fundamental meaning of baptism as the means of bestowing salvation has been established; we must now turn our attention to a series of statements in Paul that describe baptism as a salvation-event 'with Christ', as a dying with Christ and rising or being made alive with Him. In recent publications these sayings are constantly receiving prolonged reflection, because the fundamental Christian sacrament appears here in a meaningful context, most commonly designated as 'mystic'. In these cases it does not take on the appearance of a purely soteriological means of salvation but is described as a personal coming into contact with Christ. A marked emphasis falls on this 'sacramental-mysticism' in the discussion of Paul's 'Christ-mysticism'. Whereas earlier scholars were content to reproduce Paul's expressions and interpret them generally, endeavour has been made in recent times to reach a more profound understanding, a clarification of the thought processes that lie at the root of the Apostle's theology.

I. *The Religious-Historical Exposition*

In scientific research the religious-historical problem has claimed the greatest attention. Does Paul integrate Christian baptism into the Hellenistic ideas of regeneration? Does he follow the cults of the dying and rising gods? The earliest pronouncements on these issues reflect the joy of discovery on the part of scholars who plunged into the obscure and fascinating world of Greek and Oriental Mystery religions; but after initial exaggerations regarding their influence on Paul, a great deal more caution has been exercised in forming judgments. The same, or even only like, formulations as Paul's on dying and rising with Christ cannot be demonstrated. Nevertheless it was believed that similar *ideas* may be found; admittedly they do not rob the Pauline thought of its originality, but they ought to make it more understandable.

The thesis of the religious-historical school (Dieterich, Reitzenstein, Heitmüller, Brückner, Bousset etc.) may be briefly represented as follows: A similar mystical death and resurrection, such as is described by Paul as constituting the central event in Christian baptism, also takes place in many Mystery cults. The initiate suffers the death and experiences the resurrection of his god after him, and so knows a 'regeneration' that may be compared with Christian baptism. The whole idea is a familiar conception of syncretism.

It is possible to test this thesis from various sides.

1. *The similarity of the rites.* There are many kinds of washings, but none can enter into serious competition with Christian baptism. Above all the conception of a dying and rising with the divinity is not connected with any of these ablutions. They are mostly lustrations prior to the genuine initiation and serve the purpose of cultic purity. The concept of regeneration has been joined only with the 'blood baptism' of the Phrygian cult, the so-called *tauro-* or *criobolium.* For this, however, the blood is essential; the initiate makes it go into his ears, nose, etc. and greedily laps it up; obviously it was believed that special vital powers were contained in it.[1] Certain external similarities, therefore, should not be allowed to lead us astray to accept an agreement in ideas.

2. *The similarity of terminology.* Reitzenstein, following the precedent of Dieterich, endeavoured to establish the influence of the Mysteries on Paul with respect to their language, in particular with regard to certain characteristic terms.[2] The care that must be exercised when asserting a close relationship is shown by such a central concept as that of 'rebirth'.[3] It may well be that we must reckon with the possibility of considerable linguistic elements entering the Christian faith from the Mysteries, even before Clement of Alexandria, who consciously associated himself with the Hellenistic world of thought.[4] But that says nothing as to the sacramental *event.*

3. *The similarity of definite conceptual associations.* It is asserted that Paul attached the idea of *his* dying and risen Lord to the conception of the death and resurrection of a cult hero, which was central for many

[1] For the ceremony cf. Prudentius, *Peristeph.* 1011–40 (Turchi, Fontes 246); further Cumont, op. cit. 61–63; H. Gressmann, *Die orient. Relig.* 109f; Dey, op. cit. 65–81 (he denies that it really deals with 'rebirth'); Prümm *RGH* 262f.

[2] *Mysterienrel.* 81.

[3] Cf. the work of Dey and the article of Jacono, and see above § 2; for the terminology generally cf. Prümm II, 296–9; 318f (strongly denying); A. von Harnack, *Die Terminologie der Wiedergeburt und verwandter Erlebnisse in der alten Kirche*, TU 42, 3 (1918) 97ff; the same, *Mission und Ausbreitung* 249, n. 1 (positive on the terminological influence, critical on the general influence).

[4] Cf. von Harnack, *Mission und Ausbreitung* I, 253; Oepke in *ThW* I, 541–3 (he is of the opinion that the turning to Hellenism, already beginning in the latest strata of the N.T. but not yet complete, becomes an ever-increasing factor from the sub-Apostolic age on); Stauffer, *Theol.* 88; Dibelius, *Paulus und die Mystik* 6f; Prümm, *RGH* 327; O. Casel, 'Zur Kultsprache des hl. Paulus', in *ALW* 1 (1950) 1–64.

Mystery religions.[5] Since we are concerned with the salvation-event, this thesis must be tested. To do it with satisfaction would presuppose a clear working out of its meaning as given in the cults referred to; that is a complex undertaking and it would extend beyond the limits of this work. On the other hand much preparatory labour has been expended on the task; in particular the comparison with the Christian sacraments has often been drawn out, with a criticism that grows ever sharper.[6] It may be enough, therefore, if we underline several viewpoints.

(*a*) Although no formula that can be compared with the characteristic expressions of the Apostle is to be found in the Mystery religions, Bousset cannot escape the impression that the spiritual atmosphere is here provided within which the Pauline dying and rising with Christ is set.[7] He sees two given conditions that characterize it: the experience of the god and the experience of the believer.

> After briefly describing the various cults he writes: 'And so above the individual forms of the gods there grows the one figure of the suffering, dying and rising god. The individual divine form, with its definite myth, becomes less prominent. One idea manifests itself in them all and grips the piety of the Hellenistic Mysteries with a mystical power: that of the dying and rising god who brings salvation.'[8] This destiny of the cult god is transferred to the believers: 'The god with his destiny in victory and defeat becomes the type for the destiny of the believers. It is no once-for-all fact of the past that is accomplished here; it takes place ever anew.'[9]

The essential difference between this 'analogous' saving event and the Christian lies in the fact that in the Mystery religions we have to do with a myth, whereas in Christianity we are dealing with history. The root of the myth may be recognized in the ever-repeated natural succession of winter and summer. Research has established the relation of the Eleusinian Mysteries, which have long been adduced as a parallel and in which regeneration also figures, to Mother Earth and her living powers.[10]

[5] Cf. Leipoldt, *Die urchristliche Taufe* 38–63, especially 62; Bousset, *Kyrios Christos* 134ff; Reitzenstein, *Mysterienrelig.* 83ff; Dibelius op. cit. 8.

[6] On the Catholic side see Heigl 83–99; L. de Grandmaison, *Jésus Christ, sa personne, son message, ses preuves* II, Paris [16]1931, 510–32; Prümm II, 273–318; Coppens, *DB* Suppl. I, 903–20; Kuss, *Römerbrief*, 344–76; on the Protestant side G. Kittel, *Die Religionsgeschichte und das Urchristentum* 124–6; P. Althaus in NTD 6, 51–53; Hahn, op. cit. 9–22, above all against Reitzenstein; Wiencke, op. cit. 116ff concerning the conception of redemption.

[7] *Kyrios Christos* 134.

[8] Op. cit. 135.

[9] Op. cit. 138; the last sentence of the citation is in italics in Bousset's book.

[10] Cf. O. Kern in PRE XVI, 1246–50 (on the conception of regeneration see 1239); M. J. Lagrange, 'La Régénération et la Filiation divine dans les Mystères d'Éleusis', in *RB* 38 (1929) 63–81 and 201–14.

> On the Oriental cults Th. Hopfner says: 'Sagas of that kind were recounted chiefly of divinities inhabiting the depths of the earth; according to a widespread view they, like the human race itself, spring out of the earth as a grain of corn; hence the majority of the Mystery legends are connected precisely with "chthonic" deities (belonging to the earth) like Demeter and Core, Hades-Pluto, Jacchos, the Cabira, Hecate, with Adonis, Isis, Osiris-Serapis; even Mithras, later the god of the Persian Mystery-religion of the sun, was probably originally chthonic, since he was born "from the rock". Frequently sagas of this kind are nothing more than simple nature myths, based on the annual withering away and dying of the plants in summer and autumn and their germinating again in spring, as the sagas of Core, Adonis and Osiris.'[11]
>
> Correspondingly the manner of the death is also described differently from the New Testament evidence. The death of the divinity is generally an extraordinary one. Adonis is killed by a wild boar; Attis emasculates himself before he dies; Dionysus is torn in pieces and devoured by the Titans. Frequently a female divinity is introduced, who seeks the body of the one she loves and makes passionate lamentations for the dead. In contrast to that stands the sober, historical report of the death of Jesus: 'He was crucified according to the scriptures, He was buried and rose according to the scriptures' (1 Cor. xv. 3f).

The contours of the cult divinities are lost in uncertainty and therefore can be exchanged with one another; in this 'syncretism' they are fundamentally one and the same. Jesus, however, in Paul's proclamation of Him as 'the Crucified' (1 Cor. 2. 2), still bears such concrete historical features, even as *Kyrios*, that He can never exchange his place with one of these cult divinities.

(*b*) In Christian baptism, as Paul describes it, the historical salvation-event that took place in Jesus is the primary thing, and that which the believer experiences is derivative. That becomes plain in Rom. vi by the fact that Paul, instead of referring to the figures of baptism, can suddenly speak of being 'crucified with' Christ (*v*. 6). This observation did not escape Bousset; but he explains it as a 'reversion from the mysticism of the community and sacrament to the personal mysticism of Paul'.[12] But before one accepts so significant a change as this, an attempt should be made to explain the train of thought uniformly, since this is possible without presupposing the influence of the Hellenistic Mystery religions.

[11] In PRE XVI, 1323, 63–1324, 12.
[12] *Kyrios Christos* 107.

For Paul it is not the symbol but the salvation-event that is the decisive issue; it is a dying with the Christ, who once suffered the death of the cross. Paul never forgets it, and he therefore places the cross immediately beside the font.

In the Mystery religions, on the contrary, the initiate and that which happens to him occupy the central place. He actually becomes the representative, the embodiment of the divinity, the medium of the god 'who renders himself visible'. 'Nowhere in Paul's writing can the baptized man take this role on himself. Nowhere is the role of Christ exchanged with that of the baptized and then the two identified; there are always two roles—ever different, ever related to each other, but never exchangeable. That which happens to the baptized, happens to him "with Christ".'[13]

(*c*) For Paul the figurative character of baptism by immersion, which in itself is not very pronounced, is completed by the Christian *proclamation*: in whatever form it may be, if only through the confession of Christ by the baptized, the death of the Lord was made known, so that no doubt could remain concerning the relation of baptism to the death of Jesus.[14] By contrast, the consecration of the initiate in the Mysteries has above all to be self-operative. Certainly a cult legend is recounted, but more to arouse a mood than to awake faith (and at the same time to provide a reason for the cult); but it is significant that in the allegedly plainest parallel to Christian baptism, the *taurobolium*, we are left in uncertainty as to its meaning, so that scholars have also interpreted it in terms of a sacrificial offering (slaughter, blood) and not of the 'rebirth' attested by the inscriptions.[15] The mystery action obviously has to speak for itself and unfold its meaning to the initiate through the very experience. It would be a real and effective *mysterium*, even without the cult legend. To postulate the same thing of the Christian sacrament and disregard the historical act of salvation wrought by Jesus is quite impossible. For Paul the sacramental dying and rising with Christ is inseparable from the historical experience of Jesus.

The tendency of the sacred action is also decisive for the meaning of the sacramental event. The Mysteries are directed towards the gaining of a higher, natural life, a life of fulness and blessedness. The sexual moment

[13] Hahn, op. cit. 14.

[14] It is perfectly sufficient to explain the knowledge on the part of the Romans, assumed by Paul in Rom. vi. 3, that they 'were baptized to the death of Jesus'. It is unnecessary, with Bousset (*Kyrios Christos* 107) to conclude from this passage that the belief must have been present that baptism, as an act of initiation, is a dying and coming to life again, comparable in some manner to the dying and rising of Christ.

[15] Dey, op. cit. 69–72, suggests a development from an original sacrifice to Caesar to a Mystery initiation; cf. K. Prümm, *RGH* 262f.

plays a great role in these earthy views of fruitfulness and orgies. Pain and suffering are but the price to be paid for it all. In the sacramental salvation-event, as described by Paul, the emphasis falls on the ethical moment; it is a dying to sin and rising to a life for God. Certainly the thesis, at one time defended, that the Hellenistic Mysteries were morally indifferent, that they were simply actions and experiences on the level of nature religions and often performed with flagrant (sexual) immorality, has received some corrections;[16] nevertheless the ethical tendencies are so feeble, the essential direction of the rites is not touched by them. With Paul, on the contrary, the co-ordination of the sacrament with ethics is not to be abrogated. 'Baptism inaugurates a history of that continual devotion in Christ's death and resurrection that is demanded of man.'[17] For the Pauline thought an indissoluble unity is involved here: Act according to what you are! In the Mystery religions ethical demands are always secondary in comparison with the natural event of the ecstatic or magical appropriation of 'salvation', whether that event be once-for-all or renewed after a period of time.

(*d*) The sacramental interpretation of Paul remains historical in yet another sense through its prospect of the consummation, which Christ will one day bring at the parousia. Initiation into the Mysteries mediates a 'salvation' that is experienced at once, so far as that is possible, or—since it can last only a short time—one that is promised for the period following the personal death of the initiate.[18] Salvation is considered as an interior matter of the soul; admittedly it includes corporeality also, but in any case it is a natural phenomenon, an intensification of the highest vital powers in man. Frequently it is bound up with a certain hostility to the body, a despising of that which is material and earthly, which of course is the foundation of Gnosticism. In the Pauline-Christian thought this feature does not exist. Rather the prospect is held out of a redemption and transformation of the whole man (Rom. viii. 18, 23f) presented in eschatological dimensions as the work of God, an intervention from above. The strong tension between σάρξ and πνεῦμα (Gal. v. 17ff) remains as a factor only during ὁ αἰών οὗτος; yet a man cannot evade this tension by a flight into the loftier way of Gnosticism;

[16] Cf. Lietzmann, 1 *Kor.* Excursus 46f; Cumont, *Die orient. Relig.* 36–38; in particular 84f (Isis cult); 142f (Mithras cult); Kittel, *Religionsgesch. u. Urchrist.* 115; Prümm, *RGH* 296f and 323–6.

[17] Althaus, op. cit. 52.

[18] Cf. in the Isis Mysteries the clothing of the dead with the Osiris garment, worn at his initiation and preserved in a holy place (testimony of Damascius in Hopfner, PRE XVI, 1329f). The ascension of the (still living) initiate in ecstatic rapture to the godhead, and the promise of immortality, is common to all the Mysteries, cf. Hopfner, PRE XVI, 1323, 21–24; Prümm, *RGH* 298–300. The ecstasy was for the purpose of overcoming corporeality, hence the prescriptions for fasting, abstinence from drinking wine and sexual intercourse.

he must activate all possible ethical powers in the conflict. But hope presses on beyond this (frequently painful) tension to the bodily resurrection, at which this corruptible must 'put on' incorruption, this mortal immortality (1 Cor. xv. 53). By reason of the overweening attitude of the '*epoptes*' (the initiate who has 'seen'), he is often dominated by a despising of all who have not undergone initiation; in such circles the esoteric spirit of the clique is at home. Paul's social ethics are diametrically opposed to that (cf. 1 Cor. xii. 13; Gal. iii. 28; Col. iii. 11). Instead of arrogant gnosis, he demands selfless love that serves and that thought be taken for others (1 Cor. viii. 13). The divine life, graciously bestowed in the sacrament, is neither gained nor preserved through a proud renunciation of the world but through a toilsome bearing of the cross in the steps of Jesus.

These things are more than merely 'peculiar nuances of the Pauline interpretation';[19] they are distinctions that lie at the very heart of the faith. In the last analysis they stem from the fact that Christianity is a historical religion of redemption, whereas the Mystery cults set out to convey a supra-temporal mysticism that may be experienced. In the former case the thought is determined by the salvation history, in the latter it is determined by myth and mysticism. The pagan initiate is transported into another sphere by a powerful experiential process, which takes him out of the everyday world and creates for him sublime delights. Naturally the Christian is transformed in his deepest being through baptism, but it is in *this* world that he is set on a new way. Paul therefore is divided by an impassable gulf from every kind of Mystery religion piety.[20]

II. *Criticism of the Quasi-Mystery Teaching of Casel*

1. *Casel's Mystery Teaching and the Mystery Religions.* O. Casel took his point of departure from the piety of the pagan Mysteries in order to give a more profound exposition of the Christian 'cult Mystery'.[21] He has satisfied himself that it is possible to develop from the pagan Mysteries a type of 'cult mystery', though he himself admits that it 'was never fully realized' (103). He admits that 'the ancient cult in most instances remained a mere nature cult, so that the Mysteries

[19] Bousset, *Kyrios Christos* 139.

[20] On this it is still worth consulting G. Anrich, *Das antike Mysterienwesen in seinem Einfluss auf das Christentum*, 1894, especially 111f; further F. J. Dölger, *Mysterienwesen und Urchristentum* II: 'Paulus und die antiken Mysterienreligionen', *ThRev* 15 (1916), cols 433–8 (a criticism of Böhlig and Clemen); Lagrange in *RB* 29 (1920) 420–46 (criticism of Loisy); Deissner, *Paulus und die Mystik seiner Zeit* 122–30; Clemen, *Religionsgesch. Erklär. d. NT* 155–91; Schweitzer, *Mystik* 27–41; Heigl, op. cit. 99–112; Prümm, *RGH* 308–56.

[21] Cf. *Die Liturgie als Mysterienfeier* (Ecclesia orans 9), Freiburg 3–5 1923, 1–44; *Das christliche Kultmysterium* 95ff (the page numbers in the text relate to this last book).

often came to be purely animal rites and tended to repel a purified spirituality' (103). Nevertheless he desires to recognize a highly religious worth in the type of the *mysterium*, a value which, indeed, first received its true fulfilment in Christianity (103f). Here it is necessary to interpose a question, whether Casel from the very beginning has not a tendency to stylize and idealize. The early Christians, who still maintained a living contact with manifestations of this kind of piety, thought differently about it.[22]

In connection with the term *mysterium* Casel carries over the entire terminology of the Mysteries into the Church (106f), and his interpretation has called forth a lively semasiological and theological controversy on the word μυστήριον.[23] He sees in the revelation of God in the incarnate Logos (107) the chief and final *mysterium* of Christianity, the foundation and source of all Christian 'mysteries'. Since this *mysterium*, however, must be continued, the Lord creates the 'cult *mysterium*' as the last act of his life in this aeon (110). The disciples have to let the passion of their Master become ever and again a reality on the mystical plane (111). From the *mysterium* of redemption flow the other mysteries (111), in the first place baptism as a mystical-real participation in the death of the Lord for this sinful world and in his new life for God (112). It is supplemented and perfected through the anointing with the new supernatural principle of life, the *Pneuma* of Christ. The Christian now bears the *sphragis*, the seal of Christ, the supernatural assimilation to the Lord through grace. The new life in the Spirit is nourished and strengthened through the eucharist as *Pneuma*-food. The initiation of the Christian consists of these three mysteries (112). With respect to their temporal development, Casel says that this teaching is expressed with increasing plainness and clarity from the third century on, but its essential meaning was taught long before (113f).

Casel by no means overlooks the differences that exist between the nature of the pagan Mysteries and the Christian cult.[24] In saying that,

[22] Justin I *Apol.* 66. 4 (Goodspeed 275); Minuc. Felix, Oct. 22 1–4 (Halm 31f); Tatian, *Or. ad. Gr.* 8. 4 (Goodspeed 275); Origen, *C. Cels.* 6. 22–23 (Koetschau 93) etc.; above all Firm. Maternus, *De err. prof. relig.* passim, especially ch. 18.

[23] Cf. W. Prümm, '"Mysterion" von Paulus bis Origenes', *ZKTh* 61 (1937) 391–425; the same, '"Mysterion" und Verwandtes bei Hippolyt', *ZKTh* 63 (1939) 207–25; the same, '"Mysterion" und Verwandtes bei Athanasius', op. cit. 350–9; O. Casel *GGM* 118. 154; G. Söhngen, *Symbol und Wirklichkeit* 110ff; on the systematic explanation the same author, 'Das mysterium des lebendigen Christus und der lebendige Glaube', *Wissenschaft und Weisheit* 10 (1943), 126–44. On the whole subject cf. G. Bornkamm in *ThW* IV, 809ff with further literature. He concludes: 'Seen in its entirety ... it is a concept that seldom appears in the N.T., and it never permits of a relation to the Mystery cults' (831, 4f). Nevertheless he admits that there was a renewal of the cultic Mystery conception in the early Church from the time of Justin and Tertullian (832, 30ff).

[24] Filthaut, op. cit. 90f.

however, one must admit that he does not have in view a totally different structure, as given through the historical character of the saving deeds of Christ and the subordination of the Christian 'mysteries' to it; rather he believes the chief difference to lie in the revelatory character of the Christian cult: the Christian cult is of divine origin and comes 'from above', whereas all other cults, apart from that of the old Covenant, derive 'from below', from men.[25] In this way the supernatural superiority of the Christian cult, of which faith is conscious, is certainly exhibited, but not the difference in essence between pagan and Christian 'mysteries' which can be *historically tested*. The critics of Casel's theory, therefore, have some justice when they charge him with borrowing essential (natural) lines of structure for the Christian cult from the pagan Mysteries. In itself that could not constitute a ground for repudiating his theory, since there also existed in very early times a tendency to consider the natural worth of pagan culture as a preparation for the Christian faith, with a demand for an organic amalgamation (Clement of Alexandria). But it is a question of historical truth, whether we can credit this concern to Paul or not. According to his preaching of the cross, God made the 'wisdom of the world' foolishness and was pleased to save believers precisely through the foolishness of the proclamation (1 Cor. i. 18–25). He judged the pagan sacrificial system as the worship of demons (1 Cor. x. 20f) and made a clean separation between the Christian cult and all veneration of pagan 'gods and lords' (1 Cor. viii. 5f). It is, therefore, hardly probable that he associated himself, even in a minor way, with Hellenistic cults and Mysteries.[26]

2. *Casel and the sacramental dying and rising with Christ.* It is freely to be admitted that the last word is not spoken on the Pauline view of dying with Christ in baptism by such general considerations. Casel's interpretation may be characterized by the key expression 'presence in mystery'. By that he understands that the saving deeds of Jesus become present in the sacramental symbol. 'Sacrament and the original act of salvation are not two separate things but *one*, whereby the symbol is so completely filled with the reality of the original act that the latter may rightly be said to be present.'[27] A more exact definition of this 'presence in mystery' is not simple and furthermore is contested.[28] Warnach would describe it essentially as 'the appearance of the Christ event in a cult symbol, through which this event in an objectively real manner becomes present in space and time and accessible to believers, so that

[25] Filthaut, op. cit. 90 (middle).
[26] Cf. Pieper, *Paulus* 160–4; A. D. Nock, *St. Paul*, London 1938, 237ff.
[27] *GGM* 116.
[28] Cf. Filthaut, op. cit. 32ff; B. Neunheuser, 'Mysteriengegenwart', *ALW* 3 (1953) 104–22.

in dying and rising with Christ they actually accomplish it with Him, and in this manner can participate in its fruit of salvation'.[29]

These formulations become more comprehensible when they are compared with the '*effectus* doctrine' that prevails in quarters unaffected by the Mystery teaching. According to this the significance of the sacraments lies essentially in the working of grace (*effectus*), which they convey as channels of grace. The concern of the mystery theology is to change this purely causal relation into one that is inwardly meaningful. The saving work is represented in the symbol, and the effect flows from this reality.[30] It is clear that this dogmatic formulation of the question lies far from Paul. Neither the causal teaching that lies at the root of the '*effectus* doctrine', nor the idea of origin and copy required by the doctrine of symbols, can be applied without question to Paul.

But on this issue, whether in baptism, or more exactly in death and resurrection with Christ, we are presented with a Christian 'mystery event', the following remarks may be made:

1. Paul by no means considers all sacraments as a 'dying and rising with Christ'. The memorial of the death of Jesus in the Lord's Supper (1 Cor. xi. 26) is not to be linked with this conception; it stands rather in association with the thought of sacrifice and atonement: Jesus gave up his body and blood for others in order to establish a new order of salvation (*vv.* 24–25), an idea for which one will seek in the Mysteries in vain. When it is said, 'For as often as you eat this bread and drink this cup, you proclaim the death of the Lord until he comes' (*v.* 26), a 'realization' of the sacrifice of the cross is undoubtedly thereby given[31] but scarcely in the sense of the Mystery theory of O. Casel.[32] 'For Paul the ideas and mode of thought of corporate personality, when applied to the eucharist, make all speculations over the "how" of the presence of Christ's death superfluous; the presence of the representative *Kyrios* effects the presence of his saving deed.'[33] The sacramental reception of the Spirit is not to be understood primarily in the sense of a *mysterium*. It is nothing else than the fulfilment of the prophetic promise for the messianic time, an act of God, which a man by no means necessarily experiences through symbols. It is an event that is recognizable by its effects (cf. 1 Cor. xii. 3; Rom. viii. 16; Gal. iv. 6; v. 22f). Not much of the Christian 'initiation' remains, therefore, that can be compared with

[29] *ALW* 3 (1954) 347.
[30] *JLW* 13 (1933) 123.
[31] On the dogmatic side (formulation of the Tridentinum) there is an important note in Prümm, *Christentum als Neuheitserlebnis*, Freiburg i. Br. 1939, 443f; cf. G. Söhngen, *Das sakramentale Wesen des Messopfers*, Essen 1946, 9ff.
[32] Cf. P. Neuenzeit, *Das Herrenmahl*, München 1960, 127–54.
[33] P. Neuenzeit, op. cit. 154.

consecration into the Mysteries, or that can be considered as Christian 'cult *mysterium*'.

2. If, then, the 'mystery event' must be rejected as a common denominator for the understanding of Paul's sacramental teaching, it may be said on the positive side that another point of view is established, which integrates the sacrament as such into the fabric of his theology: the sacrament is the normal means of procuring the (objective and universal) salvation for the individual (cf. § 18).

3. Rom. vi is largely to be subordinated to this viewpoint. Here also Paul is concerned with the element in salvation which is (divine) life (*v.* 8). Certainly it is strongly conditioned by the ethical point of view (*v.* 4), in accordance with the tendency of the passage, and it effectively contrasts with the death for sin (*v.* 11). But Paul has no intention of representing baptism as a purely external means; he desires at the same time—and this is the characteristic element of his teaching—to bring the acquisition of salvation into closest connection with the fundamental saving deed of Jesus Christ, who as the Founder and Head of a (new) race represented all who are joined to Him. Conversely all who in baptism enter into fellowship with Him participate in that which once happened to Him for our salvation; they thus gain a share in the blessings of salvation which He acquired for us.

4. That this basic standpoint is right in Rom. vi is confirmed by the fact that Paul does not portray baptism *solely* under the aspect of dying and rising with Christ. According to the purpose he wishes to subserve, he also uses other images and viewpoints: for him baptism is a cleansing bath, an assignment to the new Lord (εἰς τὸ ὄνομα), Christ-circumcision, 'putting on Christ', incorporation into the 'Body of Christ', regeneration (Tit. iii. 5).

There are passages, therefore, which even tell in favour of an '*effectus* theory' (though certainly not in the Aristotelian sense). In Paul the sacrament always remains bound to the major purpose of mediating salvation; this it fulfils in the context of the saving history, a situation which is determined by our deliverance in principle through the cross of Christ and our waiting for salvation in fulness and glory.[34]

III. *The Hypothesis of the 'Contemporaneity' of the Christian with Christ*

W. Tr. Hahn seeks to arrive at a new understanding of the Pauline texts about dying and rising with Christ in the light of questions that are

[34] For criticism of Casel from the exegetical standpoint, see the contribution of J. Cools to the *Mémorial Lagrange*; E. Druwé, Medebegraven en-verrezen met Christus, *Bijdragen* 10 (1949) 201–23; A. Grail, La place du baptême dans la doctrine de s. Paul, *La Vie Spirituelle*, No. 352 (1950) 563–83.

being ventilated in present-day Protestant theology.[35] He first examines a thesis of K. Barth's, according to which the primitive kerygma is not to be understood in a purely historical sense; it centres upon a phenomenon that should be viewed as suprahistorical or transcending history; it is not something that can be pinned down to the here and now of the historical process, rather it is present everywhere and at all times (49). Hahn agrees with Bultmann in rejecting this thesis. The text (especially 1 Cor. xv. 7) can only be understood as an attempt to make credible the resurrection of Christ as an objective historical fact (52). Hahn adopts the pregnant conceptions of Künneth: this has to do with the perfection, concretion and singularity of the Christ event (54f). A suprahistorical fact is not a fact, but an idea or myth (49, 54).

Hahn then enters into debate with the solution suggested by Künneth himself, which loosens the unity of the cross and resurrection: the resurrection is removed from the plane of relative religious-historical occurrences, while the death of Jesus still lies in the historical plane; the resurrection is an event that transcends history (59). This, too, Hahn denies: for Paul there is no 'theology of the resurrection',[36] but only a theology of the cross (59f). Paul stresses in a uniform manner the death, burial and resurrection of Jesus as *facts*. 'All three are the history of God with his Christ and therefore fundamentally do not have a different character' (62). Moreover Hahn does not admit the procedure whereby the separation of the appearances of the Risen Lord from these three elements of the Christ-event creates an independent fourth act, as Barth has essayed to show. 'The event of the cross and resurrection as content of the preaching and traditions of Paul is a unified event, the individual acts of which comprise a compact whole; in this connection Paul does not reflect as to whether a distinct dignity is to be accorded to the individual acts or whether they belong to different planes of reality'(63). Hahn then draws a cautious conclusion: 'It is plain from this that for Paul this event is certainly a truly historical happening, but not *only* a historical one'(64). In applying this basic interpretation to the sayings about dying and rising with Christ Hahn makes a clear dividing line with respect to the Mystery cults. He also defends this view against the mystical interpretation of Deissmann's and the eschatological-mystical interpretation of Schweitzer's (68–78).

While one may agree with Hahn's fundamental aim of securing the

[35] *Das Mitsterben und Mitauferstehen mit Christus bei Paulus*, Gütersloh 1937. In what follows the page numbers of this book are indicated in brackets in our text. A view related to that of Hahn is advocated by G. Bornkamm, who expressly agrees with him (*ThBl* 18, col. 237, n. 13). Nevertheless Bornkamm avoids the modern philosophic conceptions.

[36] The Title of Künneth's book, *Theologie der Auferstehung*, München [4]1951.

historicity of the Christ event as a firm foundation for faith,[37] his positive new exposition of dying with Christ etc. does not appear so satisfactory. He himself gives his theory the name of 'contemporaneity' and briefly expresses it in the following sentences: 'The Pauline statements about dying with Christ etc. signify that one is really taken up into the once-for-all, concrete, historical suffering and death and resurrection of Christ. It means the integration of the entire existence of the Christian into this saving event' (96). He develops the idea of 'contemporaneity with Christ' in dependence on Kierkegaard and formulates it as follows (set in italics in his book): 'In this "with Christ" Paul sees himself transplanted into contemporaneity with the cross and resurrection of Jesus Christ, and in such a manner that he gains a real participation in this once-for-all event and eliminates all spatial and temporal separation' (97). What Hahn then says as to the irreversibility and uniqueness of contemporaneity on this foundation is justifiable. Similarly in his arguments concerning the possibility of contemporaneity, or more exactly concerning the Christ-*Pneuma* (115–23), he applies thoroughly Pauline conceptions; but his thesis of contemporaneity must be tested.

The chief objection to it must be that it introduces a foreign conception, gained from modern philosophy of religion, for the understanding of the texts and it is not conformable to the Pauline ways of thinking. Such conceptual bridges did not stand at Paul's disposal, or at least they cannot be proved to have been known to him.

Hahn carefully investigates the Pauline sayings regarding time; but he is constantly directed by them only to the historical factuality of the Christ event. He rightly explains the contrast of time in Rom. vi (future, of sayings relative to the ethical outworking) and Col. ii (past, because of the dogmatic tendency against the Colossian false teaching) from the respective situations of the Letters (38–42). His examination of the other sayings about dying with Christ etc. (43–45) also yields an acceptable result: this event determines the entire Christian existence and points beyond it to the consummation at the parousia.

His exposition becomes doubtful only where he relates the sayings on dying with Christ etc. to the historical plane of Christ. We may agree that Paul alludes to this historical foundation of his new life in Christ by naming the cross in Gal ii. 19b and by the context in *v.* 20b; but that he projected the union with Christ, hinted by the

[37] On the Catholic side cf. the essay of Cools.

σύν, back into the time of the death on the cross (66) is untenable in this form.

As we saw in the exegetical part, Paul here speaks, as in other texts (Col. ii. 12f; Eph. ii. 5f), in the light of the situation of his readers at their particular time (or indeed in the light of his own situation); he contrasts their (or his own) earlier walk of life with their present new life in Christ, and therefore by the σύν-sayings he doubtless refers to the point of time of becoming Christian (or in Gal. ii. 19b, the condition brought into being since that time). Hahn's formulations in this connection (66) are not entirely pertinent, since he is chiefly concerned to corroborate the *historicity* of the Christ event and its interpretation; his interpretation as to how past and present are to be united emerges only in a secondary manner.

Hahn appeals to two Synoptic texts on which to support his thesis of contemporaneity: Lk. xxiii. 32 and Mt. xxvi. 35. The former passage deals with taking out two criminals in order to be executed 'with Jesus', the latter with Peter's asseveration that he would rather die 'with Jesus' than deny him. Both occasions have in view the historical death of Jesus and concrete historical participation in it (94). In comparing the Pauline sayings with these Synoptic passages a remarkable formal agreement reveals itself. If it were not known that this dying of Paul's did not take place as it is there described, we would have to assume that Paul perished at the time when Jesus was executed (95). Hahn admittedly points out differences (95f) that modify Paul's utterances. But his fundamental interpretation remains the same.

The mistake in method here is to draw conclusions from formal similarities to agreements of content. If, therefore, we are concerned with what is immediately and naturally conveyed by such expressions, there is no need to adduce these two Synoptic passages, for in *content* they are very distant from the Pauline contexts. But the problem lies exactly at this point, that the Pauline sayings cannot be understood in a purely literal manner, since Paul did not suffer death with Jesus at the same time and place as He, nor have they done so who have been baptized at a later date. Hahn does not specify any other proofs for his hypothesis; nor could he well do so, for it is nowhere evident that Paul did away with the category of time.[38]

[38] Cf. Stauffer, *Theol.* n. 495 (p. 276): 'We die with him and live with him—"conformed" to him, as Paul puts it ... not contemporaneously with him, as is taught in Bultmann's school. To disregard the time reference at this point is to destroy the whole conception (cf. ch. 16). For the formula σὺν Χριστῷ expressly points back to the historical priority of the coming of Christ (Rom. vf) and excludes any sort of metaphysical contemporaneity.'

Yet Hahn, under the spell of his hypothesis, allows himself to give vent to views like this: 'The assertion that the Christian has been nailed to the cross with Christ and raised from the dead with Him, apart from all religious considerations, is so opposed to logical and empirical thinking that we have to face the issue: does reality reside in the world about us or in contemporaneity with Christ? Only one of the two is possible, since the one excludes the other. Paul for his part has a ready answer to the question: "The pattern of this world is about to pass away" (1 Cor. vii. 21); the cosmos has been judged in the event of the cross and resurrection and a new world has come into being; it is this reality to which contemporaneity belongs' (102f). Hahn emphasizes that such contemporaneity is given only in Christ. In this one respect alone the valid form of existence has broken through (104).

In our judgment this view is put out of court by the manner in which Paul unhesitatingly uses the future, and that not only the logical future (as in Rom. vi. 5), but also the eschatological (Phil. iii. 11; cf. also Rom. viii. 17; 2 Tim. ii. 11f). Strictly speaking, in a contemporaneity with the Christ event there could no longer be an eschatological future, an increase in the blessings of salvation. For Christ himself attained to full possession of the divine life in his resurrection.

Hahn himself perceives this difficulty and interprets 2 Cor. xiii. 4 and 1 Thess. v. 10 of the present new life (44f). On Rom. viii. 17, which, by its mention of 'inheritance', stands in an eschatological connection, he is silent; so also with regard to Phil. iii. 11, where the resurrection from the dead is expressly named, and 2 Tim. ii. 11f, which refers to the eschatological reigning with Christ. Generally speaking, his attitude to the parousia is uncertain because of his presuppositions. For him the 'new aeon' has attained an eschatological breakthrough in the Christ event (therefore in the cross and resurrection 106–11). On the other hand Paul sees the parousia still ahead of him. 'Actually, resurrection and parousia form a unity, even if they temporally fall apart from each other' (111). How can this statement come to terms with the 'contemporaneity' of the Christian with Christ, since the Christian must have entered into complete fellowship with the Christ of the resurrection?

Under the presupposition of contemporaneity with Christ, the tension of Christian existence between now and the not yet of the future must disappear; this is a tension conditioned by time. Hahn nevertheless sees and stresses the element of tension (153–63). He regards the Christian existence as dialectical: it is at the same time a having and not having, indicative and imperative, glory and suffering (163). In 'dialectic' the moment of time may be removed; in Paul it cannot be done.

Here again the basic mistake reveals itself: it is the desire to impose on Paul conceptions of modern philosophy of religion. Only by a careful interpretation of his own views out of the texts, and a cautious feeling of oneself into his conceptual world, is it possible to bring a little more light into his utterances about dying and rising with Christ.

§21. THE SACRAMENTAL DYING AND RISING WITH CHRIST AS INCLUSION IN THE CHRIST EVENT

The statements on dying etc. with Christ in baptism attest the fundamental conception that the baptized subjectively appropriates the objective and universal salvation won by Christ. The 'salvation' is attained in the fellowship of Christ. At the heart of this fellowship with Christ is baptism (along with faith, cf. above § 18). This significance should be firmly grasped in Rom. vi also, as providing the key to understanding the Pauline declarations. The movement of thought comes to rest first in *v.* 11, where it states that we are alive for God ἐν Χριστῷ Ἰησοῦ. All the foregoing statements, however important they may be to Paul in this connection, are concerned only with the process that introduces to fellowship with Christ, which is the object of his aspiration. They describe the way, for which this life ἐν Χριστῷ Ἰησοῦ is the goal. Baptism, as the virtual initiation of fellowship with Christ, has its own particular viewpoint but fundamentally it does not contain a different character. Whereas Paul elsewhere immediately mentions the effects of baptism with which he is especially concerned, namely the new being and life in Christ, he here enters in greater detail upon the way this fellowship with Christ comes into being.

In Rom. vi Paul does not consider baptism as an external condition for entering the fellowship of Christ, but he views it inwardly as an inclusion in that which happened to Christ himself. It is not only the result that concerns Christ, existence ἐν Χριστῷ, but also the event of baptism, an event σὺν Χριστῷ. In so speaking the Apostle is not concerned to lay bare that mysterious process by which our union with Christ is effected. He desires rather to draw specific consequences for the Christian life from his meditation on this theme. Dying with Christ, being crucified with Christ in baptism, stamps the whole Christian existence as a being dead for sin; and rising with Christ, which is inseparable from it, is a being alive for God, and will find its last fulfilment in the bodily resurrection. That which takes place in baptism brings the Christian into so close a relation to the crucified and risen Christ, his entire way becomes fashioned after Christ. From sacramental dying with Christ and being raised with Him grows a perpetual discipleship and conformity to the likeness of Christ, who entered the glory of God by way of the cross. Union with Christ and likeness to Christ is the real goal of Paul's christocentric piety. It is therefore comprehensible that the Apostle elsewhere characterizes the saving event in baptism as 'putting on Christ' (Gal. iii. 27), and that he can call baptism itself a 'Christ-circumcision' (Col. ii. 11). Once we are clear about that, we shall see the sacramental 'dying and rising with Christ' simply as one way along with others of representing the beginning of our fellowship with Christ, even if it be the most important and theologically most productive way.

At the same time we must not weaken this theological statement, but allow it its full realistic meaning. Yet how is the 'dying with Christ' or 'burial with Christ', that happens to the baptized person to be explained, seeing that the Lord suffered the bloody death on Golgotha long ago, once for all and unrepeatably?

From the side of Christ there is no difficulty: for the exalted Lord is identical with the historical Jesus. The concept of *Pneuma* (see § 22) makes possible an easy transition from the mode of being that Christ then had to that which He now has. But for the baptized person the question arises how he can be drawn into the once for all event on Golgotha. He enters into a real (*Pneuma*-) union with the living and present Lord, in whose name he is baptized. But for him also entrance into the fellowship of Christ goes by way of 'dying with Christ'.

Now this train of thought is joined by another from the crucified and risen Lord: Christ is to be considered, in parallelism with Adam, as the new Head of humanity, a category of thought which had just been occupying the Apostle (Rom. v. 12–21). Through Christ, the Founder of the new race, we were delivered from the dominion of sin and death and brought into the realm of the divine life. This 'Christ event' took place in two actions: in death and resurrection (Rom. iv. 25). The individual too, must sacramentally die and rise 'with Christ'. The connecting idea is obvious: that which happened to the 'One', the Founder of the race, should also happen to 'all', i.e. all who are joined to Him, the believers. They should not only receive the fruit of Christ's action, but also experience the same as Christ and together with Him, first sacramentally, then ethically and mystically, and finally eschatologically.

To grasp this mode of theological procedure on Paul's part it is necessary to realize that in his theology he avails himself of certain fundamental conceptions.

> This fact is too little heeded. The leading lines of Paul's theology become clear when we do take account of it.[39] Undoubtedly it would be false to try to understand Paul on the basis of formulae and structures; nothing would be more out of keeping with the thronging fulness, vitality and weight of his thought. Often the reality of salvation, as he sees it and personally experiences it, bursts every frame. But it must not be forgotten that he was a Rabbinically trained theologian, indebted to his teachers, and that when he became a Christian he did not simply throw away the equipment that he had gained. He used with complete freedom anything that appeared to him to be a fit means for representing elements of the Christian message. Now the Rabbinical schools were in the habit of using certain logical expedients, especially various kinds of demonstration,[40] and many theological basic principles (*theologoumena*);[41] they also coined a multitude of formal ideas and expressions, suited to catechetical teaching, as aids to memory and learning. With all this Paul is not content simply to take his position in the stream of the primitive Christian tradition, but he is himself a creative spirit, stimulating and fructifying thought. In him therefore we can distinguish: (a) logical structures (from the Rabbinic schools); (b) theological principles and leading ideas (his own theology); (c) dogmatic formulae (the theology of the Church); (d) hymns and liturgical strophes (the influence of the cultus, e.g. 1 Tim. iii. 16). We are here concerned with his own main ideas (b).

One such theological idea formed the foundation for Paul's theology of baptism generally: the Adam-Christ parallel, with which the conception of representation was closely bound (§ 17). Accordingly, a typical

[39] Cf. F. W. Maier, art. Paulus in *SThK* VIII, 36.

[40] Cf. e.g. The Rabbinic way of drawing a conclusion πολλῷ μᾶλλον, used by Paul in Rom. v. 9, 10, 15, 17; 2 Cor. iii. 9, 11. (Heb. xii. 9, 25); on this see Billerbeck III, 223–6. To the same source we must often attribute the comparison ὥσπερ-καί, Rom. v. 12, 19, 21; vi. 4 etc, as also the negative οὐχ ὡς Rom. v. 15, 16 (which in this case bursts the structure, cf. by contrast 1 Cor. xv. 22!). On the whole see H. L. Strack, *Einleitung in Talmud und Midrash*, München [5]1930, 95–109.

[41] A theologoumenon that is to be found in Apocalyptic: τὰ ἔσχατα ὡς τὰ πρῶτα. Resort was made to the paradaisical time in order to picture the future time of salvation. (The time of wilderness wanderings was considered to be a second 'typical' time, when the people were led and sustained by God). Cf. Volz. *Eschatologie* 113f and 359–61; Bousset-Gressmann, *Relig. d. Judentums* 283f; Moore, *Judaism* II, 303.

Pauline principle must be made plain if we would understand the Apostle's characteristic way of speaking about being 'buried with Christ' and 'raised with' Him, of being 'crucified with Christ' and 'living with' Him: *that which happened to Christ happens also to Christians; dying and rising with Him becomes a rule in the Christian life, which works itself out in all areas and in every aspect of life.* The Apostle has no need to borrow from the Hellenistic-Oriental cults for this representation, or to make it appear as an event after the order of the Mysteries; nor is it necessary for him to resort to philosophy, to help him over the dilemma of temporal distance from Christ. The fundamentally Semitic idea of 'corporate personality', applied to Christ, makes it possible to bring into a single perspective the salvation-event in baptism and the death and resurrection of Christ. So soon, however, as the Christian has experienced sacramentally, through grace, this 'dying and rising' with Christ in baptism, he must make this way 'through cross to resurrection' the very law of his life, in correspondence with the characteristic Christian existence 'between the times'. This he must do in ethical dying to sin, in endurance of suffering and persecution, in 'conformity with the death of Christ' (Phil. iii. 10), that so at length he may attain to the eschatological resurrection with Christ (cf. 2 Cor. iv. 11; Phil. iii. 11).

This principle, 'everything that happened to Christ happens also to the Christian', is briefly and clearly enunciated in Rom. vi. 4: ὥσπερ Χριστός-οὕτως καὶ ἡμεῖς. The rule is here applied to the sacramental sphere, but in like manner it also holds good in ethics and eschatology. For that reason the statements about dying etc. with Christ are put in the past (Rom. vi. 4; Col. ii. 12) and in the present (2 Cor. iv. 10f), in the indicative (Rom. vi. 5, 8; Col. iii. 1, 3) and, immediately adjacent thereto, in the imperative (Rom. vi. 11; Col. iii. 5), partly in the present (dying with Christ) and partly in the eschatological future (rising with Christ, Rom. vi. 8; viii. 17; Phil. iii. 10f; Col. iii. 3f; 1 Thess. iv. 14; v. 10; 2 Tim. ii. 11f). Paul is able to give this varied turn to his thought in accordance with the point of view that happens to be required; but the basis is always the same: the once for all Christ event—including death, burial, resurrection, and sometimes glorification (Rom. viii. 17), installation to the right hand of God (Eph. ii. 6) and to glory (2 Tim. ii. 12; cf. Rom. v. 17)—viewed as the event that has gone before and been determined for all who are associated with this new Founder of humanity. Sometimes the formulation affects particularly the people of Christ, sometimes more especially Christ, as in Rom. vi. 10a: 'The death that He (Christ) died, He died "to sin" (the power of sin) once for all.' This statement possesses immediately validity for those who have died with Christ in baptism (*vv.* 2, 6, 11), and here it is obviously transferred back to Christ; that explains a certain inconsequence in the sentence, which even the Fathers perceived: it can be applied to the Christ only in a figurative sense, seeing that He was never subject to sin. In this case *v.* 11 (οὕτως καὶ ὑμεῖς), to which Paul is heading, has already exercised an influence on *v.* 10.

This theological conception of Paul's is more frequently to be recognized in the formula (ὥσπερ)—οὕτως καί. In Rom. vi it appears yet again in *v.* 11: οὕτως καὶ ὑμεῖς; earlier (*v.* 10) the topic in view was the event that befell Christ, now it is carried over to Christians. Outside this primary passage the expression is to be met in 1 Thess. iv. 14—a particularly valuable testimony as coming from the oldest Letter of Paul: 'If we believe that Jesus died and rose again, so will it be (οὕτως καί) for those who through Jesus have fallen asleep;[42] God will bring them with him.' Thus in this purely eschatological context also, the expectation of Christians in the future is based on a backward glance to the Christ event of the past. The death which they experience through the will of Jesus can no more remain without the resurrection than it could in his case. Finally the same mode of expression is implied in 2 Cor. xiii. 4a-b, even if it is less apparent: in 4a Christ's dying on the cross is described, and in 4b it is added, 'καὶ γὰρ ἡμεῖς are weak ἐν αὐτῷ, but we shall live with Him (σὺν αὐτῷ) in your service'.

Along with the formula οὕτως καί there are compounds from the root μορφή that reflect this leading motif of Paul's in various contexts. First, Phil. iii. 10f is to be connected with the notion of dying and rising with Christ: Paul hopes, 'in growing conformity (συμμορφιζόμενος) with the death of Jesus', to attain to the resurrection of the dead. The statement presumes the mysticism of suffering and eschatological hope. But similar modes of expression are also found in purely eschatological contexts. A little later Paul says, '(Christ) will transform the body belonging to our humble state and give it a form like that (σύμμορφον) of his own resplendent body' (Phil. iii. 21). He uses the same word in Rom. viii. 29: 'Those whom he (God) foreknew he also ordained to have a like form (συμμόρφους) to the image of his Son, that He might be the first-born among many brothers.' Here the theme is not inclusion in the Christ event but assimilation to the form of Christ, namely the δόξα-form of the Risen Lord; but the reflection of the Adam-Christ parallel in Rom. viii. 29 shows that the same fundamental thought is in

[42] διὰ 'Ιησοῦ with κοιμηθέντες; cf. Knaberbauer, Vosté, Dibelius ad loc (against Steinmann-Tillmann).

mind. 2 Cor. iii. 18 also speaks of being 'changed' into the likeness of Christ. After the single sacramental event in baptism, the conformation to Christ can be considered as a continuous and mystical process: we are 'changed into the same image (of Christ) from splendour to splendour' (2 Cor. iii. 18).[43] This formulation shows how Paul is concerned only to lead Christians ever more deeply into the reality of Christ.

The *sequence from death to life* is variously expressed: by an introductory εἰ-sentence (Rom. vi. 5, 8; viii. 17; 2 Tim. ii. 11f), by a following ἵνα-sentence (Rom. vi. 4; 2 Cor. iv. 10, 11; Gal. ii. 19) or by a simple coordination (2 Cor. xiii. 4). Frequently this transition from death to life is made plain by the context. The thought can bear the whole representation, as in Col. ii. 12f; ii. 20–iii. 4; Eph. ii. 1–7, or it can convey a deeper ('mystical') appearance, as in Gal. ii. 19f: as one 'crucified with Christ' Paul no longer lives like the old Paul; it is Christ who lives in him. In 1 Cor. xv. 30 the thought is similar: Paul dies daily, and the context suggests that he draws power to endure this daily suffering of death from the hope of rising with Christ. As the Firstfruits of those who have fallen asleep, He has gone on before in the resurrection (*vv.* 20–23, the Adam-Christ parallel). Or 2 Cor. i. 5: as the 'suffering of Christ' richly overflows to the Apostle, so the consolation overflows 'through Christ'. The Pauline mysticism of suffering also observes the law of dying and rising with Christ.[44]

Thus this conception embraces all viewpoints of the Pauline theology. F. Prat voices the leading idea of the Pauline theology in a similar manner: 'Christ the Redeemer ... unites every believer with his death and with his life.'[45] E. Burger expresses it in this way: 'He who has been baptized has been taken up into Christ with his whole being, so that everything that is said of Christ can now be said also of the Christian ... This putting on, this growing together and being rooted in Him (Rom. vi. 5; Col. ii. 7) means actually being transferred into the reality of the crucified and risen Christ, so that the whole life of the Christian is now

[43] Windisch (ad loc) thinks that a process after the order of the Mysteries is in view; Dibelius also, *Paulus und die Mystik* 6f, adduces (with certain reserve) this very passage as an example of mystic influence: to look is to be changed! The figure of the mirror plays an important role in the ancient texts, cf. Lietzmann ad loc. Nevertheless the ideas assume different forms according as they are derived from philosophical, Gnostic or yet other circles, cf. R. Reitzenstein, *Historia Monachorum und Historia Lausiaca*, Göttingen 1916, 244–51. Close parallels are offered in *Od. Solom.* 13 and Philo, *leg. alleg.* III, 101. Allo recognizes here the great Pauline principle: L'assimilation du croyant au Christ est la grande idée fondamentale au 'paulinisme' (*2 Cor.* 97). On the idea of 'image' cf. further F. W. Eltester, *Eikon im Neuen Testament*, Berlin 1958, 23f, 165.

[44] Cf. Schneider, *Passionsmystik* 61–67.

[45] *Théol.* II. 23.

a life in Christ, a continual dying with Him and living with Him (2 Cor. iv. 10f).'[46]

> Although Burger clearly recognizes the connection of these two points of view in the unity of the living Christ, his exposition on the basis of mythical thought is unsatisfactory: 'My ego is included in the ego of the mythical figure, my here and now is included in the there and then of the mythical event.' That is characteristic of mythical thinking as it appears in the Mandaean literature.[47] For Paul Christ is not a mythical figure. His own view comes to expression in the close union of the historical (which can be proclaimed as truly historical) and the 'pneumatic', present aspects of Christ's person and work.

Moreover mysticism is no adequate point of view for these sacramental statements. Its relationship to the sacrament in general must be considered later (§ 24). Here we content ourselves with comparing the expositions of Weinel and Schneider.

> Weinel writes: 'He who is in Christ, or in whom Christ is, experiences everything with Him. From this point of view, unlike that of the religion of faith, the death of Christ is not seen as mere substitution. The believer, who has become a single life with Him, has died on the cross with Him, Gal. ii. 19.'[48] If the death of the believer is referred back in such a mystic fashion to that of Christ and blended with it, the dying of Jesus likewise continues on in the mystic: 'Paul so seriously regards his body as a vessel in which Christ lives and works, that he looks on his suffering as the putting of Jesus to death, and that He is, as it were, first truly martyred in him.'[49]

There is no need to dispute that this mystical point of view holds good for Paul's so called mysticism of suffering; but to try to explain in

[46] Op. cit. 53. Good statements of this are also to be found in Bornkamm: 'He (Christ) dies our death, and inasmuch as He dies, He brings sin to its death and does not allow us any more to die our godless, destructive death, but takes us with Him into his own death. This takes place in baptism: it is the appropriation of the redeeming death of Christ' (ThBl 17, 50). 'The death that the baptized and Christ die is only one, i.e. the death of Christ himself, and precisely this death takes place through the baptism of the believer' (ThBl 18, 235). Further cf. K. H. Schelkle, 'Taufe und Tod'. On the exegesis of Rom. vi. 1–11, *Vom christlichen Mysterium* (Gedenkschrift für O. Casel), Düsseldorf 1951, 9–21, especially 10: 'In baptism the concern of each man with the cross is brought to actuality and he is drawn into the death and resurrection of Christ'; similarly Ph. Seidensticker, *Lebendiges Opfer* (Röm. xii. 1) (NtlAbh XX, 1–3), Münster i. W. 1954, 240f.

[47] Op. cit. 59.

[48] *Bibl. Theol.* 244f.

[49] Op. cit. 245.

this way the *sacramental* dying etc. with Christ is not feasible. In Weinel a reversion is possible, but in the Pauline texts the historically rooted Christ event always maintains its primary and immovable place. Paul never says that Christ is killed, buried or raised *with us*, but always that we are crucified and raised *with Christ.*

The mystical exegesis of Schneider's also does not deal with the heart of the sacramental texts.

Schneider first of all rightly objects to an unsatisfactory doctrinaire exegesis which weakens the texts as follows: 'to suffer, *as it were*, the death of Christ oneself'; '*as if*, because of ours ins, we had suffered death as the punishment of our sins', etc.[50] Against that Schneider contends for the mystical interpretation of βαπτίζειν εἰς Χριστόν (on this see above § 4), and he describes the mystical fellowship of death with Christ in baptism: 'Baptism is not only an immersion into the death of Christ, but through baptism into death a burial with Christ takes place. The grave of Christ and baptism come together in the mystical experience as a contemporaneous event.'[51]

Whereas Hahn thought in terms of a *metaphysical* 'contemporaneity', here a *mystical* contemporaneity is in mind. Paul, however, gives no indication that the sacrament has to do with a 'mystical experience'. Any 'mystical temperature' is lacking; not a word is to be found in the 'I'-style, as in the mysticism of suffering. The sacrament is a salvation-event for all Christians. The mystical experience of fellowship with Christ in death and resurrection with Him can be associated with it, but that does not form the kernel of the objective, sacramental event.[52]

Something different is intended by the language of many exegetes, especially Catholic, who characterize the close *Pneuma*-union of the baptized with Christ as 'mystical'. By that is meant an objective and factual condition. The expression 'mystical', however, can easily be misleading.

In conclusion we may say: the basic idea of the sacramental dying and rising with Christ depends on the conception, peculiar to Paul yet explicable on the basis of Jewish presuppositions, that Christ represented

[50] Op. cit. 40.

[51] Op. cit. 42f. Cf. also J. Schneider, *Die Taufe im N.T.* 45: 'Our death in baptism and the death of Christ become one in the sense of mystical contemporaneity.' Nevertheless Schneider would now understand that more in the sense of the Mystery teaching of O. Casel and V. Warnach, cf. *ThW* V, 194f.

[52] Cf. Bornkamm, ThBl 17, 50: 'It is not to be understood in a mystical way; it is grounded in the event of his own death, and the change that commences in baptism and in faith possesses the character of an historical and eschatological relation between Christ and the believer.'

us as the second Adam and as our Representative took death on himself and attained to resurrection for our sake. When we join ourselves in faith to the new Founder of the race and in baptism become members of the 'Body of Christ', we gain a share in his death and resurrection and step with Him from death to life. This event of grace and sacrament then becomes a task for moral effort on our part (death for sin, life for God) and a rule for our entire Christian existence; in the discipleship of suffering we are to become mystically conformed to his likeness, that at the last we might attain to the eschatological resurrection and so possess in fulness the form and being of the glorified Lord. 'Death and resurrection with Christ' therefore, becomes a basic conception for the whole Pauline theology; its formulation is the original work of the Apostle.

§22. THE SACRAMENTAL DYING AND RISING WITH CHRIST AS UNION WITH THE *Pneuma*-CHRIST

That Paul can look on Christ at one and the same time as an historic Figure and present Power, as the Messiah who died and rose and as the ever living Lord, is based on the fact that he knows that the Lord moved into a *Pneuma*-existence after his resurrection, a fact which accorded equally with his corporeality. Because the Lord is πνεῦμα (2 Cor. iii. 17) He can, without losing his nature as a concrete, historical person, enter upon an intimate fellowship with one who believes on Him, grow with him to a unity unimaginably close, and nevertheless not impugn his own personal nature nor yet that of the believer. To this end it is necessary that the believer also gain a share in the *Pneuma*-existence, in order that the Lord and he may be united. Therefore the idea of the *Pneuma*, as the place for meeting Christ and the subjective attainment of salvation, is of fundamental importance for baptism. Only if a man is filled with *Pneuma* in the sacramental salvation-event is the union of the baptized with Christ possible, and that union is described as an abiding and inward fellowship (especially Gal. ii. 20).

This significance of the *Pneuma* for the Pauline 'Christ-mysticism' is today generally admitted;[53] only discussion is still vigorous as to the nature of the Spirit, the origin and development of this conception in Paul, the personality of the *Pneuma*, and his relation to the person of

[53] P. Gächter, 'Zum Pneuma-Begriff des hl. Paulus,' *ZKTh* 53 (1929) 345–408, takes a quite different way in connection with the *Pneuma*-concept: he sets out from the triadic statements, whose number he extends as far as possible, and sees in them the revelation of the Trinity. He himself, however, perceives the difficulty of coming to terms on this view with passages in which πνεῦμα appears alongside δύναμις, and others where πνεῦμα appears in opposition to σάρξ and γράμμα (403). Against this cf. Bertrams, op. cit. 28–76; Wikenhauser, *Christusmystik*, 48–56; F. Hermann, *Kyrios und Pneuma*.

Christ. For us, however, the special question arises whether Paul connects the impartation of the *Pneuma* with the salvation-event in baptism, as it is described in Rom. vi. That baptism in itself mediates the Spirit is, according to 1 Cor. xii. 13, not to be doubted. But why do we not find ἐν πνεύματι in association with συνετάφημεν etc.?

First, in considering 1 Cor. xii. 13 it should be observed that the mention of the Spirit in this passage has a special meaning (cf. above § 5); a like reason is not present in Rom. vi. Moreover the *Pneuma* foundation of the whole process can be perceived in another way, namely through the ζωή-concept. Certainly in Rom. vi all the emphasis falls on the ethical *walk* in life, corresponding to the practical tendency of the passage; nevertheless in *v.* 5 ἀναστάσεως hints of something more than an ethically transformed life. The resurrection of Christ was a transformation affecting his very being, and we should participate precisely in that. In *v.* 4 the expression ἐν καινότητι ζωῆς bears a character of transition: it has in view especially the outworking of the new life in the ethical shaping of existence, but it presupposes the new divine life as a reality affecting one's very being. In *v.* 5 some quite general statements are made, on the basis of our union with Christ, concerning the passage from death to life, from dying with Christ to rising with Christ. But *v.* 8 speaks very plainly: συζήσομεν certainly does not merely signify a present 'life with' Christ, the future denoting a logical consequence; it includes the future perfect possession of life. This 'life', however, is not the earthly, natural life; to Paul it is the *Pneuma*-life, that one day will be manifested ἐν δόξῃ (Col. iii. 4). In *v.* 11 the ethical and practical point of view again stands in the foreground.

In our passage, therefore, the fact of the possession of the *Pneuma*-life is only apparently concealed. It is perverse to set forth the alternatives: Paul interprets the sacramental effects as *either* purely ethical *or* purely ontological.[54] In reality he looks on both as indissolubly one, since the divine life is bestowed in a manner affecting the being of the believer and carries in itself (without affecting the free decision of the man) a tendency and bent to transform the walk of the Christian in accordance with the will of God.

Two chapters later Paul expounds this in connection with the concept of the *Pneuma*. In Rom. viii. 12–14 the connection between ζωή and πνεῦμα is also made indubitable: Christians really 'live', i.e. continually and in the full sense, only when 'in the Spirit' they put to death the

[54] E. Sokolowsky, *Die Begriffe Geist und Leben bei Paulus*, Göttingen 1903, especially 40–79' interprets the possession of life one-sidedly as ethical only; cf. H. J. Holtzmann, *Theol.* II, 163ff. Contra Bertrams, op. cit. 54–60; 91–95.

works of the flesh (*v.* 13b). To live after the flesh is not genuine 'life', as Paul understands it, namely life from the fulness of the divine life; life after the flesh passes away, and it leads to death (*v.* 13a). But the Spirit, who lives in the Christian (*v.* 11), drives (*v.* 14) and urges him on to 'walk in the Spirit', as Gal. v. 16–18, 22–23 describes in greater detail. For Paul, therefore, to 'walk in newness of life' (Rom. vi. 4) and to 'walk in the Spirit' (Gal. vi. 16) are synonymous, and the ethical outlook has its basis in the Christian's possession of life or Spirit. In Rom. vi the Apostle speaks of 'life', instead of 'Spirit', because it fits more exactly the idea of resurrection (and 'death'), whereas in Gal. v he is concerned to oppose the 'walk in the flesh' by the 'walk in the Spirit'.

Since in Rom. vi 'life' appears as a condition or element of salvation, it is needful to take into consideration the *impersonal Pneuma*-power. The expression ζῶντας in *v.* 11 is especially worthy of note; if it were desired to reproduce it in terms corresponding to πνεῦμα, we should have to write ἐν πνεύματι ὄντας (cf. Rom. viii. 9).

We now have to face the question as to the role played by the *Pneuma* in the process of dying and rising with Christ. Is the πνεῦμα first imparted, the salvation-event then taking place ἐν πνεύματι, or is the baptized person first drawn into this process and because of it gains the possession of the Spirit? Or, as a third possibility, is the receiving of the Spirit a parallel event to the dying with Christ?

> It is difficult to gain any clear impression about this from Casel. He writes, 'The *Pneuma* of Christ or, more exactly, the *Pneuma*-Lord, is present in the mysteries, and through them He is continually at hand and active in the Church.'[55] 'This *Pneuma*-presence of Christ, however, stands in closest relation to his historical act of salvation; it makes the latter present in a *Pneuma*-fashion and conveys its fruits of grace to the Church.'[56] The difficulty lies in Casel's conception of 'presence in the mysteries'. It is hard to imagine how the historical act of salvation becomes present in a *Pneuma*-fashion. A more exact definition as to how the Christian comes into possession of the *Pneuma* is not suggested.

Since the Spirit and life belong together, it must be concluded that the baptized person first gains the Spirit when he is 'made alive' with Christ, i.e. in his resurrection with Christ. On the other hand the *entire* process of dying etc. with Christ takes place on a plane that belongs to the *Pneuma*-sphere: it is the *Pneuma*-Lord who meets the baptized man. It is the same problem that appears in the juxtaposition of ἐν Χριστῷ

[55] In *JLW* 8 (1928) 162. [56] Op. cit. 163.

and σὺν Χριστῷ (Col. ii. 12; Eph. ii. 6). The formula σὺν Χριστῷ describes the sacramental procuring of salvation, the formula ἐν Χριστῷ the perpetual fellowship of Christ. In Col. ii. 12 it is written, 'In Him (Christ) you have also been raised with Him ...'. But the Christ-life and fellowship of Christ should be obtained through being raised with Him! In Col. ii ἐν Χριστῷ (ἐν ᾧ) plays a leading role in the whole passage: 'in Him' the entire fulness of the Godhead dwells (*v.* 9), 'in Him' Christians have attained to fulness (*v.* 10), 'in Him' they have been circumcised (*v.* 11), 'in Him' they have also risen from the dead (*v.* 12). *Christ is, as it were, a sphere in which all this has become possible*, including being buried with Him in baptism (*v.* 12a)[57] and rising with Him in faith (and in baptism—*v.* 12b).

The explanation concerning the *Pneuma* could lie in a similar direction. In a wider sense the whole process of dying etc. with Christ takes place in the sphere of the *Pneuma*: Christ is buried and rises 'with' the baptized, and actually lives only as the exalted *Pneuma*-Lord (*v.* 10b). This *Pneuma*-Christ also draws the baptized to himself and imparts his *Pneuma* to him. The process of dying etc. with Christ, in so far as it takes its rise from God and brings the baptized into relation with the *Pneuma*-Lord, is to be characterized as 'pneumatic'—borne by the *Pneuma*. But in a narrower sense the result of this sacramental event is the possession of the Spirit by the baptized.[58] Under no circumstances can it be maintained that the Spirit is first bestowed, and the dying etc. with Christ then takes place by this possession of the Spirit. Rather, in so far as the process is the gift of salvation, it is *parallel* with the bestowal of the Spirit. In each case the sacramental event is described from a different viewpoint. But the dying etc. with Christ is possible only on the ground that Christ is πνεῦμα ζωοποιοῦν (1 Cor. xv. 45) and unites the baptized with himself through the same.

A certain tension exists between the process of dying etc. σὺν Χριστῷ, that takes place in individual phases, and the acquisition of the Spirit, conceived of as a single act. But Paul also considers the entire event of dying and rising with Christ to be a unified and indivisible whole. Manifestly it lies far from his purpose to convey the impression that 'first' a death for sin takes place in immersion, in being buried with

[57] Lohmeyer (ad loc p. 111) thinks that Paul could never say of baptism that it takes place 'in Him' (Christ). He relates the 'Christ-circumcision' to the sacrifice on the cross; but συνταφέντες is *also* independent of ἐν ᾧ. Lohmeyer would escape the difficulty if he understood ἐν ᾧ in a removed sense. Dibelius groups the various saving deeds together: ' "In Him" three things are gained: circumcision, the gift of life and liberation from the powers of darkness (ii. 11, 12b, 15).'

[58] The reserve of Büchsel (*Geist Gottes* 426f) with regard to the reception of the Spirit in baptism is unjustifiable for Paul.

Christ, and 'then' life is gained. To him both belong together; he only emphasizes these two stages with regard to the single Christ event (death-resurrection) and the double effect for the baptized (death for sin—life for God).

Further, in other passages incorporation into the 'Body of Christ' takes place through the *Pneuma* (1 Cor. xii. 13), but on the other hand the *Pneuma* is also considered as a gift (Tit. iii. 6; cf. Rom. v. 5) or as 'earnest money' (Eph. i. 14; 2 Cor. i. 22; v. 5).

Finally, to understand the connection between dying etc. with Christ and the impartation of the Spirit, a word should be said on the connection between resurrection and the possession of the Spirit. The exalted Lord Himself is a *Pneuma*-being only after his resurrection (Rom. i. 4; 1 Tim. iii. 16), and from that time He imparts the *Pneuma* to others.[59] It is significant that they who believe in Him also attain to a 'resurrection' that puts them in possession of the Spirit. This 'life in Christ' (Rom. viii. 9) admittedly is not yet the glorified mode of being that the risen Lord possesses. For the present, Christians still remain in the earthly existence (cf. Gal. ii. 20b), in 'this aeon' (cf. 1 Cor. iii. 18; vii. 29ff); but through the *Pneuma* that dwells in them they will also attain to the resurrection of the body at the end (Rom. viii. 11) and be given to share the likeness of the glorified Christ (Rom. viii. 29; 1 Cor. xv. 49; Phil. iii. 21).

§23. THE SACRAMENTAL DYING ETC. WITH CHRIST AS THE WORK OF GOD ON MAN

For the understanding of the sacramental salvation-event that Paul describes as a dying and rising with Christ, it is important to bear in mind that God is always considered as its Author. This fact comes to expression in a twofold manner in the texts:

(a) Through passive expressions:

συνετάφημεν Rom. vi. 4	συνταφέντες Col. ii. 12a
σύμφυτοι γεγόναμεν Rom. vi. 5	συνηγέρθητε Col. ii. 12b
συνεσταυρώθη Rom. vi. 6	συνηγέρθητε Col. iii. 1

cf. also the non-sacramental sayings:

συνεσταύρωμαι Gal. ii. 19

[59] Neither the pre-existent nor the historic Christ was a 'Spirit-being' in this sense, cf. Prat, *Théol.* II, 353; Wikenhauser, *Christusmystik* 53. In his messianic work Jesus was *in possession of* the Spirit, cf. Mk. i. 10, 12 par; Lk. iv. 18. 21; Mt. xii. 28, but He did not yet possess the *mode of being* of πνεῦμα and δόξα. Only after the resurrection does He also give the πνεῦμα, cf. Jn. vii. 39; xx. 22. Cf. further Feine, *Théol.* 262; Deissner, *Auferstehungshoffnung* 40ff; Schweitzer, *Mystik* 163–5; Hahn, op. cit. 115f; I. Hermann, op. cit. 61–63, 143f; H. D. Wendland, Das Wirken des Heiligen Geistes in den Gläubigen nach Paulus, *ThLZ* (1952), cols 457–70; E. Schweizer in *ThW* VI 417, 1–9.

ἐσταύρωται Gal. vi. 14
συμμορφιζόμενος Phil. iii. 10

(b) Through active expressions that have God as subject:

συνεζωοποίησεν Eph. ii. 5 } God's action yet more particularly underscored through χάριτί
συνήγειρεν Eph. ii. 6 } ἐστε σεσωσμένοι Eph. ii. 5
συνεκάθισεν Eph. ii. 6 }
συνεζωοποίησεν Col. ii. 16—cf. χαρισάμενος Eph. ii. 5

With these are to be classed expressions that are neutral in themselves but in the context imply the passivity of the human attitude:

ἀπεθάνομεν σὺν Χριστῷ Rom. vi. 8
cf. νεκροὺς τῇ ἁμαρτίᾳ Rom. vi. 11
ἀπεθάνετε σὺν Χριστῷ Col. ii. 20
ἀπεθάνετε Col. iii. 3

By contrast συναπεθάνομεν 2. Tim. ii. 11 is not sacramental, as the parallel expression ὑπομένομεν *v*. 12 shows; it contains an active moment, in so far as the moral power of perseverance and endurance is in prospect.

Where the sacramental view passes over into the ethical, as in Rom. vi. 4 (περιπατήσωμεν); vi. 12–14; Col. iii. 1–2, 5, active expressions naturally are found. In Gal. v. 24 σταυροῦν is also to be interpreted as having an ethical significance. The mystical and eschatological statements do not fall to be considered here.

We may conclude, therefore, that the sacramental dying etc. with Christ is described throughout as the work of God that a man suffers to be done on himself. We can, however—and this is significant for the idea of dying etc. with Christ—take a step further back and find the same form of expression used in relation to the Christ event. In Paul, of course, the resurrection of Jesus is always described as an activity of the Father, so this mode of expression in the sacramental texts about dying etc. with Christ would not portend anything special.[60] But in Rom. vi. 4 Paul expressly adds διὰ τῆς δόξης τοῦ πατρός. The power and glory of the Father are revealed in the resurrection of Jesus. This mighty working of God continues its action on men in the sacramental salvation-event, so that in this respect also the Christ event and baptism share a common feature. The addition in Col. ii. 12, accordingly, is not without significance, that we were raised with Christ 'through faith in the power of God, who raised Him (Jesus) from the dead'. The inclusion in the Christ event and conformation to the likeness of Christ go back to God Himself. This whole gracious and miraculous event is to be understood

[60] The intransitive ἀνέστη 1 Thess. iv. 14; Rom. xiv. 9 v. l. can also stand for the passive, cf. Polyc. ix. 2 ὑπὸ θεοῦ ἀναστάντα.

solely as a work of God and therefore to be apprehended only by faith. The object of this faith is nothing other than receiving God's action for our salvation in Christ. In the resurrection of Christ God has made 'visible' his power to call the dead to life (Rom. iv. 17) and caused it to abound for our blessing (Rom. iv. 24f).

The Letter to the Ephesians is rooted in this theocentric view. Paul cannot sufficiently emphasize God's will to save and his saving work in our being 'made alive together with Christ' (cf. ii. 4, 5, 7, 8). This placing of all emphasis on God's action, however, similarly applies to Christ's resurrection and exaltation. The author describes the resurrection of Christ as God's mighty deed by expressions that tumble over one another and are heaped high (i. 19f).

What consequences then, are to be drawn from this stressing of the action of God in the sacramental salvation-event?

1. The difference from the Mystery cults again comes to the fore. Admittedly, a certain passivity is demanded of the initiate in these cults also: he must let the manifold rites of consecration be performed on him. But at the same time he is in strong measure actively participant with all his powers of soul. Lucretius, at his consecration into the Isis Mysteries, describes the wandering through the kingdom of the dead and the world of the lower and upper gods by means of active expressions; it is above all a beholding.[61] The *mystes* is exposed to the terrors of death and must learn to overcome them.[62] In Christian baptism something fundamentally different takes place; it is a supernatural event, effected by God, and to its essential nature the baptized can add nothing. The chief means of the Mysteries was ecstasy, and to induce this many natural means were applied.

Cumont describes it as follows: 'They produce this ecstasy either through the nervous exhaustion that follows continuous mortifications and strenuous contemplation, or by material means; e.g. the priests of the "Great Mother" (= Cybele) resorted to dances that caused dizziness, exciting music, or even to taking alcoholic drinks after long abstention.'[63]

Consonant with this the priests (mystagogues) play a great role in the oriental cults. They import meaning into the rites, apply the various material means, and in the dramatic performances dress up and act out pantomimes. We hear nothing of all this human activity in Paul. Certainly it is presupposed, in distinction to Jewish baptisms, that an administrator of baptism is present to carry it out; but as the Acts shows

[61] Apuleius, *Metam.* XI, 23 (Turchi, Fontes 209. 8–12); cf. Dibelius, *Die Isisweihe bei Apuleius* 25.
[62] Dibelius, *Isisweihe* 27; Wendland, *Die orientalischen Religionen* 45.
[63] *Die orient. Relig.* 27.

that others besides Apostles baptized (e.g. Philip, viii. 12, 13, 16, 38), so Paul sees no Apostolic reservation at this point (1 Cor. i. 17). In Christian baptism the decisive thing is not what man does but what God does.

2. The sacrament, therefore, is apprehended as really constituting a saving event for man. It is a soteriological occurrence that applies to the individual God's universal work of salvation, his cosmic act of reconciliation (2 Cor. v. 19; Col. i. 20). The order in which Paul describes the cosmic and sacramental salvation-event, whether as a reconciliation with mankind first and then with the individual (cf. Rom. v with vi) or in the reverse order (cf. Col. ii. 11–13a with 13b–15), is irrelevant in this connection.

Something of God's creative, indeed, new-creation activity is manifested in this. Where God is at work a new thing happens (2 Cor. v. 17). There is a constant connection between God's cosmic act of reconciliation in Christ and the awakening of the individual to a new life (Rom. vi. 4). An unbroken series of divine acts takes place from God's elective decree to justification and glorification (Rom. viii. 28–30). The way which we men have to tread is marked out beforehand in Christ. The 'image' to which we are led by God is that of his Son in the glory of the resurrection. God joins us to Him.

3. Accordingly, sacramental magic is excluded. The sacraments are and remain means of salvation in the hand of God. He avails Himself of them to fulfil his saving work on us. The believing man suffers himself to be seized by God, to be immersed in the water and filled with his *Pneuma*. That this may be represented as a dying and rising with Christ is a particular point of view that remains subordinate to the dominant one of bestowal of salvation by God. In this supernatural, theocentric view, dying etc. with Christ loses all title to being a mystical-magical transaction. Since God's gifts are always at the same time tasks laid upon us, great obligations grow from the sacramental event, namely of holding firmly the peace with God that has been made and of preserving the life of God in the service for God yielded in our earthly walk (Rom. vi. 13).

4. Nevertheless man is no dead puppet object of the divine work of salvation. Faith and co-operation are necessary. As Christ had to utter an obedient 'Yes' to his dying, so man must render the obedience of faith, i.e. to do in faith everything that is demanded of him. But God effects the salvation entirely. 'You are saved through grace.' The hope of final salvation is built on this foundation and is made all the more certain through God's work of salvation that already has been begun

(Rom. v. 1–11). The revelation of the glory of the Risen Lord to his brethren on earth is still awaited; but it lies in the plan of divine action that God at the last will crown the process of dying etc. with Christ through our glorification with Him (cf. Rom. viii. 17; Col. iii. 4).

Thus in the sacramental salvation-event, as Paul represents it, a wonderful harmony with God's general work of salvation is revealed, a continuation of that saving work that He began with the sending of his Son.

EXCURSUS—THE ORIGIN OF THE FORMULA σὺν Χριστῷ

I. *Passages relating to the Future (Lohmeyer's view)*

Along with the interpretation of Paul's intention in employing expressions relative to dying and rising with Christ, the question as to how he came to use the formula σὺν Χριστῷ is of interest. E. Lohmeyer, in investigating this problem of origin, endeavours to come to grips with the Pauline conception that lies behind all these statements.[64] Starting from Diessmann's discussion of the formula ἐν Χριστῷ he puts under the microscope the formal expression σὺν Χριστῷ, which occurs only twelve times in Paul.[65] After dealing with it briefly and in all the essential connections (218–34), he enquires after its origin and comes at once to the negative conclusion: a comparable view to this is found neither in the Greek translation of the Old Testament (224–6), nor in the field of Greek language and literature (226–9). Greek writings, it is true, offer a fulness of testimonies for σὺν θεῷ or θεοῖς; but the essential idea is different from the Pauline. 'The Pauline formula "with Christ" appears to be solitary and to stand without clear historical connection. It cannot be derived from an original tradition of Israelite religion, nor from Greek or Hellenistic religion, even if its application may perchance have been influenced by the expression σὺν θεῷ' (229).

On the other hand Lohmeyer thinks that where it does appear in Paul its meaning is assumed to be known, and in 1 Thess. iv. 17 it is perhaps dependent on the traditional wording of a Dominical saying (229). The idiom presupposes a definite Christology: Christ was a divine Being, who descended from heaven to earth to undergo the span of an earthly life, and after the end of this life was exalted again to God (230). As a positive linguistic connecting link Lohmeyer examines the phrase οἱ σὺν Ἰησοῦ ὄντες and others approximating to it (e.g. Mk. ii. 26; Lk. v. 9; viii. 15; ix. 32; xxii. 56; Acts iv. 13; they do not appear in Mt. and Jn.).

[64] Σὺν Χριστῷ, 218–57. In the text the page numbers of the book are added in brackets.

[65] Rom. vi. 8; viii. 32; 2 Cor. iv. 14; xiii. 4; Phil. i. 23; Col. ii. 13, 20; iii. 3, 4; 1 Thess. iv. 14, 17; v. 10. Rom. viii. 32 ('with Christ God will lavish all his gifts on us') is a special use and does not belong to the context of this view.

'But the sense of this designation is here purely historical; it connotes being together in time and space, not beyond all times and places' (231). Lohmeyer also adduces expressions with μετά which avoid 'the solemnity of the preposition σύν' (232), e.g. the saying of Jesus to the penitent thief: 'Today you will be with me in Paradise' (Lk. xxiii. 43). Actually it is more suitable here, because it speaks of the continuation of an historical association in a transfigured living σὺν Χριστῷ. But this also, in his view, does not explain the peculiar formula he is investigating. On the contrary, he believes that the formula (μετὰ Χριστοῦ) is to be encountered with a variety of significance in the Revelation of John (233). Lohmeyer pursues this tradition farther back into the Apocalyptic-Gnostic literature (234ff), and he sees the view that underlies it clearly reflected in the proclamation of Zarathustra and its development in the Avestas (239); its origin, therefore, is not in Hellenistic mysticism but in Iranian and Jewish apocalyptic. To this end he cites especially the Book of Enoch (241–5). Many Synoptic, and above all Johannine, sayings become comprehensible in its light (245ff). This eschatological 'being-with-the-Lord' is linked in all the testimonies with the figure of the 'Son of Man' (246). Lohmeyer finds a particular contact with the martyr's yearning to attain to fellowship with the Lord, especially in Phil. i. 23 (247). A primitive Christian tradition lies here, 'the elements of which have been prepared for in the apocalyptic of late Judaism, developed under Iranian influence. The Johannine Seer still stands firmly rooted in it, while Paul reflects it only occasionally' (248).

Against this hypothesis Hahn has offered the criticism that μετά nowhere relates to the Christ event; on the other hand a like relation of σύν in connection with the verbs ἀναιρεθῆναι and ἀποθανεῖν, which manifestly comes close to Paul's utterances, is known to the Synoptics. Accordingly we have no right to gloss lightly over the Synoptic σύν.[66]

Hahn provides an important hint in this criticism. But he does not observe that Paul himself does not connect the formula σὺν Χριστῷ with Christ's death and resurrection in *any* passage; the Apostle uses it in a transcendent sense, and in a certain way it does permit comparison with passages in the Book of Revelation;[67] this transcendent 'being-with-Christ' is seen in 1 Thess. iv. 17b; Phil. i. 23; Col. iii. 3. A reminiscence of the Synoptic expression, 'those with Jesus',[68] could plausibly be

[66] Op. cit. 94.

[67] Rev. iii. 4, 20, 21; xvii. 14; xx. 4, 6 (cf. also Rev. xxi. 3 ter).

[68] (Mk. ii. 26, not from Jesus); Lk. v. 9; viii. 1, 38, 45 (only individual mss.); ix. 32; xxii. 14, 56; (xxiv. 24 not from Jesus); xxiv. 29 (33 not from Jesus), 44. But cf. also in Mt. and Mk the phrase μετ' αὐτοῦ, e.g. Mt. xxvi. 18, 20, 23, 29 (table fellowship), 51, 69, 71; xxviii. 20; Mk. iii. 14; in Lk. xxiv. 29 μετά and σύν can still be exchanged.

acknowledged in 1 Thess. v. 10; but perhaps also there is a bridge leading to the eschatological fellowship, 1 Thess. iv. 17.

It may well be that these passages should be associated with the tradition recognized by Lohmeyer; preponderately they have in view the eschatological condition (εἶναι) or the transcendental life 'with Christ' after the death of the individual (Phil. i. 23). The statements that give expression to the beginning of this eschatological fellowship are related to them: God will bring us to life 'with Christ' (1 Thess. iv. 14); we shall be manifested in glory 'with him' (Col. iii. 4), though in this last place another tendency is already perceptible. In the Book of Revelation the abiding heavenly fellowship of life with Christ is represented in the formula μετὰ Χριστοῦ (iii. 20), or as fellowship in sovereignty (iii. 21; xx. 4, 6).

J. Dupont has investigated in a monograph the passages which treat of our future life 'with Christ'.[69] He confirms the conclusion of Lohmeyer, that the formula does not derive from Hellenism, but rather is to be explained from Jewish and Christian apocalyptic. Especially noteworthy is his thesis that behind 1 Tim. ii. 11f, as indeed Tit. iii. 4–8, stand Christian hymns and catechetical traditions that Paul found and took over. The formulation 'to die with Christ, in order to live with him', however, goes back to Paul himself.[70] Dupont holds that the eschatological prospect of our 'living and reigning with Christ' is primary, and that the baptismal sayings are derived from it. Unfortunately he has not yet published the second part of his research, which will deal with the statements that have to do with the present.

II. *Statements Relating to the Present*

Passages which speak of a present dying etc. with Christ must be considered as a group by themselves. The baptismal affirmations, like Rom. vi. 4, 5, 6, 8; Col. ii. 13, 20, are characteristic for these passages, but those like Rom. viii. 17; Phil. iii. 10; Eph. ii. 5f; 2 Tim. ii. 11f should also be noticed. 2 Cor. xiii. 4 includes the idea of 'life with Christ' while here on earth—influenced evidently by the conception of dying etc. with Christ.[71] The same view has also affected the eschatological passages 1 Thess. iv. 14; v. 10; 2 Cor. iv. 14; Col. iii. 4. Nevertheless there is no trace in the Book of Revelation of this conception of dying etc. with Christ, which is so prominent in Paul. Because the Pauline sayings hark

[69] J. Dupont, Σὺν Χριστῷ. *L'union avec le Christ suivant saint Paul I*: '*Avec le Christ' dans la vie future*, Bruges 1952.

[70] J. Dupont, op. cit. 107–10.

[71] In itself a relation to the eschatological future, as in 2 Cor. iv. 14, is not to be excluded: 'nevertheless the addition εἰς ὑμᾶς makes the relation to the present certain' (Windisch ad loc).

back to the historical Christ event, the relation can never be reversed; yet in Rev. iii. 20 we read: δειπνήσω μετ' αὐτοῦ καὶ αὐτὸς μετ' ἐμοῦ. Possibly the writer's thinking about the Lord's Supper has produced an after effect; but the immediate reference is to a meal that fulfils it in the next world, not the 'sacrament'. The characteristic dying etc. with Christ in *baptism* is nowhere mentioned or evaluated in the Book of Revelation.

This relation of the formula σὺν Χριστῷ to the *sacrament* is perhaps the weakest spot in Lohmeyer's hypothesis. Certainly, sacramental experience and eschatological hope belong together (253); 'life with Christ' in the consummation of the times is the fulfilment of the 'resurrection with Christ' that is indicated in the sacrament (and to a certain extent already realized in it). Meanwhile the eschatological formula does not shed any light on the double significance of *dying* and rising with Christ that is of the essence of the sacrament. With regard to bodily death, 1 Thess. iv. 14 significantly states not κοιμηθέντες σὺν τῷ 'Ιησοῦ but διὰ τοῦ 'Ιησοῦ. The formula σὺν Χριστῷ therefore does not allow a backward projection from eschatology to the sacramental plane.

Numerically the texts that speak of dying etc. with Christ occupy the leading place, whether they have in view a sacramental, ethical or mystical relation. The passages in which the formula σὺν Χριστῷ occurs are as follows: Rom. vi. 8; 2 Cor. xiii. 4; Col. ii. 13, 20; (iii. 3). But to these, which have been selected only because of the formal occurrence in them of σὺν Χριστῷ, a rich material must be added, wherein the σύν is combined with the verb.

> Lohmeyer has paid too little attention to this material. He remarks on it: 'The statistics that we have brought forward could be increased thereby to the extent of a few examples, but they would not actually involve any change.'[72] He freely observes[73] that the circle of thought can be 'made complete only by the conception of being "crucified with Christ" and "buried with Christ"'. But this fact deserves to be noted, because it falls outside the eschatological framework.

In view of its extent this material deserves our urgent attention.[74] Of the many compounds with σύν those ought to be eliminated that do not relate to the union between Christ and the Christian, such as συναθλεῖν (Phil. i. 27; iv. 3), συναναμίγνυσθαι (1 Cor. v. 9, 11; 2 Thess. iii. 14),

[72] Op. cit. 220.
[73] Ibid., n. 1.
[74] It has been assembled by F. Prat, *Théol.* I. 21. From his list o–s should be excluded; cf. further in the text.

συνεσθίειν (1 Cor. v. 11; Gal. ii. 12) etc.; those too, (against Prat) which admittedly have a relation to Christ but demand as the immediate complement of σύν not Christ, but Christians in Christ; see the compounds in Eph. ii. 22; iii. 6. In Eph. ii. 21 and iv. 16 also the σύν serves only to strengthen the verb.

The following occurrences then remain over:

συμπάσχειν Rom. viii. 17
συναποθνῄσκειν 2 Tim. ii. 11
συσταυροῦσθαι Rom. vi. 6; Gal. ii. 19
συνθάπτεσθαι Rom. vi. 4; Col. ii. 12
συνεγείρειν and pass. Eph. ii. 6; Col. ii. 12; iii. 1
συζωοποιεῖν Eph. ii. 5; Col. ii. 13
σνζῆν Rom. vi. 8; 2 Tim. ii. 11
συγκαθίζειν Eph. ii. 6
συνδοξάζεσθαι Rom. viii. 17
συμβασιλεύειν 2 Tim. ii. 12
συγκληρονόμος Rom. viii. 17
συμμορφίζεσθαι Phil. iii. 10
σύμμορφος Rom. viii. 29; Phil. iii. 20
σύμφυτος Rom. vi. 5

We could be tempted to assign one or other of the expressions in this table to the eschatological aspect earlier mentioned, especially συγκληρονόμος or συμβασιλεύειν but the context in all places shows that the leading idea is union with Christ and that which He experienced.

A closer examination of these terms leads to the observation that Paul is using them in a special sense, peculiar to him alone. The following verbs also occur lexicographically in other passages of the New Testament.

συμπάσχειν	1 Cor. xii. 26
συσταυροῦσθαι	Mt. xxvii. 44 = Mk. xv. 32; Jn. xix. 32
συναποθνῄσκειν	Mk. xiv. 31; cf. 2 Cor. vii. 3
συζῆν	2 Cor. vii. 3
συγκαθίζειν	Lk. xxii. 55
συμβασιλεύειν	1 Cor. iv. 8
συγκληρονόμος	Eph. iii. 6; Heb. xi. 9; 1 Pt. iii. 7

The other terms are also to be met in ancient literature with the original literal meaning that σύν suggests (cf. Bauer, *Wörterbuch*); only συζωοποιεῖν is a purely Pauline formation. It is particularly interesting that Paul himself uses this non-specific meaning with συναποθνῄσκειν and συζῆν in 2 Cor. vii. 3. These compounds cannot be found anywhere in ancient literature in the metaphorical (Pauline) sense, not even in the language of the Mysteries and the Hermetic mysticism. They are most closely integrated with the Pauline Christology and soteriology. The suggestion lies to hand, therefore, that they should be regarded as an original Pauline formation.

But how has Paul arrived at this view? Here we cannot advance beyond conjecture. Doubtless his theological guiding principle, as developed in § 21, is fundamental. On the linguistic and formal side the following considerations may perhaps be adduced:

1. Anyone who thinks up a key idea or a favourite conception searches also for an appropriate linguistic form of expression. Exactly that was offered to the Greek-speaking Apostle in the preposition σύν; it possessed a certain air of solemnity in the religious terminology, and it was capable of reproducing both the idea of making like another and temporal and spatial togetherness. 1 Cor. xii. 26 offers a good example of this linguistic possibility in Paul:

'If one member suffers, all the members suffer with it (συμπάσχει); if one member receives honour, all the members rejoice with it (συγχαίρει).'

An organic union is here in mind, a destiny in solidarity. But Christians also stand in a solidary union with Christ, the Founder of the new race to which they belong, and with Him they experience that which He himself went through. Paul could well have formed the σύν-compounds with this consideration in mind, as E. Best clearly sees: 'The formula "with Christ" suggests to us the inclusion of Christians in Christ; what happens to Him—death, resurrection etc.—happens to them; in this they are "solid" with Him.'[75] In distinction to 1 Cor. xii. 26, however, it must be stressed that Christ possesses a peculiar and inexchangeable place, as Founder and Head of the new humanity.

2. A linguistic dependence on Synoptic statements about being crucified with Christ (Mk. xv. 32) and dying with Him (Mk. xiv. 31) is not ruled out, even if the idea itself is raised to another plane. Its application in a similar sense in 2 Cor. vii. 3 tells in favour of this, as also the fact that the Pauline declarations about dying etc. with Christ stand on the solid ground of the historical event (cf. Rom. vi. 6). It is well to observe this also in 2 Cor. iv. 14. There Paul mentions the historical resurrection of Jesus and continues: God will raise up also us—not σὺν Χριστῷ, but σὺν Ἰησοῦ.

3. The original Pauline conception of dying etc. with Christ entered upon a process of blending with the idea of eschatological fellowship of life σὺν Χριστῷ, a process which can still be observed in several places.

[75] *One Body in Christ*, p. 57.

On account of this many nuances manifest themselves under the cover of σὺν Χριστῷ.

1 Thess. v. 10: 'Christ *died* for us that we ... might *live*'. The addition, '(that we might live) *with him*', presupposes that Christ also lives. The unabridged train of thought would therefore be:

'Christ died for us and lives; through his death we also should attain to life, and that to a life *with Him*.

An indication that the statements about dying etc. with Christ are not derived from the eschatological formula of 'life with Christ', but rest on the historical Christ event, and indeed conversely influence the eschatological form of the sayings, is provided by 1 Thess. iv. 14. Ἄξει σὺν αὐτῷ appears to be wholly in the line of tradition: God will bring those who have fallen asleep with Christ at the parousia. But the particular accent in this short sentence is determined by that which precedes it: 'We believe that Jesus died and rose again.' The meaning is 'Those who have fallen asleep in fellowship with Jesus God will (raise from the dead and) bring *together with Him and exactly as Him*'.

In 2 Cor. iv. 14 the connection σὺν Ἰησοῦ ἐγερεῖ shows the strength of the Pauline idea of participation in the destiny of Jesus. There can be no question of a resurrection of Jesus in the eschatological future; but *our* resurrection is described in association with the resurrection of Jesus, which has already happened and influences the mode of expression.

A variety of motives are mingled together in Col. iii. 3–4. Here also the opposition of death and life is undeniable. We died with Christ (iii. 3a; cf. ii. 20), but our life in the glory is hidden 'with Christ' in God. That is transcendentally conceived of, similarly as in Phil. i. 23, since the passage also stands under the contrast of 'below' and 'above' (iii. 1–2). Nevertheless, we participate even now inwardly ('mystically') in the life of the exalted Lord; in *v.* 4 Christ is described as 'our life'. But the glory of the life that will proceed from our dying with Christ is still held in reserve and will first become manifest at the parousia 'with Christ' (an eschatological motif).

Finally, the connection between sayings relating to the present and those that relate to the future is seen in 2 Tim. ii. 11ff. In this context the 'dying with' Christ means above all toil and suffering (cf. *vv.* 1–10), and it leads to 'living with' Christ, even as 'endurance' in hardship and battle leads to 'reigning with' Him. The same thought appears in Rom. viii. 17. The joint 'rule' is an old apocalyptic motif (cf. Dan. vii. 18, 27;

Rev. v. 10; xx. 6; xxii. 5); the Apostle takes it up and sets it forth as a sure hope in virtue of the present 'suffering and dying with Christ'.

Since the influence of the conception of dying etc. with Christ is already observable in 1 Thessalonians, the Apostle must have fashioned this idea very early, even if its maturest expression belongs to the later Paulines. With regard to the σὺν Χριστῷ sayings, however, it emerges from the beginning in effective competition with the old eschatological σὺν Χριστῷ idea that in all probability had come down in the tradition. If, therefore, the formula σὺν Χριστῷ does not show an entirely uniform origin and sphere of use, it merely shares in that respect the fate of the other and much more richly used formula ἐν Χριστῷ.[76] Paul nevertheless is attracted to these quasi-formal coinages, because in their terseness they are suitable means of expressing and holding together his own ideas. It is plain that both formulae have their own sphere of validity. But each formula offers room for varied applications in its own area.

[76] Against the unitary interpretation of Deissmann (*Die ntl. Formel 'in Chr. J.'* 97f) and others, see Mundle, *Das rel. Leben* 73, n. 1; O. Schmitz, op. cit. 240–2; Büchsel, *Geist Gottes* 293; Sommerlath, op. cit. 65–68; Prat, *Théol.* II, 477–9; Oepke in *ThW* II, 537f; Wikenhauser, *Christusmystik* 6–14; Meinertz, *Theologie des N.T.* II, 135f.

CHAPTER THREE

Consequences from the Baptismal Theology of Paul for his Total Theology

§24. THE 'MYSTICAL' AND 'MYSTERY' ELEMENTS IN THE THEOLOGY OF PAUL

I. *Baptism and Personal 'Christ-Mysticism'*

From the second decade of our century the mysticism of Paul has been a focal point of scientific discussion. The debate on how far it is permissible to speak of mysticism in Paul was given a strong impetus through the book on Paul by A. Deissmann ([1]1911), and it has been taken up in ever widening circles. Research by the religious-historical school into the philosophic mysticism of Hellenism and the Mystery religions contributed much to the mystical interpretation of Paul, while the lively interest in mystical questions is partly explained by the trend of the times after the first world war. In the course of the scientific discussion it became apparent how difficult it is to determine the concept of 'mysticism' itself.[1] Nevertheless the expression 'Pauline Christ-mysticism' naturalized itself and several works are devoted to this theme.[2] It was precisely the penetrating examination of the Pauline texts and comparison of them with literature outside Christianity, however, that sharpened the perception of what was characteristic and peculiar in his devotion to Christ, and it increased the number of voices that objected to the inclusion of Paul among the mystics.[3] The present situation may be indicated in the words of M. Dibelius:

> 'It will be understood, therefore, that the theme "Paul and Mysticism" at the present time possesses a validity within theology

[1] Cf. Deissmann in the 2nd edition of his work on Paul (Tübingen 1925) 117–23; further Deissner, *Paulus und die Mystik seiner Zeit* 1–17; H. Korn, *Die Nachwirkungen der Christusmystik des Paulus in den Apostolischen Vätern* (Diss. Berlin), Leipzig 1928; 1–11. From the Catholic standpoint see M. Grabmann, *Wesen und Grundlagen der katholischen Mystik* [2]1924; E. Krebs, *Grundfragen der kirchl. Mystik* 1921.

[2] W. Mundle, *Das religiöse Leben des Paulus* (1923); E. Sommerlath, *Der Ursprung des neuen Lebens nach Paulus* (1923); W. Weber, *Christusmystik* (1924); O. Schmitz, Die *Christusgemeinschaft des Paulus* (1924); E. Wissmann, *Das Verhältnis von ΠΙΣΤΙΣ und Christusfrömmigkeit bei Paulus* (1926); A. Wikenhauser, *Die Christusmystik des hl. Paulus* (1928); A. Schweitzer, *Die Mysiik des Apostels Paulus* (1930).

[3] Deissner (see above n. 1); E. Brunner, *Die Mystik und das Wort* (1924); G. Heinzelmann, *Glaube und Mystik* (1926); H. E. Weber, *Glaube und Mystik* (1927); the same, *Eschatologie und Mystik im N.T.* (1930). Cf. also Dibelius, *Paulus und die Mystik im N.T.* (1930).

only with considerable limitations. Some would not allow the term "mysticism" to be used at all in connection with Paul, others would modify it through additions and speak about "reacting" or "objective" mysticism, of "faith mysticism", or "formative" (in distinction to "deforming") mysticism, and finally of "eschatological" mysticism.'[4]

A major reason for this controversy is that since A. Ritschl Protestant theology has regarded the characteristic feature of mysticism to be the *experience* of becoming one with God, especially in the extraordinary experience of ecstasy.[5] By contrast, Catholic theology sees the essential thing to be the unity itself, so that it can describe the process of becoming united with God in one's being, without any special feelings being involved, as mystical. In this sense almost all Catholic exegetes speak of the mystical or mystical-real union with Christ, and they extend this concept to the union of Christians with each other in Christ. The 'mystical Body of Christ' has become an established concept in present day Catholic theology. Nevertheless, there is a danger in this use of 'mystical', since the term has too much the sound of 'mysterious' for many people, and by its means theologians all too easily excuse themselves the difficult task of defining more exactly the reality that stands behind the Pauline sayings.

Our own concern is not with a description of the Pauline mysticism as such, but with the relation of the sayings that are usually designated as 'mystical' to the baptismal texts. The question at once arises whether the sacramental dying and rising with Christ (Rom. vi. 2–11; Col. ii. 12), 'putting on' Christ (Gal. iii. 27), being 'imbued' with the one Spirit (1 Cor. xii. 13b) and 'rebirth' (Tit. iii. 5) are to be reckoned among the mystical statements. Here a distinction, which has a foundation in the Pauline texts themselves, is necessary. In baptism Paul uses the plural; it belongs by its nature to all believers. The foundational Christian sacrament is administered in the context of worship, or at least it always possesses a 'public' character, and it is related to the community. If it be wished to subsume it under the mystical viewpoint, then it would be necessary to speak rather of 'cult-mysticism'; how far this is justified in Paul will be estimated below (under II). Against it are ranged the non-sacramental texts, or at any rate those that do not expressly link the experience to the sacrament. In these texts Paul prefers to speak in the 'I' style; with all the 'objectivity' that can be affirmed of them, i.e. the validity that applies in principle to all Christians, they yet possess an

[4] *Paulus und die Mystik* 2.
[5] Cf. Wikenhauser, *Christusmystik* 2.

undeniable relation to experience that is not only personal, but original and unique to him. This applies especially to the so-called 'mysticism of suffering',[6] which takes up a considerable space among these utterances. This mysticism, in which the element of experience is much stronger, is called 'personal' mysticism, to distinguish it from other kinds. Among all the Letters of Paul, 2 Corinthians affords the richest mine for it (after which Philippians is most valuable); it is the Letter in which Paul speaks as in no other of his personal sufferings for Christ (xi. 22–33), and that in which, as in no other, he describes his Apostolic life—his toil, disappointments and sorrows, and also his joys and hopes—as the suffering of Christ and the consolation of Christ (i. 3–7), as dying and rising with Christ (iv. 7–18), as being weak and being quickened with Him (xiii. 4). Here it is seen that the mysticism of the Apostle Paul 'in its ultimate depths is a mysticism of the Passion. The κοινωνία τοῦ Χριστοῦ extends to fellowship with his suffering and death. It can be said that this Passion-mysticism is the heart of the Pauline piety.'[7]

It might be anticipated that in Paul sacrament and personal mysticism exist in tension. By its nature mystical experience is something inward, something belonging to the soul. In the hidden sanctuary of the soul there awaken voices and feelings, from which grow the ardour of rapture or the garnered power of suffering and sympathy with the personal Lord. Men of such inner concentration and depth of experience are little inclined to external ceremonies and cultic actions; for this reason a certain disregard for and depreciation of the sacrament appears in Deissmann, to whom this experiential piety and mystical fervour of Paul's surpasses everything.

> He holds that for Paul himself it was not baptism but the Christophany about Damascus that was the decisive thing.[8] 'After the *altissimum* of Damascus follows the normal life in Christ that moves on a steady line of personal experience, but in the times of distress and renewal of consecration it rises again to a passionately intensified communion of prayer with the Saviour.'[9] But for Christians generally it holds good: 'It is God who brings about fellowship with Christ. He takes the initiative in the mystical initiation. Not that every Christian has an experience equal to that of a Damascus hour, but every one who possesses the living Christ or the Spirit has received the gift from God Himself, or is "apprehended" by Christ Himself.' Deissmann then continues, 'The assertion that in Paul baptism is the means of access to Christ, I

[6] Cf. Mundle, op. cit. 78, and the works of Schneider and Wilson.
[7] J. Schneider, op. cit. 12. [8] Paulus 115. [9] Op. cit. 112.

take to be incorrect.... I think it is more correct to say that baptism does not bring about but only sets the seal on the fellowship of Christ.'[10]

Weinel, it is true, considers that in the sacraments we have a way of salvation that equally encompasses the whole of religion as do the other two of faith and mysticism. He characterizes it, in distinction from mysticism, by the assertion that here everything is experienced on the sensuous plane. In itself it has the same result: Christ and the Spirit are received. But he perceives therein a danger for religion: 'Whereas the inwardness of mysticism easily unites with a religion of faith, the introduction of the sacraments to morally weak men signifies a *danger*—the danger of its foundering on the magic of the sacrament.'[11]

> Weinel thinks that this danger was already a burning one in Corinth. These 'Gnostics' denied the resurrection of the body, but they so strongly believed on the sacrament that they had themselves baptized for their dead (1 Cor. xv. 29); and from the sacrament, that works *ex opere operato*, they drew the immoral conclusion, 'everything is allowed', not only with regard to food and drink but also the sexual life (1 Cor. x. 23, viii. 1; vi. 12). In his reply Paul had no other resort than to hark back to the religion of the Law and give that bold exposition of the Exodus narrative, according to which the Israelites at that time had had sacraments. 'Here in Paul appears that fusion of *sacrament and religion of Law* that later stamped Catholicism.' Weinel finally comes to the conclusion that sacraments are a foreign body in the religion of Paul, a remnant of the outworn religious stage of the Mysteries. 'In him mysticism penetrates the whole of life, but the sacrament does not.'

Both in Deissmann and in Weinel the sacrament is brought into a tension with mysticism that is unknown in the Pauline texts. The positive grounds adduced for this tension are not convincing: it is urged that Paul spoke but seldom of the sacraments; in the Letter to the Romans he refers to baptism on a single occasion only (vi. 3ff) and makes no mention of the Lord's Supper; and according to 1 Cor. i. 17 he regarded baptism as unessential. The sacramental texts in Paul, taken in their totality, are nevertheless of considerable weight and cannot be torn out of his proclamation. Even if Rom. vi. 3ff is the single passage that deals with baptism in this major dogmatic Epistle, by its content it is yet of great significance, sufficient to cancel out any far-reaching consequences

[10] Op. cit. 115. [11] *Bibl. Theol.* 249–51.

drawn from 1 Cor. i. 17. It must be granted to Deissmann that the Damascus event brought about Paul's conversion and afterwards decisively influenced his personal piety and also his theology; but for that very reason it is the more remarkable that he never conducted a polemic against the sacraments—at most he opposed a false sacramental piety (1 Cor. x. 1ff).

J. Schneider does more justice to the fact when he characterizes baptism as fellowship with Christ in his death, burial and resurrection—an objective-real event, through which a man is transplanted into the sphere of Christ.[12] The salvation-event in baptism is the foundation for the entire Christ-formed life of the Christian. It is not mystical experience that stands at the beginning of the Christian way, but the act of God's grace in the sacrament; in the further course of his life, however, the Christian has also to experience and realize in a personal manner the 'dying and rising with Christ'. It is, therefore, incorrect to pose the alternatives: mysticism or sacrament; Paul was capable of holding both in unity.

It is possible to go a step farther and affirm: what Paul knew as a very deep personal experience, that once (in the Damascus hour) he was seized by Christ as one that fled from Him (Phil. iii. 12), and what was to *him personally* a thought that ever moved him, a power that strengthened him in suffering, and a motive that spurred him to Apostolic action, *that* he saw as a real possibility and necessity for *all Christians*—first sacramentally through baptism (Rom. vi. 5), then ethically as a task, in a complete death to the power of sin and decisive living for God (Rom. vi. 4, 11), and finally in the personal endurance of suffering (Rom. viii. 17; cf. v. 3f; 2 Tim. ii. 11f; cf. iii. 12). The Apostle never states that the life and suffering of Christians must possess as intensive an *experience* of unity with the Crucified Lord as his own; but the connection of thought in Gal. ii implies that he expects of every Christian that he will live his earthly life as one crucified with Christ and bound most closely with the living Christ, who loved him and gave Himself for him (Gal. ii. 19f). Paul has lifted the conception of dying and rising with Christ from the purely personal realm to possess a general, objective validity, and to be a rule of Christian standing in this era of the world. For this reason the real foundation that baptism creates was important to him. In individual cases Christians could then also experience the fellowship of suffering and resurrection with Christ, even to that mystical ardour that occasionally strikes us in Paul's Letters; but fundamentally this occurrence was loosed from the uncertainty and

[12] *Leidensmystik* 36f.

inconstancy of personal experience and transferred to the plane of objective reality. From the mysticism of experience came the mysticism of being.[13]

This close union of mysticism and sacrament also makes it possible to discover a relation between mysticism and *mission*; to this theme M. Meinertz devotes attention in a lecture.[14] He weighs the motives that proceed from the peculiar kind of Pauline mysticism and that led to his drive for mission, and with this he contrasts the individualistic Hellenistic mysticism. According to a dictum of Reitzenstein, the (Hellenistic) πνευματικός founds θίασοι but not lasting communities, least of all a Church; Paul, however, is the Apostle of the consciousness of unity in and through the Church.[15] The bridge that facilitates this step from personal, mystical and close fellowship with Christ to unity in the Church can be perceived at once, namely baptism (cf. Gal. iii. 27f). It is consonant with this glance at mission and community, its use and construction, that Paul did not highly esteem extraordinary mystical phenomena, like visions and ecstasies (2 Cor. xii. 1–10), and that he sought to put a restraint on exuberant *Pneuma* conditions (1 Cor. xii. 14).

Conversely M. Dibelius explains the limitations which Paul the mystic lays on himself from his call to mission. It seems to him at first sight surprising that a man who had so unusual an inner life, who knows *gnosis*, ecstasy, vision and personal experiences of a mystical kind, could yet with a light heart declare all this to be of secondary importance on the ground that the community or even only the weak brother cannot take a full share in it. He gives the answer from the viewpoint of Paul's missionary thinking: at his conversion Paul had been touched first as a man of religious experience; but that which was revealed to him changed in his consciousness into the demand for mission to the heathen.[16]

Thus in Paul sacrament and mysticism are harmoniously united; that is due to the peculiarity of his mysticism. The factors that limit his mystical experience are different. Dibelius alludes to something of importance when he emphasizes the relation of the Christian faith to the Christ event that has already happened and to the still impending parousia and breaking in of a new world. Nevertheless his statement can be approved only in part.

[13] H. Korn, op. cit. 19, speaks of the completion of individual mysticism through social mysticism. For criticism of works that depreciate the objectivity of the sacrament in favour of mysticism or personal experience, cf. especially the excursus in Mundle, *Glaubensbegriff* 140–9.

[14] 'Mystik und Mission bei Paulus', in *Ztschr. f. Missionswiss.* 13 (1923) pp. 1–12.

[15] Op. cit. 8.

[16] Op. cit. 19.

> 'The consciousness of the redemption that in part has happened and in part is awaited as a consequence of this event is so overpowering that it is *almost irrelevant* as to how the individual appropriates it to himself—whether he inserts himself into this accomplished work by faith or whether he grows together with it in the manner of mysticism—so long as it becomes reality for him and his life.'[17]

Here the recognition is rightly made that for Paul it is not (as in Hellenistic mysticism) the blessed experience of oneness with God within the soul that is the decisive thing, but the actuality of a salvation which supports itself on the historical coming of Christ. But the manner of the appropriation is not unimportant. In order to ensure that the individual gains salvation, a way must be shown that can be taken by all. Such a way is provided in the means of salvation in the sacraments, to which mystical experience can be subjoined in varying degrees of vigour.

II. *Baptism and 'Cult-Mysterium'*

The thesis of the 'cult-*mysterium*' has been developed especially by O. Casel (see above § 20). He falls back on the results of religious-historical research, which particularly directed attention to the significance of the cultus, and at the same time he associates himself with a wider circle of historians of the liturgy, who wish to see the life of the primitive Church, including Paul, in organic connection with the liturgical development of the post-Apostolic era.[18] These scholars, however, by no means stand on the ground of Casel's mystery theory.[19] The cultic element is stronger in Paul than was earlier supposed;[20] but that he interpreted the Christian cultus mystically or as a mystery is a strongly contested thesis.

> Although Deissmann esteems so highly the personal experience of Paul and lays such strong emphasis on personal mysticism, he also gives an affirmative answer to the question of a cultus mysticism. For him the Christ-cult serves as a presupposition for the cultus.[21]

The decision as to the question of a 'cult-*mysterium*' is finally settled in connection with the celebration of the eucharist. The Christian community gathers at it; in distinction from baptism, that essentially belongs to its performance. In the Lord's Supper there is not only the administration of a sacrament, i.e. the impartation of salvation to the individual

[17] Op. cit. 18.

[18] Cf. the works of Schermann, Baumstark, Leclerq, Brinktrine, Arnold, Lietzmann, etc.

[19] Cf. J. M. Hanssens, 'Estne Liturgia cultus Mystericus?' *Period. theol. mor. can. lit.* 23 (1934) 112–32, 137–60; Brinktrine 'Zur sog. Mysterientheorie', *ThGl* 28 (1936) 349–51, 472–6.

[20] Cf. Schweitzer, *Gesch. d. paulin. Forschung* 129.

[21] Paulus 92.

through outward signs; a sacred event also takes place at which the community thinks on its Lord who has died for it and in worship is exalted by it. At this memorial of death the exalted and living Lord is present and comes into close relation with the whole community. When the Lord's Supper is celebrated the sacramental and cult conceptions meet, in the sense of communal worship and union with the exalted Lord.

That Casel, in laying the Biblical foundation of his thought, especially seizes on baptism is manifestly due to the fact that in Rom. vi baptism appears more plainly as a *mysterium* of dying and rising with Christ. He would lift the idea of the Christian 'cult *mysterium*' out of Rom. vi and transfer it to the Lord's Supper. Here, however, it is only the memorial of Christ's *death* that is spoken of (1 Cor. xi. 26); but Casel is concerned with the full 'cult-*mysterium*', in which the *resurrection* of Christ is also present.[22] As to baptism, it appeared to us that Rom. vi is not to be explained along the lines of the Mysteries but from other original presuppositions of the Apostle's own thinking, (cf. § 21). A cultus after the fashion of the Mysteries does not arise from the fact that all Christians are included in the death and resurrection of Christ and gain a share in their saving effects; in any case 'after the fashion of the Mysteries' is a dubious expression for Paul.[23] Admittedly, that is not to say that the celebration of the eucharist does not permit of being considered as a Christian cult-*mysterium*, for here we have to do with a genuine cult-celebration of the community, in which something is done 'in memory' of the Lord, and in which the death of Christ is 'proclaimed'—'till He come' (1 Cor. xi. 23–26).

To investigate this question goes beyond the bounds of the present work. We content ourselves with saying this: primitive Christian worship in its basic features stands certainly on Old Testament-Jewish ground.[24] The conception of 'cultic representation' is not foreign to the cult of Israel; it especially plays a part at the feast of the Passover. According to the Passover Haggada, whenever the Israelites celebrate this feast, they should identify themselves with the generation of the

[22] Casel himself perceives this problem, since the tradition 'exclusively mentions the *Passion* as object of memory', and he seeks to resolve it under various points of view, see *JLW* 6 (1926), 202–4. Ever and again he returns to baptism (Rom. vi): 'If it (mankind) has mystically died, yet it lives with Christ for God. Therefore the mass must also be the sacrament of the resurrection; otherwise it would stand back and lag behind baptism, which simply prepares for this *mysterium* and yet also applies the grace of the resurrection' (203f).

[23] Cf. Cools, op. cit. 295, n. 1. He does not desire to introduce the expression 'after the order of the Mysteries' (mystérique). 'Comme étranger, je ne me risquerai pas a essayer d'introduire un tel néologisme.'

[24] Cf. W. O. E. Osterley, *The Jewish Background of the Christian Liturgy*, Oxford, 1925, especially 194ff.

Exodus: 'In every age each man is obliged to look on himself as if he himself had gone out of Egypt.'[25] Taking this as his starting point W. D. Davies would take the Passover conception as a guide not only for the Lord's Supper but for the entire σύν-sayings of Paul. Paul considered Christians as the new Israel that has experienced the new Exodus with redemption through Jesus Christ. Paul 'was the κῆρυξ not of a new mystery, but of a new Exodus and all that that implied.... This comes out clearly in the eucharist, where the rite is designed not merely "in memory" of Christ but εἰς τὴν ἐμὴν ἀνάμνησιν, with a view to recalling Him, i.e. appropriating Him as present reality. It is in the light of this that we are to understand the dying and rising with Christ.'[26] Davies rightly sees the significance of the conception of 'corporate personality'; but he probably overestimates the influence of the Passover rite. The ideas that resound in the Passover feast are undoubtedly also a fruit of the Semitic thought of solidarity; but for Paul this offers only a general guide, in accordance with which he develops his own conceptions about Christ, the second Adam. The Passover rite does not possess any immediate significance for baptism and the σύν-compounds.[27]

The idea of 'memorial' occupies a broad place in the cult life of Israel, going beyond the Passover festival (cf. the Psalms), and it constantly leads to 'cult representation'. The primitive Christian ἀνάμνησις must be connected not with the Hellenistic memorial of the dead but with the Old Testament Jewish idea, to which very close attention has been paid in recent years.[28] On the other hand, it is also necessary to consider the early Christian proclamation that attested Jesus Christ as the Crucified and Risen One and so bestowed on the 'memorial' its own character.[29] How the representation of the death of Christ, that ensues from the proclamation and liturgical event at the celebration of the eucharist, is to be more fully explained remains uncertain. P. Neuenzeit in a thorough investigation attains to the result: 'An objective representation of the crucifixion of Christ in the Lord's Supper does not permit of proof from the proclamation and memorial conceptions of the Old and New Testaments. The Pauline utterances also are too brief to yield anything on the question as to the manner of the representation, beyond

[25] Mishna Pesachim X, 5b. The passage is lacking in the Budapest Mishna codex, but it is old, cf. G. Beer, *Pesachim*, Giessen 1912, 195f; in greater detail Davies, *Paul and Rabbinic Judaism* 102f.

[26] Davies, op. cit. 108.

[27] For criticism cf. P. Neuenzeit, *Das Herrenmahl.* 148f.

[28] N. A. Dahl, 'Anamnesis', in *StTh* 1. (1948) 69–95; L. L. Honor, 'The Role of Memory in Biblical History' (M. M. Kaplan, Jubilee Volume), New York 1953, 417–35; W. Marxsen, 'Repräsentation im Abendmahl?' *Monatsschrift für Pastoraltheologie* 41 (1952) 69–78.

[29] Cf. O. Michel in *ThW* IV, 678–87.

that of the one effective Presence.'[30] He also rejects for the eucharist a 'mystery-presence', in the sense of Casel and Warnach, as unprovable.

Hence a 'cult-*mysterium*', in the sense of the Benedictines of Maria Laach, remains uncertain, even for the celebration of the eucharist. Nevertheless the discussion over it is not yet concluded. On the whole, especially with respect to baptism, it is better not to talk about 'cult-mysticism' or 'cult-*mysterium*' in connection with Paul. Paul is not a theologian who thinks in terms of liturgy or mysteries. First and foremost he is and remains a preacher of the Gospel; that is his calling (1 Cor. i. 17) and that is his unwavering concern with regard to all the churches (cf. Rom. i. 11; 2 Cor. v. 20; Phil. i. 25; Eph. vi. 19f; Col. iv. 3f). In this respect he belongs rather to the 'prophetic type' (Dibelius).

§25. SACRAMENT AND ETHICS IN THE THEOLOGY OF PAUL

I. *The religious-moral, non-magical Character of Baptism*

In connection with the thesis maintained by the religious-historical school, that Paul's sacramental thought depends on Hellenistic sacramental conceptions, the objection is continually being raised against the Apostle that he has opened a door for 'sacramental magic'. W. Heitmüller, through his brief but trenchant work, *Taufe und Abendmahl bei Paulus* (1903), was chiefly responsible for stirring up the lively discussion on sacraments in Paul; although he wished to root them without limitation in the Hellenistic sphere, he himself did *not* draw this conclusion. His basic idea is that for Paul the ethical-spiritual sphere is not conceivable without a foundation in the natural order; in the Apostle's thinking ethical and natural are not clearly separated (17). Life ἐν Χριστῷ is not to be interpreted as merely ethical but as also, and at the same time, mystical (20). To convey this idea he employs the expression (not a happy one from the point of view of Catholic theology), the 'physical-hyperphysical new creation of existence in its entirety' (20). In his judgment 'the real seed bed for the sacrament is the area where the ethical-personal and the natural-sensual merge without clear borders into one another' (21).

> Heitmüller aroused considerable attention at that time by his application of the Catholic scholastic expression *ex opere operato* to the Pauline sacraments, as he understood them.[31] In answering attacks against him on this account he said: 'I know and knew very well that the vulgar Protestant polemic commonly understands and makes use of (the concept *ex opere operato*)... in such a manner

[30] Neuenzeit, *Das Herrenmahl* 145.

[31] *Taufe* I, 15.

that the idea is given of a magical working of the sacraments.'[32] He added: 'The concept and the objection of magic is in any case not contained in this scholastic technical phrase nor is it justified.'[33] In his later writing, *Taufe und Abendmahl im Urchristentum* (1911), he emphasizes that for Paul the sacraments do not work magically, since in his teaching faith forms the presupposition of the sacraments (19).

Since that time understanding of the sacraments has grown on the Protestant side and the objection of magic is seldom heard.[34] The chief reason for the change is the stress on faith, without which the sacrament cannot exist. It is in accord with the same tendency that a too strong 'natural' mysticism is rejected for Paul; his mysticism is genuinely Christian, a 'faith-mysticism'.[35]

Catholic theology has always firmly held to the view that the sacraments, even in Paul, are self operative through the application of the sacramental sign (*ex opere operato*), hence that they do not receive their essential power from the subjective attitude of the recipient or administrator, nor are they exhausted in their moral influence. To have prepared a way for such an estimate of the sacrament in Paul in wider, non-Catholic circles is a positive result of the religious-historical research, even if the derivation from the Hellenistic sacramental conception is unacceptable. Catholic theology, however, has at all times with equal decision repudiated the objection of 'sacramental magic', despite the objectification and 'materialization' of the means of grace.

First, it is necessary to be agreed as to what 'magic' is. However difficult it may be to give a universally satisfactory definition, the essential feature lies in the view that mysterious, superhuman powers dwell in particular objects, and that from these things the powers are transferable by means of certain practices for the use or injury of others.[36] At most the Christian sacraments have a very superficial likeness to that, in so far as the recipient through them is equipped with new, supernatural powers. But the essential difference must not be overlooked: the divine power, the new life (πνεῦμα, ζωή) does not come from the sacraments as such, but ultimately from God, though mediated through them. The binding of the sacrament to the divine working is an essential

[32] In *ThStKr* 78 (1905) 462.

[33] Op. cit. 463.

[34] On this cf. Schlier, *Taufe* 345 and in *ThLZ* 72 (1947), 326.

[35] H. E. Weber, *Eschatologie und Mystik* 12ff; Oepke, *Gal.* p. 49. cf. P. Althaus, *Römerbrief* p. 50: 'For Paul baptism has to do with neither a magical nor a historical nor a mystical event... All reality between God and man in the work of redemption is personal, i.e. it is actually only for us when we with the judgment of faith seize it as such.'

[36] Cf. Bertholet in RGG ²III, 1839ff.

feature of Pauline thought (see § 16 and 23). For Paul the sacrament is not simply a sign, the validity of which is appointed by God; he represents God Himself as working in the sacramental event. What the sacrament outwardly indicates, that God inwardly works on a man. To that extent man is not dealing with a mere 'instrument' of salvation but stands confronted with the action of God. Only this meeting with the divine working in the sacramental sphere is withdrawn from any subjective uncertainty, since this sign is objectively efficacious. With its application a man is certain that God is acting and imparting his blessings of salvation to him. The sacraments are not simply symbolic corroborations of his finding God in faith, or moral stimuli for the strengthening and increase of faith; nor are they merely a secondary track for faith, but the proper means of the gift of salvation provided by God.

> That this significance of the sacraments is approved by Protestants today is illustrated by the words of P. Althaus: 'In the baptismal act we are not dealing with an inner experience but with the power of the act as such coming from God, independently of the attitude and experience of man. But this power has nothing to do with a magical effect of baptism. God's act in baptism has the personal manner of all his redemptive action on man.'[37]

With Paul the *Christian* sacrament gains its characteristic feature through the fact that it unites us with God by *Christ*. Christ shows Himself as the way to the Father, not only in the knowledge of faith but also in the sacramental sphere. Through baptism we are transplanted into existence ἐν Χριστῷ, and in fellowship with Christ we also gain fellowship with God. In this respect the Pauline thinking most closely approaches the Johannine (cf. Jn. vi. 57). Paul does not know any formulae about a 'God-mysticism' in its own right, but he makes the line of communication go further—beyond Christ to God (cf. 1 Cor. iii. 23; Rom. viii. 29; Eph. iv. 5f). The *Pneuma* that unites us with Christ is the Spirit of God (Rom. viii. 9), or the Spirit of Him who raised Jesus from the dead (Rom. viii. 11), so that with this *Pneuma* God Himself is operative in us (1 Cor. xii. 6) and receives us as his sons (Rom. viii. 15; Gal. iv. 6).

It becomes plain, therefore, that in the theology of Paul the sacraments create a strong *personal connection* with Christ and with God—with Christ as the living way to fellowship with God, and with God as the One who alone effects salvation and is the final goal of all endeavour after salvation. Because of this personal connection, this significance of

[37] *Römerbrief.* 51.

creating fellowship with God and nothing more, the Christian sacrament is religious-moral according to its very nature. It can never be employed for other men's use or injury. In 1 Cor. x. 1–13 Paul decisively rejected a false 'magical' interpretation of the sacrament. He is thereby seen in the difficult position of 'having to combat the unauthentic sacrament by the authentic sacramental conception, of contesting sacraments with sacrament, of refuting sacramental superstition with sacramental faith.'[38] But this struggle with the Corinthian libertines leads to the whole problem of redemption by grace and moral obligation (see below II).

The personal connection which the sacrament makes between God and man, however, demands from man a certain active participation. The sacrament is co-ordinated with *faith*. Christians are not asked for a faith in magical miraculous powers, a faith in the successful operation of applied signs and means (without which the Mystery cults and pagan sorcery could not exist), but rather faith in Jesus the Christ and Mediator of salvation. This faith, however, is essential. 'If the redemptive activity of God is prior to faith and independent of it, it is, nevertheless, at the same time only *for* it.'[39] Because Christological faith is the presupposition for the sacrament, accompanies it, and remains effective alongside it and beyond it, the operations of salvation can be imparted to it exactly as they are to the sacrament. The goal, in which faith and sacrament fall together, is always the *Pneuma*-fellowship with Christ. In Christian faith, which is quite other than the special 'magic-faith' of pagan cults, the personal link with Christ and God is underscored, and with it the religious-moral character of the sacrament from the side of the recipient. Its objective efficacy, which depends solely on the action of God, and its subjective presupposition, namely faith, are the two great pillars which ensure its religious-ethical permanency.

Thus the kernel of the sacramental teaching that later came to be developed and conceptually clarified is recognizable in Paul. The Apostle offers a true sacramental view, though without elaborate concepts, and by it concentrates attention on Christ and God.

II. *The Drive of the Sacramental Effect to Ethical Fulfilment*

The sacrament offers a further difficult problem from the ethical point of view: is not a man's own ethical effort diminished by the objective efficacy of the sacrament to impart salvation? Does not the action of divine grace take the place of ethical action? And does not sacramental religion promise even to a scoundrel a comfortable salvation that falls

[38] H. von Soden, *Sakrament und Ethik bei Paulus* 23. [39] Althaus, *Römerbrief* 51.

effortlessly into his lap? The question had already occupied pagan thinkers who opposed the teaching of the Mystery religions. The latter unconditionally promised rebirth and salvation to initiates, provided they but trod the way of initiation and conscientiously fulfilled all the prescriptions and rites of the secret cult. Plutarch cites an (otherwise lost) saying of Sophocles: 'Thrice blessed are the men who ascend to Hades after beholding these rites of initiation. To them alone is a life there given, and to the rest nothing but misery.' When Diogenes heard something similar he replied: 'What are you saying? Will the thief Patecio have a better fate than Epaminondas after his death, because he has been initiated?'[40]

Again, the Pauline teaching stands in sharp contrast to this kind of Mystery piety. Whereas many ethical currents may have existed in the communities practising the secret cults, especially in the Isis and Mithras cults, they were not inwardly bound up with the Mystery event. The Persian and Egyptian forms of piety, even in this time of syncretism, still throve on the ancient inheritance of their religious and highly ethical native soil,[41] but they brought no fresh developments of ethics to light of day. With Paul, on the contrary, the ethical obligations of the Christian position flow immediately from the sacramental salvation-event. From that which the Christian has become through the sacramental act of God's grace he emphasizes with strong motives the duty of fashioning one's own life ethically in accordance with that which has taken place, often using the same formulations but with the imperative instead of indicative. The kernel of thought in Rom. vi, where the Apostle enters into discussion with false libertine deductions drawn from his doctrine of justification, lies in this contention: you have died *sacramentally* to the power of sin, consequently you can no longer *ethically* live to sin; you have entered into a new, divine sphere of life and must reflect this in your walk of life. For Paul it is unthinkable that the sacramental event should be purely external; rather it should effect a stepping out of the old circle of doom and an actual stepping into a new order of existence.

Does that mean, then, that the Apostle looks on the sacrament ultimately as an act of man, an expression of his repentance and his new faith? Even if this consideration does play a part, it does not reach the heart of the Pauline view. For him the sacrament remains essentially an act of God's grace; but the effect of this act of grace *presses on out of*

[40] Plutarch, Quomodo adolescens poetas audire debeat c. 4; Tafel-Osiander-Schwab, *Griech. Prosaiker in neuen Ubers.* Bd. 33, Stuttgart 1828, p. 64.

[41] Cf. Prümm, *RGH* 296f.

itself to ethical fulfilment. The powers that are here bestowed by God on man work to produce a different walk of life. For this the decisive factor again is the *Pneuma* idea. When the Corinthians were still pagans they were 'driven on' to the dumb idols. Now, however, they are possessed of the Spirit of God and He inspires the confession, 'Jesus is Lord' (1 Cor. xii. 2f). Undoubtedly this is only a rule to enable the 'distinguishing of Spirits'; but behind it stands the view that the Spirit of God is a living, driving power in them, just as the evil spirits were formerly. In fact, the Apostle does speak of 'being driven by the Spirit of God' (Rom. viii. 14; Gal. v. 18). Only this impulse ought not to be thought of as physical or irresistible; these sayings are formulated as imperatives and serve the parenesis. We are no longer 'in debt' to the σάρξ, to live after the manner of the *sarx* (Rom. viii. 12); through the Spirit, which we possess as an operative power, we can and should put to death the (sinful) works of the body (Rom. viii. 13).

In this allowing oneself to be led by the Spirit of God lies the really ethical moment in the Christian life.[42] It is no longer a grim and hopeless struggle with purely human resources against the power of sin, as it was under the sovereignty of the Law, but a victory in principle through the power of God; we have to hold it fast by working with the divine powers of salvation and prove it in fresh struggles. For Paul the Christian, therefore, the moral imperatives are more far reaching and even occupy a considerable place; but they are not the same exhortations as the commands of the *nomos* that cannot be fulfilled. A quite different law, that of the Spirit, is operative in us on the ground of our fellowship of life with Christ Jesus, and it no longer drives us into the clutches of sin and death but rather to God (cf. Rom. viii. 2).[43]

This fundamental moral attitude, which is built entirely on the experience of salvation, was greatly misunderstood and misused even in Paul's time. For this reason the Apostle never wearies of hammering home to his readers his basic thought in ever new ways. Hence arises the juxtaposition of appeal to God's powerful deed of salvation and of moral exhortation, as we find it especially in Rom. vi. 1–4; viii. 9–17; 1 Cor. vi. 8–11; 2 Cor. v. 17–21; Gal. v. 25; Col. i. 9–15. For Paul the sacrament stands at the narrow junction where divine justification and response

[42] H. Windisch, 'Das Problem des paulinischen Imperativs', *ZNW* 23 (1924), 277f likewise rejects the conclusion 'that the Spirit is a divine power that irresistibly takes the man, in whom it enters, out of the sphere of the flesh, or which radically suppresses in him the power of the flesh'. Rather (he contends) the context regularly implies 'that this supernatural Spirit, when it wills to achieve its work in man, needs the co-operation of man or must be set in motion through a decision of the will of man'; Paul causes the divine and human factors to work together in indissoluble union.

[43] Cf. S. Lyonnet, *Liberté chrétienne et loi nouvelle*, Rome, 1953.

of the human will come together. In the final sentence of Rom. vi. 4 he modifies the soteriological statement about gaining the divine life and makes it fit the ethical setting of the new walk of life; similarly in *v.* 11 he introduces the ethical 'ought' as a consequence (λογίζεσθε) of the sacramental salvation-event, and so leads on to the parenesis of *v.* 12. But in the sentence of *v.* 14, that clinches the preceding argument, he turns the attention back again to the objective event of grace, through which the deprivation of sin's power and liberation from the old order of Law came about.

From the fact that Paul on the one hand joyfully proclaims to his churches the good tidings of deliverance and salvation through faith in Jesus Christ, and on the other hand emphatically enjoins the duties of the Christian position, the impression constantly arises of a tension between the indicative of the declarations of salvation and the imperative of moral exhortation. It is called forth by the Christian existence in this world. This is the viewpoint from which the 'problem of the Pauline imperative' must be considered. The long discussion in Protestant theology over the compatibility of Paul's teaching on justification and his ethics[44] appears, after the sharp illumination of the 'contradictory' texts, to have led to the reflection that the deep rift between the two series of statements does not have its basis in the Pauline thought; it is rooted rather in our attitude to the salvation history, and so it is apprehended by Paul.[45]

Whereas Bultmann and Windisch, in their articles in *ZNW* 23 (1924), especially make Rom. vi–viii and Gal. v their point of departure, H. von Soden, in his study *Sakrament und Ethik bei Paulus* (1931), examines 1 Cor. viii–x: he rejects the commonly favoured interpolation hypothesis for these chapters and attempts to resolve the tension between sacrament and ethics from a higher

[44] P. Wernle, *Der Christ und die Sünde bei Paulus* (1897); H. Windisch, *Taufe u. Sünde* (1908); R. Bultmann, 'Das Problem der Ethik bei Paulus', *ZNW* 23 (1924), 123–40; H. Windisch, *ZNW* 23 (1924) 265–81; A. Oepke, *Gal.* 109f; P. Althaus *Röm* 53–55. W. Mundle, 'Religion und Sittlichkeit bei Paulus in ihrem inneren Zusammenhang', in *ZsyTh* 4 (1927) 456–82; Ch. Hauge, *Die sittliche Rechtfertigungslehre des Paulus*, Halle 1957. On the Catholic side see especially A. Kirchgässner, *Erlösung und Sünde im Neuen Testament*, Freiburg i. Br. 1950, 147–57.

[45] Windisch in *ZNW* 23 p. 281 is of the opinion that Paul did not succeed in integrating his 'most original creation', the doctrine of justification by grace, into the rest of the traditions, on which he laid the same value; or better, he did not succeed in giving these their proper place in it. The change of view that has taken place is seen in Althaus, op. cit. 54: 'The ethics rest on the absolute, pre-ethical statements. The doctrine of redemption and ethics belong essentially together.' Cf. also Büchsel, *Theol.* 137: 'This double sidedness corresponds exactly to the fact that justification is in truth a present possession, but at the same time an object of hope, that salvation is a fact, but only in the hope that the man lives at the same time in the Spirit and in the flesh.' G. Bornkamm (ThBl 18, 239ff) believes the necessity of the exhortation to be grounded on the hiddenness of the new life.

> religious-ethical point of view. To him the difficulty is that in 1 Cor. x. 14ff Paul introduces a 'second, quite different and less worthy motive', namely fear of demons, and thus 'through the superstitious-magical reminder of their own dangers the nerve of the ethical appeal is drawn'. (22). Von Soden removes the barb from this view, in that he takes the motive that lies at the basis of this section to be not danger to self, but care for the glory of God and union with Christ the Lord (24f). This section, therefore, also stands in the light of genuine and religiously grounded morality. Von Soden comes to the conclusion that Paul maintains a critical attitude to the sacramental conception of time and the deification of gnosis (35). The Pauline ethic, however, is sacramental, a specifically theological ethic and an ethical theology (36).

Since the tension between sacrament and ethic has been viewed as grounded above all in the Christian existence, another viewpoint comes more definitely into the field of view—the eschatological. The breach does not run through the thought of Paul but through the situation of the present time, seen under the aspect of the salvation history. As justified men Christians belong *in principle* to a new era; they have already been raised with Christ and installed in heaven (Eph. ii. 6). The coming aeon rises to view in the old aeon. In Christ and with Christ the entire salvation has been imparted even now to believers. Through the mercy of God they have been snatched from their walk in sin 'according to the aeon of this world' (ii. 2), and are 'firmly grounded in Christ for good works, which God prepared beforehand that we should walk in them' (ii. 10). And yet 'the boundless riches of the divine grace' will not be disclosed till the coming aeon. One perceives how the thinking of the writer hangs on the consummation and how he is nevertheless conscious of still standing in the old aeon. It makes the Christian no longer under the domination of sins and passions, but holds him existentially firm. The Christian cannot escape it. Col. iii. 3f declares that our true life is even now hidden with Christ in God, but it will be revealed in its glory only at the parousia. Till that time the ethical task is to fix our eyes on that which is 'above' (iii. 1f) and 'kill' the members which are still on earth (iii. 5), i.e. to flee from the works of these members: unchastity, impurity, passion, evil desire, covetousness. In such passages it becomes plain that the moral imperative is necessary through the peculiarity of the 'time between' in which we stand, the intermediate time of the salvation history. The sacraments, it is true, continually convey to us the blessings and powers of the salvation that belongs to the future aeon; but they do not bring to us the aeon itself. Therefore they necessarily need the moral imperative beside themselves; indeed, it is dangerous to delude oneself into security by a false (magical) conception of the sacraments. Paul expounded that with all sharpness to the Corinthian libertines, using the example of the generation in the wilderness. The Christian in this aeon always lives under a threat. 'Let him who stands see that he does not fall!' (1 Cor. x. 12). But again, Paul knows, 'God is faithful; he will not let you be tempted beyond your powers' (*v.* 13). Paul never comes out of this existential-theological tension. It gives to his theology of salvation its dynamic application to ethics, and his ethics the energizing certainty that with God's power the victory is to be won. In this situation of man's salvation and doom, sacrament and ethics are directed to each other.

Only under the point of view afforded by the salvation history is the danger avoided of depreciating the indicatives and the imperatives of the Pauline statements. 'In fact at times the indicative has been idealistically evaporated—as in the speculatively influenced theology of the nineteenth century, and at times it has been coarsened in a naturalistic manner, so that the Pauline system appeared to teach the sinlessness of Christians, as in the religious-historical theology.... A really penetrating understanding is possible only when the peculiar Pauline consciousness of time is recognized. Between this aeon and that which is to come Paul knows the *eschatological reality* as a condition of transition and suspense.'[46] Von Soden declared that the ethic of Paul is 'historically, Christologically and eschatologically related'.[47] Althaus also sees therein the final solution: 'The new aeon does not yet replace the old one. But it shows its reality as a continuous "No" of battle to the old. That is: just because the Christian is removed with Christ into the new aeon, he fights in the old by its aid.'[48] Here the interrelation of sacrament, ethics and eschatology is shown,[49] conditioning a constantly fruitful tension and a dynamic development.

Yet these lines that tend to separation are brought together in the reality of Christ. It is the same Christ, with whom we are united through baptism into a real fellowship and whose complete fellowship (σὺν-Χριστῷ-εἶναι) we still await and long for in the day of his parousia. This complete—yet incomplete—fellowship with Christ is also the foundation of the Pauline ethic and provides it with its most powerful motive.[50]

[46] Oepke, *Gal.* 109. [47] Op. cit. 36. [48] *Römerbrief* 54f.

[49] Cf. H. E. Weber, *Eschatologie und Mystik* 105: 'The "mystical" opposition of the old and new condition of life is "ethical"'; and 160: primitive Christian piety is 'expressly eschatological; it remains so also in its "mystical" application.'

[50] This is hinted at, but unfortunately developed in an exegetically unsatisfactory manner, by G. Staffelbach, *Die Vereinigung mit Christus als Prinzip der Moral bei Paulus* (Diss.), Freiburg 1932. He speaks of an 'Interimsethik' (13).

It holds the Apostle continually in tension: it transports him with ringing jubilation and gratitude, and it consumes him with yearning; it compels him to humble prayer on his knees, and it snatches him up to restless Apostolic labour; he knows that he has been seized by Christ, and yet he pursues after Him that he may gain Him (Phil. iii. 12). So with unfailing power he stretches every nerve—truly an example for all his churches—that he may win the victor's prize of God's heavenly calling in Christ Jesus (*v.* 13).

§26. THE THEOLOGY OF PAUL AS CHARACTERIZED BY THE SALVATION-HISTORY AND ESCHATOLOGY

In the course of our investigation we have had to emphasize frequently that Paul's baptismal and sacramental theology does not receive its stamp from a supratemporal-mystical or mystery kind of thinking, but from one dominated by the salvation-history. Baptism links the believer with that which happened historically to Jesus Christ, namely with his crucifixion and resurrection. From the fact that this event, in itself once for all and settled (Rom. vi. 9f), wins for the whole future a saving significance, it is transformed from being a purely historical event to one conceived of in terms of soteriology and the salvation-history. Christ is the Beginning and Head of a new humanity which, in contrast to the Adamitic humanity, has attained again to peace with God, the divine life and all other divine blessings of salvation (Rom. v. 12–21). The thought characterized by the salvation-history, however, has yet another viewpoint, extending to the future, namely the parousia of Christ and the consummation of salvation. If the sacramental view of Paul is to be completely integrated into the construction of this theology of the salvation history, the relation of the sacramental salvation-event to the parousia must also be shown.

A question is thrown up thereby which, under the viewpoint of 'eschatology and mysticism', has occupied New Testament research, both from the side of Biblical theology and from that of the history of religions. K. L. Schmidt, in an article, Eschatologie und Mystik im Urchristentum,[51] briefly outlined the prevailing view of that time (1922) in the following manner: 'A rapid survey of primitive Christianity would represent it in this way: Jesus and the first community at Jerusalem are to be classified as eschatological; the fourth Evangelist, standing at the close of primitive Christianity, is a mystic; Paul who comes between is a contested figure. In any case at the beginning of early Christianity there is eschatology, at its end mysticism' (280). But even

[51] In *ZNW* 21 (1922) 277–91.

at that time Schmidt set over against this view two theses: 1. Primitive Christianity remained an eschatological religion right up to the time that it entered its so-called Hellenistic period: 2. The characteristic elements of mysticism, as we find them in the Hellenistic period, reach into the very earliest beginnings of Christianity (286). A warning is thereby given to research against any one sided characterization of the piety of the Church in the Jerusalem period and of the Pauline and Johannine theology. But the difficulty is also illustrated of assigning to the Apostle Paul, standing as he does in the stream of the early Christian development and at the same time strongly personally stamped in his own religious experience, the right place between Jewish and Hellenistic piety, between views that are bound by the tradition and those that are pressing onward, between thought dominated by the salvation history and that which is supratemporal and 'mystical'. In the centre of this question stands his sacramental teaching, which on the one hand seems to guard the traditional deposit and bear testimony to the early Church's reverence for institutions and cultic actions handed on to it, and on the other it awakens in many scholars the impression of a new 'unJewish' type of religion. This question, already repeatedly raised, warrants a final decision precisely from the eschatological point of view. Undoubtedly the Hellenistic Mystery piety is closely bound up with faith in personal immortality, but it does not know an eschatology as primitive Christianity understood it. This eschatology is rooted in the ground of late Judaism and its apocalyptic writings, but in spirit it links on to Old Testament religion, with its thought about the salvation history, its prophecy and its messianic expectation. The question therefore should be raised: to what extent does the eschatological viewpoint provide the key to the Pauline teaching on the Sacraments?

The sacramental salvation-event is brought formally into connection with the parousia of the Lord in the celebration of the eucharist. In 1 Cor. xi. 26 Paul says that the Christian Church at the Lord's Supper proclaims the death of Jesus 'till he comes'. The importance of this Pauline saying cannot be weakened by suggesting that it is explicable from the eschatological outlook of Jesus Himself at the Last Supper and therefore is secondary for the specifically Pauline theology of the sacrament. For it does not stand in Paul's recital of the tradition but is a commentary from the Apostle, though it is freely to be admitted that in making it he desires to be in accord with the view of the Lord as to the meaning of this celebration.[52] The eschatological direction of his thinking is confirmed a few verses later in the allusion to the judgment.

[52] Cf. Neuenzeit, *Das Herrenmahl* 221–9.

The Lord's Supper is fundamentally distinguished from all pagan cult-meals by the fact that the Christian Church here meets its Lord Jesus Christ, who died for it once, gave it this holy institution for his 'remembrance', and binds Himself most closely here with all its members to be present with them, till one day He comes in glory. Only *that* is the whole 'reality of Christ'. Since this picture of Christ is essential for Paul, and determines his entire thought, reflection and aspiration, the Lord's Supper cannot be deprived of this perspective. The Lord's Supper is fellowship with Christ, as it is now possible 'between the times', between the aeon of ruin that still exists, but which for the Christian has been deprived of its power, and the aeon of salvation, which is future but which already looms in this in its reality and power—actually, and yet veiled, granting real participation in Christ and yet only promising and preparing the way for the final and full fellowship.

If this relation to the eschatological fulfilment comes to expression at the eucharist in an unmistakable manner, it is equally presupposed in baptism, only not so obviously. The practical tendency of Rom. vi and the attention which the Apostle pays to the life for God that is ethically fruitful interrupts this line of thought, but any reader of the Pauline Letters can draw it out for himself. We have risen with Christ in baptism, sacramentally to a new life (Col. ii. 12) and ethically to a new walk of life (Rom. vi. 4); but it is not yet the full life of the divine glory. We believe that we also shall live with Christ (Rom. vi. 8); to this Rom. viii adds a more detailed exposition: if the Spirit of Him who raised Jesus from the dead dwells in us, then He, who raised Christ Jesus from the dead, will also make our mortal body alive through his Spirit who dwells in us (*v*. 11). The δόξα essentially belongs to the living and exalted Christ. If we suffer with Him, we shall also be glorified with Him (*v*. 17). This glorification has been determined for us by God along with our justification (*v*. 30); or, Christologically considered, it is a certain possession for us at the end (so far as we prove true ethically), since Jesus, who is enthroned at the right hand of God, intercedes for us (*v*. 34).

In the Letter to the Galatians, which is characterized by the 'theology of the cross', the prospect of the consummation is not lacking. It is reproduced here from the point of view that as sons of God we are also heirs. Our sonship to God, which rests on faith and baptism (iii. 26f), gains its full meaning only by virtue of our having become the heirs of the promise (iii. 29). We possess the Spirit as the real pledge, the foundation for this (iv. 6f); He bears testimony to our sonship to God and guarantees our claim on the inheritance.

In the Prison Epistles this prospect of the eschatological perfection becomes clear in another way. Our hope is described in Eph. i. 18f with exuberant language and in *vv.* 20ff it is grounded on the position of supremacy that Christ has, 'not only in this aeon, but also in that which is to come' (*v.* 21); although baptism is not mentioned, it is not doubtful that it stands in the background as the entrance into the fellowship of Christ in the light of Eph. ii. 5f. The peculiarity of this view consists in the fact that this earthly world seems almost to be forgotten and those who have become alive with Christ already count as raised with Him and installed in heaven with Him. However true it be that the Apostle has to set the possession of salvation already secured in Christ (Col. ii. 10–12) before the eyes of the Colossians, who have been hoodwinked by a false teaching, he never for a moment forgets that the fellowship of Christ and the possession of salvation are still imperfect. If they are already raised with Christ (namely in baptism, ii. 12), their true life is nevertheless hidden still with the exalted Christ in God and will first become manifest with the parousia of Christ in divine glory (iii. 1–4).

The provisional nature and imperfection of the present enjoyment of salvation becomes especially clear in the possession of the Spirit. The πνεῦμα desires to manifest his deepest nature as δόξα. In 2 Cor. iii. 18 the beginning of a δόξα-transfiguration is ascribed to the present condition of Christians, but it is only a gradual process of change into the likeness of the glory of the risen transfigured Lord; it is a process of transformation ἀπὸ δόξης εἰς δόξαν. From another point of view the Spirit is bestowed simply as an 'earnest money' (2 Cor. i. 22: v. 5), as a payment in advance on the future inheritance (Eph. i. 14). We have been 'sealed' through the Spirit for the day of redemption (Eph. iv. 30). So surely as we have received the Spirit of adoption and in Him cry 'Abba' (Rom. viii. 15), we nevertheless possess Him only as 'initial gift' (ἀπαρχή) and sigh in ourselves in expectation of the sonship (Rom. viii. 23). Only when our corporeality has been penetrated by the reality and glory of the Spirit of God, when the 'transformation' has taken place (1 Cor. xv. 51f), will our salvation be perfected. For it is the divine plan and will that this corruptible should 'put on' incorruptibility and this mortal immortality (1 Cor. xv. 53). Not till then will the final victory be achieved over the ruinous powers of death and sin (1 Cor. xv. 54ff). This glimpse into the bodily resurrection is a Jewish inheritance.[53]

If, therefore, the impartation of the Spirit is bound up with baptism, then the provision of this sacrament is incontestably directed to the

[53] Cf. J. Jeremias, 'Flesh and Blood cannot inherit the Kingdom of God', *NTS* 2. (1955–6) 151–9.

consummation in the last times, the day of baptism presses on to and calls for the day of the Lord, the 'day of redemption'. The sacramental dying and rising with Christ imperiously demands the (bodily) resurrection with Christ at his parousia.

In this sense A. Schweitzer is right: 'Separated from his eschatology, the Pauline sacraments would become meaningless and ineffectual. They are confined to the time between the resurrection of Jesus and his parousia, when the dead shall rise. Their power depends on the fact that is past and on that which is still impending. In this sense they are "historically conditioned".'[54]

With all this relating of baptism to the eschatological perfection, there still remains an unresolved residue. Any desire to consider the present salvation, as mediated in baptism, as but a preliminary stage of the salvation of the end, would not do justice to the character of tension which is inherent in the theology of Paul. The new creation of man, which is given with entrance into the fellowship of Christ (2 Cor. v. 17; Gal. vi. 15), is in principle an eschatological declaration (Rev. xxi. 5); it already appears in the prophecy of Isaiah (xliii. 18; lxv. 17f), and in the language of the Rabbinic schools it is applied to the present saving action of God, the forgiveness of sins.[55]

> Billerbeck remarks: 'It is particularly noteworthy that the Rabbinic scholars, when speaking of the new creation of man, nowhere have in view his *moral* renewal in the sense of the New Testament regeneration. On the Rabbinic view the moral renewal of man belongs to the future, which alone can bring the promised new spirit or the new heart.'[56] For Paul and primitive Christianity, however, it is characteristic that the outpouring of the Spirit takes place even now, in the present time of salvation (1 Cor. vi. 11; Tit. iii. 5f), and that accordingly the aeon of salvation has broken into this.

Since research has increasingly come to recognize that this tension in Paul is not to be explained by the contrast 'mysticism and eschatology',[57] inasmuch as in his view both have indissolubly flowed together, attempts are made to give other theological answers. The general framework of

[54] *Geschichte der paulin. Forsch.* 169.
[55] Billerbeck II, 421f and III, 519; Moore I, 533.
[56] II, 421.
[57] Cf. on this the work of H. E. Weber, op. cit. On the one hand he characterizes this mysticism as 'the mysticism of hope' (18f) and on the other he seeks to give validity to the mystical element alongside the eschatological, especially with reference to the Lord's Supper, which is the 'representation of Jesus the Lord in the prospect of his coming, with the living consciousness of unity with Him' (158), but also with reference to baptism (159f).

the salvation-history, within which the solution is doubtless to be sought, appears insufficient to some and they seek other special categories for the eschatological statements.

E. Stauffer, who regards Paul as a realist alongside fanatics and scoffers,[58] interprets the 'new creation' in terms of the judgment of God. 'So far as one's actual being is concerned, everything can remain within the old order. That is the antecedent clause that preserves us from fanaticism. But everything has become new—*forensically*. That is the consequent clause that delivers us from nihilism.'[59] This thesis has been too one-sidedly influenced by the doctrine of justification, and that in the sense of the Lutheran theory of imputation. If the representatives of the 'mystical' interpretation laid excessive emphasis on the role of the *Pneuma* in the piety and theology of Paul, and thereby sought to draw the Apostle into the circle of Hellenistic mystical views, conversely there appears in Stauffer a lack of understanding of the Pauline *Pneuma*-texts that have reference to being. He links the Spirit above all to that which man experiences in prayer and moral struggle.[60] Of the possession of the Spirit (Rom. v. 5, 1 Cor. ii. 12, 17) or the indwelling of the Spirit in us (Rom. viii. 11; 1 Cor. iii. 16) he scarcely speaks. In this Stauffer does not do justice to the present possession of the Spirit; also it is not true that so far as our being is concerned everything has remained within the old order. We have been filled with a new divine power. To Paul Spirit and power belong very closely together. O. Schmitz has worked this out very well.[61] Paul, he says, speaks in objective terms of the Spirit's action and in such contexts sees δικαιοσύνη, ἁγιασμός and ἀπολύτρωσις as synonyms.[62] To him this power is a truly *present* possession of the believer, but at the same time it is also truly an object of hope in the consummation.[63] This view approximates to that which has been always defended by Catholic theology, namely that the Pauline teaching on justification and sanctification has its basis in *life*. Catholic exegesis certainly does not deny the partly forensic *mode of speech*.[64] But the formula of a purely presumptive possession of salvation in the present says too little.

Other Protestant theologians speak of the paradoxical and dialectical

[58] *Theol.* 120.
[59] *Theol.* 122f.
[60] *Theol.* 145.
[61] O. Schmitz, 'Der Begriff δύναμις bei Paulus,' *Festg. f. A. Deissmann*, Tübingen 1927, 139–67.
[62] Op. cit. 164.
[63] Op. cit. 167.
[64] Cf. Lagrange, *Rom Exc*, p. 133: 'According as believers are righteous, God holds them as righteous; but the first thought is the chief one and the root of the second.' Further Tobac, op. cit. 211–3; Prat, II, 297f; Amiot, I, 222.

character of the reality of Christ.[65] They endeavour to emphasize in equal measure mystical presence and eschatological future as two poles between which the Pauline existence is in continual movement. This way of looking at the matter has the great merit that it makes plain the *unity in tension* between indicative and imperative, between initial and final salvation. Only it must be clearly recognized that the dialectical scheme of thesis, antithesis and synthesis is not a Pauline category of thought.

> Steiger describes this 'dialectical existence' in the following manner: 'The characteristic of a life so formed is a peculiar movement, which to a certain extent oscillates between the utmost possibilities of realization, in order to reach at the last a rest in a potentiality that lies beyond all these possibilities and tendencies.'[66]

As to the nature of this 'dialectical thinking', the same thing applies as Burger affirms with regard to every one-sided schematizing of Paul's thought: 'The reality of the living Christ does not permit of being imprisoned in a category of our thinking; nor does it permit of being buried in a concept, because it is a living reality.'[67]

This reference to the living Christ gives the finest answer. Christ is Past, Present and Future. He offers Himself to the believer even now, in a fellowship which Paul is especially fond of characterizing by the brief formula ἐν Χριστῷ. But He promises a still closer, unlimited fellowship, no longer hindered through the body and the world, denoted by the Apostle as σὺν Χριστῷ. For the totality of believers he expects it at the parousia (Col. iii. 4; 1 Thess. iv. 14); it is called a 'being with the Lord' (1 Thess. iv. 17b), a 'joint reign' with Him (2 Tim. ii. 12). But in principle he knows that he and all other Christians have already been transferred into this kingdom of Christ (Col. i. 13).

In his yearning after Christ Paul ever and again desires to overleap the bounds that still exist, and this affects the peculiar dynamic of his utterances. Theologically they can be placed in juxtaposition, on calm reflection be brought into harmony with each other, and to some extent be defined in relation to each other. Nevertheless they lie in a continual tension. Paul lives his theology, and he takes his theological conceptions from the reality of Christ he experiences. He can never be satisfied with

[65] R. Steiger, *Die Dialektik der paulinischen Existenz* (Unters z. N.T. 20), Leipzig 1931; Burger, op. cit. 61–70; further the work of W. T. Hahn.

[66] Op. cit. 17; cf. also his arguments on 34ff. On baptism: 'In baptism the Christian experiences what Paul knew in his conversion, *the inbreaking of the Christological dialectic* into his existence' (44).

[67] Op. cit. 68.

the present possession of salvation. Everything that appeared to him of worth before his meeting with Christ he holds to be a loss, now that he has won Christ (Phil. iii. 8); he is therefore conscious of his inestimable riches in Christ. But at the same time he desires to win Christ (also Phil. iii. 8), and to that end he does not shrink from any trouble or suffering. Once more, as with his ethics, we are confronted with the driving power of his religious spirit—his living faith in Christ. Paul is not a fanatic, torn hither and thither by extreme tensions, nor is he a thinker tortured by the modern distress of existence; he is a man of faith, pressing on to his heavenly Lord with a force born of love.

At bottom, therefore, the question whether Paul adhered to Jewish or Hellenistic thought is falsely posed. It is undeniable that his point of departure was Jewish theological territory, as is seen above all in the manner of his thinking along the lines of the salvation history. But that does not exclude an advance into the Hellenistic world of his Gentile mission churches. In the last resort, however, his orientation is neither to Judaism nor to Hellenism but to Christ, who for him is the most living reality. The peculiar tension of his theology arises because this actuality of Christ 'according to its nature is a divine event that has already happened, faith's present reality and a hope of consummation directed to the end'.[68] Into this fulness of life the Christian is planted, and in it he should grow ever more strongly, till at the end 'all things are freely given' to him 'with Christ' (Rom. viii. 32).

[68] Burger, op. cit. 69. O. Cullmann, *Christus und die Zeit*, Zollikon-Zürich [2]1948, 92ff, 107ff.

RECAPITULATION

As we look back we can confirm that baptism possesses a permanent and assured place in Paul's world of thought. It is no intrusive matter, requiring hard work on the Apostle's part to be united with his deeper 'mystical' associations of thought, or that can only clumsily be fitted into the framework of the salvation history; rather it is a component well suited to the construction of his total theology. For him the proclamation of the one great Christ event, already given in the primitive Apostolic kerygma, is fundamental: Jesus died, was buried and has risen according to the Scriptures (1 Cor. xv. 3f). The foundation for it is Paul's profound Christology of the pre-existent Son of God: He emptied Himself of the form of God and humbled Himself to the death on the cross, but precisely for that reason He was exalted by God and as the living Lord sits enthroned at the right hand of the Father (Phil. ii. 4–11); one day He will come again as the glorified Lord and as Victor over the powers at enmity with God, and at the end He will deliver up the sovereignty to the Father (1 Cor. xv. 24–28). The soteriology is essentially bound up with this Christology, for this whole *descensus* and *ascensus* of the eternal Son of God has in view the goal of saving men from eternal perdition (Rom. viii. 32). Paul's attention, therefore, is concentrated on the crucifixion and its deep significance, grounded as it is in God's all-wise plan and which consists in liberating men from the ruinous powers of sin and death, from the Law that promotes them, and from their sphere of operation, the *sarx* that is sunk in sin. In the light of the resurrection victory of Christ, the fearful death of shame and annihilation that the Son of God endured on the cross has completed this deliverance objectively, in principle and on a cosmic-universal scale. But this soteriology has to be applied to the individual in his concrete situation. Fundamentally that has become possible through the fact that Christ died and rose again as the Head of a new humanity. As Adam was the founder of physical mankind, so Christ is such for the spiritual, redeemed mankind. In God's sight, what happened to Him happened representatively for the whole of mankind; Christ was but the Firstborn of an entire succession.

Now the question at the heart of the 'subjective doctrine of redemption' is: how does the individual gain the salvation that Christ has won? Or, otherwise expressed, how does the individual step into fellowship with Christ, in order that through Him and in Him he might win the divine life and the divine glory? Paul answers; through faith and baptism. To him faith in Jesus the Christ is the great formula of unity over against the Jewish way of justification through the Law. Paul finds baptism already existing as an institution in the primitive Church, but for him it is self-evident that the believer should affirm this outward sign that mediates salvation and submit to baptism.

From that, however, a theological concern grows in Paul's mind to exhibit baptism in its saving power and in its significance for union with Christ. First, employing the concept of the impartation of salvation, it is for him a washing away of sin (1 Cor. vi. 11). In so representing it he adheres to its original symbolic content and to the oldest baptismal theology of the primitive Church. Later he deepens this theological line and directs it towards the Church: the Church as a whole has been through this bath (Eph. v. 26). In Tit. iii. 5 Paul calls it a 'bath of regeneration'; it is not entirely excluded that in that expression he also takes account of a conception widely known in the pagan world. Nevertheless he wants nothing more from it than a terminological accord; in concept and content he remains wholly on the ground of his theology of Christ and the Spirit, which, along with its original Christian taproot, possessed its strongest roots in the Old Testament (Tit. iii. 6). His own endeavours after a theology of baptism are more clearly recognizable where he seeks to represent baptism as a means of union with Christ. If with the formula 'in the name of Jesus' (1 Cor. i. 13) he adheres to a still more primitive Church tradition (Acts xix. 5), he makes an original contribution by describing this act of reception into the new people of God as 'Christ-circumcision' (Col. ii. 11). He first gives expression to his inner concern, however, when he emphasizes as the result of baptism not alone the outward belonging to Christ but a personal union with Christ that affects our very existence. In this sense he calls baptism a 'putting on Christ' (Gal. iii. 27).

Yet the Apostle reaches the height of his christocentric baptismal theology in the conception of 'dying and rising with Christ' (Rom. vi 1–11, Col. iii. 11f). In baptism the believer in Christ is drawn into the Christ event; he accompanies his Lord through death to resurrection. Starting out from 'being buried with Christ', Paul infers also a resurrection to a new divine life and a corresponding walk of life for God. The depth of this thought lies here, that it all happens 'with Christ', who once was crucified for us and rose again. It is not simply a question of remembrance and becoming like Him, but rather a participation in Christ's cross and resurrection, so that everything that Christ went through for our salvation also happens to the baptized, and he thus obtains the fruit of Christ's dying. These statements are not explained through 'mysticism', nor are they rightly described as a 'cult-*mysterium*', nor are they really comprised in the category of 'contemporaneity'. Rather they are founded on a Semitic idea, according to which the founder of a people is inseparably bound up with those who are joined to him; he represents and takes the place of his followers, and these again share his destiny. Baptism is the place where this union of believers with Christ, the Founder of a new humanity, is established, and therefore they die 'with Him' and live 'with Him'. The entire process takes place in them sacramentally by grace.

At the same time the baptized are incorporated into the fellowship of all who belong to Christ, i.e. into the *Church*. Paul understands the Church also not only in an outward manner as an earthly and visible community, but as the 'Body of Christ', fashioned and built up by the Holy Spirit, to which new members are joined in baptism (1 Cor. xii. 13, 27). This ecclesiological view is likewise an inalienable ingredient of the Pauline theology of baptism. It also explains the importance of baptism along with faith. Inward faith and outward confession, personal fellowship with Christ and incorporation into the 'Body of Christ', belong together inseparably. The new existence which the believer in Christ gains is also life in a new community, in which all distinctions that hitherto existed lose their significance (Gal. iii. 28; 1 Cor. xiii. 12; Col. iii. 11).

Accordingly, in Paul the salvation-event in baptism is set within the frame of Christology and soteriology, and theologically it is concentrated in the actuality of Christ. The most profound and characteristic expression of the theology of baptism, that of dying and rising with Christ, at the same time leads on to other aspects of Pauline thought—to ethics, mysticism and eschatology. That which the Christian has become in a sacramental and real manner, through grace and the mighty deed of God, he must now ethically strive after, mystically experience in life and suffering, and hope for eschatologically. On the foundation of what happened in baptism an edifice of further conceptions is raised; the sacramental 'dying and rising with Christ' must perpetuate itself in the life of the Christian. The sacrament calls for ethical application and preservation, and the ethic cannot exist without the power of the sacrament, i.e. without the *Pneuma*. 'Mysticism' is conformity with Christ on the deepest level, especially in suffering; but it is accompanied by ethical sobriety and by its peculiar nature offers itself as a way for *all*. But the eschatological direction of thought is absolutely essential for all these points of view: for baptism, in order to consummate the God-given salvation; for ethics, to give the right position and motivation between the times; for mysticism, to provide the promise of its deepest longing.

A complete 'system' of Pauline theology cannot be framed. This man, who has been apprehended by Christ, is too full of life and tensions and of seeking and striving to be able to give expression to the fulness of his faith in Christ. But his theology is not without construction and inner connection; it is thought out and carefully fashioned, even to its linguistic formulations. No one is more conscious than Paul himself of the inadequacy of verbal clothing and of the difficulty of confining within words the whole reality of Christ. But the ardour of his faith makes itself felt through the imperfect form. To conduct men to the real and living Christ and to lead them into fellowship with Him, that is the real intent of the Apostle's labour; as he himself puts it so incomparably: 'I suffer the pangs of child-birth again, till Christ win his form in you '(Gal. iv. 19).

Bibliography

Abel, F. M., *Grammaire du Grec biblique*, Paris 1927
Abbott, T. K., *Epistles to the Ephesians and to the Colossians* (Int. Crit. Comm.), Edinburgh 1897, repr. 1922
Allo, E. B., *Première épître aux Corinthiens*, Paris 1934
—— *Seconde épître aux Corinthiens*, Paris 1937
Althaus, P., *Der Brief an die Römer* (NTD 6), Göttingen [5]1946
Ambrosiaster, *Komm. zu den paulinischen Briefen*: Migne, PL 17, 45ff
Amiot, F., *L'enseignement de S. Paul*, 2 vol., Paris 1938
Aquinas, Thomas, *In Pauli Apost. epistolas commentaria*, ed. L. Vivès, Paris I 1870; II 1874
Bachmann, Ph., *Der 1. Brief des Paulus an die Korinther* (Zahns Komm. 7), Leipzig [2]1910
—— *Der 2. Brief des Paulus an die Korinther* (Zahns Komm. 8), Leipzig 1909
Bandas, R. G., *The Master-Idea of St. Paul's Epistles or the Redemption* (Diss. Lov.), Bruges 1925
Barrett, C. K., *A Commentary on the Epistle to the Romans*, London 1957
Barth, M., *Die Taufe—ein Sakrament?* Zollikon-Zürich 1951
Bauer, W., *Griechisch-Deutsches Wörterbuch zu den Schriften des NT und der übrigen urchristlichen Literatur*, Berlin [5]1958
Belser, J. E., *Der 2. Brief des Apostels Paulus an die Korinther*, Freiburg 1910
—— *Der Epheserbrief des Apostels Paulus*, Freiburg 1908
Benoit, A., *Le baptême chrétien au second siècle*, Paris 1953
Best, E., *One Body in Christ*, London 1955
Billerbeck, P., *Kommentar zum Neuen Testament aus Talmud und Midrasch*, 4 vols, München 1922–28
Blass, E.-Debrunner, A., *Grammatik des neutestam. Griechisch*, Göttingen [9]1954
Bonnard, P., 'Mourir et vivre avec Jésus-Christ selon s. Paul', *RHPhR* 35 (1956) pp. 101–12
Bonsirven, J., *Le judaïsme palestinien au temps de J. Chr.*, 2 vols., Paris 1934–35
Bornkamm, G., 'Die ntl. Lehre von der Taufe', *ThBl* 17 (1938), cols 42–52
—— 'Taufe und neues Leben bei Paulus', *ThBl* 18 (1939), cols. 233–42
Bousset, W., '1 u. 2 Kor u. Gal': *Die Schriften des NT*, hrsg. v. J. Weiss, II Göttingen [3]1917
—— *Kyrios Christos*, Göttingen [4]1935
Bousset, W.-Gressmann, H., *Die Religion des Judentums im späthellenistischen Zeitalter* (Handb. z. NT 21), Tübingen [3]1926
Büchsel, F., *Theologie des NT*, Gütersloh [2]1937
Bultmann, R., *Theologie des NT*, Tübingen 1953
Burger, E., *Der lebendige Christus* (Tübing. Stud. z. syst. Theol. 2), Stuttgart 1933
Burton, E. de Witt, *The Epistle to the Galatians* (Int. Crit. Comm.), Edinburgh 1921
Casel, O., *Das christliche Kultmysterium*, Regensburg [2]1935
—— *Glaube, Gnosis, Mysterium*, Münster 1941 ((= *GGM*) *JLW* and Filthaut)
Catenae graecorum Patrum in NT, ed. J. A. Cramer, Oxford 1844ff

Cerfaux, L., *La théologie de L'Eglise suivant S. Paul*, Paris ^{2}1948
Chrysostomus, J., *Komm. zu den paulin. Briefen*, ed. de Montfaucon IX–XI, Venedig 1741
Clemen, C., *Religionsgeschichtliche Erklärung des NT*, Giessen ^{2}1924
Cools, J., 'La présence mystique du Christ dans le baptême', *Mémorial Lagrange*, Paris 1940, 295–305
Cornely, R., *Epistola ad Romanos* (Curs. Script. S.), Paris 1896
—— *Prior epist. ad Corinthios*, Paris 1909
—— *Epist. ad Corinthios altera et ad Galatas*, Paris 1892
Crehan, J. H., *Early Christian Baptism and the Creed*, London 1950
Cullmann, O., *Die Tauflehre des Neuen Testaments*, Zürich 1948
Cumont, F., *Die orientalischen Religionen im römischen Heidentum* (bearb. v. A. Burckhardt-Brandenburg), Leipzig-Berlin ^{3}1931
—— *Die Mysterien des Mithra* (transl. Gehrich), Leipzig ^{2}1911
Cyril of Alexandria, *Komm. zu den paulin. Briefen*, Migne, PG 74
Cyril of Jerusalem, 'Cat. myst'. *Monumenta eucharistica et liturgica vetustissima*, collegit J. Quasten (Floril. Patr. VII, 2), Bonn 1935
Davies, W. D., *Paul and Rabbinic Judaism*, London 1955
Deissmann, A., *Die ntl. Formel 'In Christo Jesu'*, Marburg 1892
—— *Bibelstudien*, Marburg 1895, *Neue Bibelstudien* 1897
—— *Licht vom Osten*, Tübingen ^{4}1923
—— *Paulus*, Tübingen ^{2}1925
Deissner, K., *Paulus und die Mystik seiner Zeit*, Leipzig ^{2}1921
—— *Auferstehungshoffnung und Pneumagedanke bei Paulus*, Leipzig 1912
Dey, J., Παλιγγενεσία (Ntl. Abh. XVII, 5), Münster 1937
Dibelius, M., *An die Kolosser, Epheser, an Philemon* (Handb. z. NT 12), Tübingen ^{2}1927; ^{3}1953 bearbeitet von H. Greeven
—— *Die Pastoralbriefe* (Handb. z. NT 13), Tübingen ^{2}1931; ^{3}1955 bearbeitet von H. Conzelmann
—— *Die Isisweihe des Apulejus* (SAH 4), Heidelberg 1917, S. 45ff
—— *Paulus und die Mystik*, München 1941
Dieterich, A., *Eine Mithrasliturgie*, Leipzig-Berlin ^{3}1923
Dobschütz, E. v., 'Sakrament und Symbol im Urchristentum', *ThStKr* 78 (1905), 1–40
Dodd, C. H., *The Epistle of Paul to the Romans*, (Moffatt NT Comm.), London 1932 (repr. 1954)
Dölger, F. J., *Ichthys, das Fischsymbol in frühchristlicher Zeit*, I Rom 1910 (^{2}Münster 1928); II Münster 1922
—— *Sphragis*, Paderborn 1911
Dupont, J., Σὺν Χριστῷ. *L'union avec le Christ suivant s. Paul I*, Bruges 1952
Estius, W., *In omnes D. Pauli epistolas comm. I u. II*, Mainz 1858f
Ewald, P., *Die Briefe des Paulus an die Epheser, Kolosser und Philemon* (Zahns Komm. 10), Leipzig 1905
Feine, P., *Theologie des NT*, Berlin ^{8}1951
Filthaut, Th., *Die Kontroverse über die Mysterienlehre* (Diss.), Warendorf i. W. 1947
Flemington, W. F., *The New Testament Doctrine of Baptism*, London 1948
Gaugler, E., *Der Brief an die Römer*, 2 vols. Zürich 1945–52
Gesenius, W.-Buhl, F., *Hebräisches und aramäisches Handwörterbuch über das AT*, Leipzig ^{14}1905

Gewiess, J., *Die urapostolische Heilsverkündigung nach der Apg* (Bresl. Stud. z. hist. Theol., N.F. 5), Breslau 1939
Grail, A., 'La place du baptême dans la doctrine de s. Paul', *La Vie Spirituelle* nr. 352 (1950) 563–83
—— 'Le baptême dans l'Epître aux Galates (III, 26-IV, 7)', *RB* 58 (1951) 503–20
Gressmann, H., *Die orientalischen Religionen im hellenistisch-römischen Zeitalter*, Berlin-Leipzig 1930
Gutjahr, F. S., *Der Brief an die Römer*, Graz-Wien 1923
—— *Die zwei Briefe an die Korinther*, Graz-Wien ²1921
Hahn, W. Tr., *Das Mitsterben und Mitauferstehen mit Christus bei Paulus*, Gütersloh 1937
Harnack, A. von, *Mission und Ausbreitung des Christentums I*, Leipzig ⁴1924
Heigl, B., *Antike Mysterienreligionen und Urchristentum* (BZfr XII 11–12), Münster 1932
Heitmüller, W., *Im Namen Jesu* (FRLANT I, 2), Göttingen 1903
—— *Taufe und Abendmahl bei Paulus*, Göttingen 1903 (Taufe I)
—— *Taufe und Abendmahl im Urchristentum* (Religionsgesch. Volksbücher) 1911 (Taufe II)
Henle, F. A. von, *Der Epheserbrief des hl. Apostels Paulus*, Augsburg ²1908
Héring, J., *La première épître de s. Paul aux Corinthiens*, Neuchâtel-Paris 1949
—— *La seconde épître de s. Paul aux Corinthiens*, Neuchâtel-Paris 1958
Hermann, I., *Kyrios und Pneuma. Studien zur Christologie der paulinischen Hauptbriefe*, München 1961
Holtzmann, H. J., *Lehrbuch der ntl. Theologie*, 2 Bde, Tübingen ²1911
Huby, J., *Epître aux Romains* (Verb. salutis I), Paris ²1940
—— *Première épître aux Corinth.* (Verb. sal. XIII), Paris 1946
—— *Les épîtres de la captivité* (Verb. sal. VIII), Paris 1935
Jeremias, J., *Die Kindertaufe in den ersten vier Jahrhunderten*, Göttingen 1958
Jülicher, A., Röm. (in *Schriften des NT, hrsg.* v. J. Weiss II), Göttingen ³1908
Käsemann, E., *Leib und Leib Christi* (Beitr. z. hist. Theol. 9), Tübingen 1933
Kelly, J. N. D., *Early Christian Creeds*, London ²1960
Kirchgässner, A., *Erlösung und Sünde im Neuen Testament*, Freiburg i. Br. 1950
Kittel, G., *Die Religionsgeschichte und das Urchristentum*, Gütersloh 1932
—— 'Die Wirkungen der christlichen Wassertaufe nach dem NT', *ThStKr* 87 (1914) 33–42
Knabenbauer, J., *Epist. ad Eph., Phil., Col.* (Curs. Script. S.), Paris 1912
—— *Epist. ad Thess., Timoth., Tit., Philem.*, Paris 1913
Koch, W., *Die Taufe im NT* (BZfr III, 10), Münster 1910
Kühl, E., *Der Brief des Paulus an die Römer*, Leipzig 1913
Künneth, W., *Theologie der Auferstehung*, München ²1934
Kuss, O., 'Zur paulinischen und nachpaulinischen Tauflehre im NT', *ThGl* 42 (1952), 401–25
—— *Der Römerbrief*, 1. und 2. Fascicles, Regensburg 1957–59
Lagrange, M. J., *Epître aux Romains*, Paris ²1922
—— *Epître aux Galates*, Paris 1918
—— *Le Judaïsme avant Jésus-Christ*, Paris 1931
Lampe, G. W. H., *The Seal of the Spirit*, London 1951
Lapide, Corn. a., *Comm. in omnes S. Pauli epistolas*, ed. A. Padovani, Turin I 1909; II 1911

Leenhardt, F. J., *Le Baptême chrétien, son origine, sa signification*, Neuchâtel-Paris 1946
—— *L'Epître de S. Paul aux Romains*, Neuchâtel-Paris 1957
Leipoldt, J., *Die urchristliche Taufe im Lichte der Religionsgeschichte*, Leipzig 1928
—— *Sterbende und auferstehende Götter*, Leipzig 1923
Levy, J.-Goldschmidt, L., *Wörterbuch über die Talmudim und Midraschim*, 4 Bd., Berlin-Wien ²1924
Liddell, H. G.-Scott, R., *A Greek-English Lexicon*, Oxford ⁹1940
Lietzmann, H., *An die Römer* (Handb. z. NT 8), Tübingen ⁴1933
—— *An die Korinther* (Handb. z. NT 9), Tübingen ³1931; ⁴1949 ergänzte von W. G. Kümmel
—— *An die Galater* (Handb. z. NT 10), Tübingen ²1923
Lock, W., *The Pastoral Epistles* (Int. Crit. Comm.), Edinburgh 1924
Lohmeyer, E., *Der Brief an die Philipper* (H. A. W. Meyers Komm. ⁸IX, 1), Göttingen 1928
—— *Die Briefe an die Kolosser und an Philemon* (H. A. W. Meyers Komm. ⁸IX, 2), Göttingen 1930
—— Σὺν Χριστῷ, in *Festgabe* f. *A. Deissmann*, Tübingen 1927, pp. 218–57
—— *Grundlagen paulinischer Theologie*, Tübingen 1929
Lundberg, P., *La typologie baptismale dans l'ancienne Eglise*, Lund 1942
Maier, A., *Komm. über den Brief Pauli an die Römer*, Freiburg 1847
—— *Komm. über den 2. Brief an die Korinther*, Freiburg 1865
Maier, F. W., 'Paulus', *LThK* VIII, 27–43
Marsh, G. H., *The Origin and Significance of the N.T. Baptism*, Manchester 1941
Meinertz. M.-Tillmann, F., *Die Gefangenschaftsbriefe des hl. Paulus*, Bonn ⁴1931
—— *Die Pastoralbriefe des hl. Paulus*, Bonn ⁴1931
—— *Einleitung in das NT*, Paderborn ⁵1950
—— *Theologie des Neuen Testamentes*, 2 vols., Bonn 1950
Michaelis, W., *Pastoralbriefe und Gefangenschaftsbriefe* (Ntl. Forsch. I, 6), Gütersloh 1930
—— *Einleitung in das NT*, Bern ²1954, Ergänzungsheft 1961
Michel, O., *Der Brief an die Hebräer* (H. A. W. Meyers Komm. ⁷XIII), Göttingen 1936
—— *Der Brief an die Römer* (H. A. W. Meyers Komm. IV¹⁰), Göttingen 1955
Mittring, K., *Die Heilswirklichkeit bei Paulus*, Gütersloh 1929
Moore, G. F., *Judaism in the first centuries of the Christian era, the age of the Tannaim*, 3 vols., Cambridge 1927 and 1930
Moulton, J. H.-Milligan, G., *The Vocabulary of the Greek Testament illustrated from the Papyri and other non-literary sources*, 8 vols. 1914–29
Moulton, J. H. (-Thumb, A.), *Einleitung in die Sprache des NT*, Heidelberg 1911
Mundle, W., *Das religiöse Leben des Apostels Paulus*, Leipzig 1923
—— *Der Glaubensbegriff des Paulus*, Leipzig 1932
Nygren, A., *Der Römerbrief*, Göttingen 1951
Oecumenius, *Komm. zu den paulin. Briefen*, Migne, PG 118, 323ff
Oepke, A., *Der Brief des Paulus an die Galater* (Theol. Handkomm. z. NT 9), Leipzig 1937
Origenes, *Komm. zu den paulin. Briefen* (transl. Rufinus), Migne, PG 14, 837ff
Passow, F., *Handwörterbuch der griechischen Sprache*, 4 vols., Leipzig ⁵1841–57
Percy, E., *Die Probleme der Kolosser- und Epheserbriefe*, Lund 1946
Philo of Alex., *Opera omnia ed. L. Cohn-P. Wendland*, 7 vols., 1896ff

Pieper, K., *Paulus* (Ntl. Abh. XII 1–2), Münster [2–3]1929
Plummer, A., *Second Epistle of St. Paul to the Corinthians* (Int. Crit. Comm.), Edinburgh 1915
Prat, E., *La Théologie de S. Paul*, 2 vols., Paris [28]1938 and 1941
Preisigke, F., *Wörterbuch der griechischen Papyrusurkunden*, 3 vols, Berlin 1925–31
Prümm, K., *Der christl. Glaube und die altheidnische Welt*, 2 vols, Leipzig 1935
—— *Religionsgeschichtliches Handbuch für den Raum der altchristlichen Umwelt*, Freiburg 1943 (*RGH*)
Radermacher, L., *Ntl. Grammatik* (Handb. z. NT 1), Tübingen [2]1925
Reitzenstein, R., *Die hellenistischen Mysterienreligionen*, Leipzig [3]1927
—— *Die Vorgeschichte der christlichen Taufe*, Leipzig 1929
Riessler, P., *Altjüdisches Schrifttum ausserhalb der Bibel*, Augsburg 1928
Robertson, A. T., *A Grammar of the Greek NT in the light of historical research*, New York 1919
Robertson- (H. Stocks), *Kurzgefasste Grammatik des ntl. Griechisch*, Leipzig 1911
Robertson, A.-Plummer, A., *First epistle of St. Paul to the Corinthians* (Int. Crit. Comm.), Edinburgh 1911
Sanday, W.-Headlam, A. C., *The epistle to the Romans* (Int. Crit. Comm.), Edinburgh [5]1902, repr. 1920
Schelkle, K. H., *Paulus Lehrer der Väter. Die altkirchliche Auslegung von Röm 1–11*, Düsseldorf 1956
Schlatter, A., *Die Theologie der Apostel*, Stuttgart 1910 ([2]1922)
—— *Gottes Gerechtigkeit* (*Ein Komm. zu Röm*), Stuttgart 1935
—— *Paulus der Bote Jesu* (*1 u. 2 Kor*), Stuttgart 1934
Schlier, H., *Christus und die Kirche im Eph* (Beitr. z. hist. Theol. 6), Tübingen 1930
—— *Der Galaterbrief* (H. A. W. Meyers Komm. [10]VII), Göttingen 1949
—— 'Die Taufe nach dem 6. Kapitel des Röm', *EvTh* 1938, 335–47
—— 'Zur kirchlichen Lehre von der Taufe', *ThLZ* 72 (1947) cols. 321–36
—— *Der Brief an die Epheser*, Düsseldorf 1957
Schmid, J., 'Der Epheserbrief des Apostels Paulus' (*BSt* XXIII, 3–4), 1928
Schmidt, Tr., *Der Leib Christi*, Erlangen 1919
Schmitz, O., *Die Christusgemeinschaft des Paulus im Lichte seines Genitivgebrauchs* (Ntl. Forsch. I, 2), Gütersloh 1924
Schnackenburg, R., 'Todes- und Lebensgemeinschaft mit Christus. Neue Studien zu Röm 6, 1–11', *MüThZ* 6 (1955) 32–53
Schneider, J., *Die Passionsmystik des Paulus* (Unters. z. NT 15), Leipzig 1929
—— *Die Taufe im Neuen Testament*, Stuttgart 1952
Schwarzmann, H., *Zur Tauftheologie des hl. Paulus in Röm 6*, Heidelberg 1950
Schweitzer, A., *Geschichte der paulinischen Forschung von der Reformation bis auf die Gegenwart*, Tübingen 1911 ([2]1932)
—— *Die Mystik des Apostels Paulus*, Tübingen 1930
Seeberg, A., *Die Taufe im NT*, [2]1913
Sickenberger, J., *Die Briefe des hl. Paulus an die Korinther und Römer*, Bonn [4]1932
Sieffert, F., *Der Brief an die Galater* (H. A. W. Meyers Komm. [9]VII), Göttingen 1899
Soden, H. von, *Sakrament und Ethik bei Paulus* (Marb. theol. Stud. 1), Gotha 1931
Söhngen, G., *Symbol und Wirklichkeit im Kultmysterium*, Bonn [2]1940
—— *Der Wesensaufbau des Mysteriums*, Bonn 1938
Sommerlath, E., *Der Ursprung des neuen Lebens nach Paulus*, Leipzig 1923

Staab, K., *Pauluskommentare aus der griechischen Kirche* (Ntl. Abh. XV), Münster i. W. 1933
Stanley, D. M., 'The NT Doctrine of Baptism', *ThSt* 18 (1957) 169–215
Stauffer, E., *Die Theologie des NT*, Stuttgart ^{3}1947
Steinmann, A.-Tillmann, F., *Die Briefe an die Thessalonicher und Galater*, Bonn ^{4}1935
Straub, W., *Die Bildersprache des Apostels Paulus*, Tübingen 1937
Stricker, S., 'Der Mysteriengedanke des hl. Paulus nach Röm. 6, 2–11', *Liturg. Leben* 1 (1934), 285–96
Stromberg, A. von, *Studien zur Theorie und Praxis der Taufe*, Berlin 1913
Theodoret, *Komm. zu den paulin. Briefen*, in Migne, PG 82, 43ff bzw. ed. Noesselt III
Theophylact, *Komm.* in Migne, PG 124
Thomas, J., *Le mouvement baptiste en Palestine et Syrie 150 avant J. Chr.–300 après J. Chr.* (Diss. Lov.), Gembloux 1935
Thornton, L. S., *The Common Life in the Body of Christ*, London ^{3}1950
Tobac, E., *La problème de la justification dans s. Paul* (Diss. Lov.), Lovanii 1908
Turchi, N., *Fontes historicae Mysteriorum aevi hellenistici*, Roma 1930
Volz, P., *Die Eschatologie der jüdischen Gemeinde im ntl. Zeitalter*, Tübingen ^{2}1934
Warnach, V., 'Taufe und Christusgeschehen nach Römer 6', *ALW* III/2 (1954) 284–366
—— 'Die Tauflehre des Römerbriefes in der neueren theologischen Diskussion', *ALW* V/2 (1958) 274–332
Weber, H. E., 'Eschatologie' und 'Mystik' im NT (*BFchTh* II, 20), Gütersloh 1930
Weinel, H., *Biblische Theologie des NT*, Tübingen ^{4}1928
Weiss, B., *Der Brief an die Römer* (H. A. W. Meyers Komm. ^{9}IV), Göttingen 1899
—— *Lehrbuch der Biblischen Theologie des NT*, Stuttgart-Berlin ^{7}1903
Weiss, J., *Der erste Korintherbrief* (H. A. W. Meyers Komm. ^{9}V), Göttingen 1910
—— *Die Gefangenschaftsbriefe* (Schriften des NT II), Göttingen ^{3}1917
—— *Das Urchristentum*, Göttingen 1914 and 1917
Wendland, H. D., *Die Briefe an die Korinther* (NTD 7), Göttingen ^{4}1946
Wichmann, W., *Die Leidenstheologie, eine Form der Leidensdeutung im Spätjudentum*, Stuttgart 1930
Wiencke, G., Paulus über den Tod Jesu (*BFchTh* II, 42), Göttingen 1939
Wikenhauser, A., *Die Christusmystik des Paulus*, Apostels Freiburg i. Br. ^{2}1956
—— *Die Kirche als der mystische Leib Christi nach dem Apostel Paulus*, Münster ^{2}1940
—— *Einleitung in das Neue Testament*, Freiburg i. Br. ^{2}1956
Wilson, E. W., The Development of Paul's Doctrine of Dying and Rising again with Christ, *Exp. Times* 42 (1931), 562–5
Windisch, H., *Taufe und Sünde im ältesten Christentum bis auf Origenes*, Tübingen 1908
—— *Der zweite Korintherbrief* (H. A. W. Meyers Komm. ^{9}VI), Göttingen 1924
Wissmann, E., *Das Verhältnis von* Πίστις *und Christusfrömmigkeit bei Paulus* (FRLANT N.F. 23), Göttingen 1926
Wohlenberg, G., *Die Pastoralbriefe* (Zahns Komm. XIII), Leipzig 1906 (^{2}1911)
Wrede, W., *Paulus*, Halle ^{2}1907
Zahn, Th., *Der Brief des Paulus an die Römer*, Leipzig 1910 (^{3}1925)
—— *Der Brief des Paulus an die Galater*, Leipzig ^{2}1907 (^{3}1922)

Indices

I. SCRIPTURE REFERENCES

A. OLD TESTAMENT

B. NEW TESTAMENT

C. ANCIENT JEWISH LITERATURE

D. ANCIENT CHRISTIAN LITERATURE

E. OTHER ANCIENT WRITINGS

2. SUBJECT INDEX

3. INDEX OF AUTHORS